"With the sophistication of a scholar and the savvy of a Washington insider, Evan Michelson reveals the research and policy roles of the Woodrow Wilson International Center's Project on Emerging Nanotechnologies. In doing so, he creates much-needed perspective on the role of NGOs in the anticipatory governance of nanotechnology and other emerging technologies."

David H. Guston, Professor and Founding Director, School for the Future of Innovation in Society, Arizona State University, USA

"In this meticulously documented yet engaging work, Michelson details how recent networked, non-governmental alternatives to US government technology assessment provide superior long term governance of emerging nanotechnologies and synthetic biology. The book compellingly argues that new anticipatory non-governmental approaches 'proactively address the multidimensional, interconnected societal impacts of science and technology advancements.'"

Barbara Herr Harthorn, Director, Center for Nanotechnology in Society, University of California at Santa Barbara, USA

"This is an extremely interesting and timely book. Evan Michelson has placed his hands on one of the most challenging policy issues today: how to anticipate technology advancements in order to adjust governance systems appropriately. He skillfully uses the examples of two 'hot' fields, nanotechnology and synthetic biology. An outstanding job. Must read!!"

Nicholas S. Vonortas, Professor of Economics and International Affairs, Center for International Science and Technology Policy & Department of Economics, The George Washington University, USA

"This is an eminently readable account of how decentralized approaches have been used to consider future societal impacts of nanotechnology and synthetic biology. The book gives us rich insights into the development of the Project on Emerging Nanotechnologies among other non-governmental efforts to address key aspects of technology assessment."

Jan Youtie, Director, Program in Science, Technology, and Innovation Policy, Georgia Institute of Technology, USA

"Evan Michelson has done the policy and research communities an important service. *Assessing the Societal Implications of Emerging Technologies: anticipatory governance in practice* demonstrates the critical role of systematic efforts to imagine different futures and then understand what this means for how we perceive and act in the present. Not only does this study lay out the utility of futures thinking but it also reviews and explains how it is done. Michelson's message is clear: decision makers need to engage in broad based processes that use the future to leverage collective intelligence – without this knowledge the potential of human genius may not only be wasted but could do significant harm."

Riel Miller, former Head of Foresight, UNESCO, France

Assessing the Societal Implications of Emerging Technologies

A growing problem of interest in the field of science and technology policy is that the next generation of innovations is arriving at an accelerating rate, and the governance system is struggling to catch up. Current approaches and institutions for effective technology assessment are ill suited and poorly designed to proactively address the multidimensional, interconnected societal impacts of science and technology advancements that are already taking place and expected to continue over the course of the twenty-first century.

This book offers tangible insights into the strategies deployed by well-known, high-profile organizations involved in anticipating the various societal and policy implications of nanotechnology and synthetic biology. It focuses predominantly on an examination of the practices adopted by the often-cited and uniquely positioned Project on Emerging Nanotechnologies in the United States, as well as being informed by comparisons with a range of institutions also interested in embedding forward-looking perspectives in their respective area of innovation. The book lays out one of the first actionable roadmaps that other interested stakeholders can follow when working toward institutionalizing anticipatory governance practices throughout the policymaking process.

Evan S. Michelson is a Program Director at the Alfred P. Sloan Foundation, USA.

The Earthscan Science in Society Series

Series Editor: Steve Rayner
Institute for Science, Innovation and Society, University of Oxford
Editorial Board: Jason Blackstock, Bjorn Ola Linner, Susan Owens, Timothy O'Riordan, Arthur Petersen, Nick Pidgeon, Dan Sarewitz, Andy Sterling, Chris Tyler, Andrew Webster, Steve Yearley

The Earthscan Science in Society Series aims to publish new high-quality research, teaching, practical and policy-related books on topics that address the complex and vitally important interface between science and society.

A full list of titles in this series is available at: www.routledge.com/series/ESSS

Assessing the Societal Implications of Emerging Technologies

Anticipatory governance in practice

Evan S. Michelson

Routledge
Taylor & Francis Group

LONDON AND NEW YORK

from Routledge

First published 2016
by Routledge

2 Park Square, Milton Park, Abingdon, Oxfordshire OX14 4RN
711 Third Avenue, New York, NY 10017

Routledge is an imprint of the Taylor & Francis Group, an informa business

First issued in paperback 2017

British Library Cataloguing-in-Publication Data
A catalogue record for this book is available from the British Library

Library of Congress Cataloging-in-Publication Data
A catalog record for this book has been requested.

ISBN: 978-1-138-12343-4 (hbk)
ISBN: 978-0-8153-5578-6 (pbk)

Typeset in Bembo
by Florence Production Limited, Stoodleigh, Devon, UK

A sense of the future is behind all good politics.
Unless we have it, we can give nothing—either
wise or decent—to the world.

(Attributed to C. P. Snow by John Gibbons
in the Office of Technology Assessment
Annual Report to the Congress, March 1984)

To Ilysa, Mira, and Seth:
You make the future brighter every day.
I love you, love you madly.

Contents

Illustrations

Figures

Tables

Acronyms and abbreviations

CERCLA	Comprehensive Environmental Response, Compensation, and Liability Act
CBEN	Center for Biological and Environmental Nanotechnology
CLIP	component-level implementation process
CNS-ASU	Center for Nanotechnology in Society at Arizona State University
CPI	Consumer Products Inventory
CPSC	Consumer Product Safety Commission
DEFRA	Department of Environment, Food, and Rural Affairs
DIY	do-it-yourself
ECAST	Expert and Citizen Assessment of Science and Technology network
EDF	Environmental Defense Fund
EHS	environmental, health and safety
EPA	Environmental Protection Agency
FDA	Food and Drug Administration
FIFRA	Federal Insecticide, Fungicide and Rodenticide Act
GAO	Government Accountability Office
GMO	genetically modified organism
ICON	International Council on Nanotechnology
iGEM	International Genetically Engineered Machine Foundation
Nano	nanotechnology
NGO	non-governmental organization
NIOSH	National Institute for Occupational Safety and Health
NISE Net	Nanoscale Informal Science Education Network
NNI	National Nanotechnology Initiative
NSF	National Science Foundation
OECD	Organization for Economic Cooperation and Development
OSTP	Office of Science and Technology Policy
OTA	Office of Technology Assessment
PCGCC	Pew Center on Global Climate Change
PEN	Project on Emerging Nanotechnologies
PES	public engagement with science

PIFB	Pew Initiative on Food and Biotechnology
PUS	public understanding of science
PVM	public value mapping
RCRA	Resource Conservation and Recovery Act
RTTA	real-time technology assessment
STIP	Science and Technology Innovation Program
Synbio	synthetic biology
TSCA	Toxic Substances Control Act
US	United States
WPMN	Working Party on Manufactured Nanomaterials

Acknowledgements

Producing a study of this scope would not be possible without numerous people who generously provided their assistance, support, and encouragement throughout the research and writing process. In particular, three stand out. First, Rogan Kersh offered unparalleled guidance with usual insight and grace, and he has been a mentor, friend, and sage. Second, David Guston suggested invaluable input, conceptual leadership, and all around encouragement from the very beginning. Third, David Rejeski contributed endless time and unfiltered access to the main case study materials from the very beginning, and he encouraged the reporting of open and honest results throughout the process.

Thanks also go to Maria Damon, Daniel Sarewitz, Shankar Prasad, Michael Gorman, and Stefaan Verhulst who made helpful comments on earlier versions of this manuscript. A big, heartfelt thank you also goes to Julia Moore, who encouraged me to pursue this kind of research and whose reassurance never wavered as the years rolled by. I am indebted to Dietram Scheufele and Doo-Hun Choi from the University of Wisconsin-Madison, who openly and willingly shared their database of nanotechnology newspaper articles that is analyzed in Chapter 6. Evan Faber and Angela Kissell provided helpful research assistance and proofreading, respectively, on earlier drafts, and David Jenkins and Andrew Bryant assisted in interview transcription. Many thanks go to Steve Rayner for being willing to take on this project and Helen Bell from Routledge for her editorial assistance. I also appreciate the help from the evaluation team at The Pew Charitable Trusts, who graciously shared all relevant requested materials. None of the organizations discussed in this book had any say in or control over the final results.

I am deeply grateful to all of the individuals who took considerable time out of their busy schedules to be interviewed for this study. This analysis would not have been possible without their assistance. While almost all individuals agreed to allow their names to be quoted, I decided that, out of an abundance of caution and respect for their opinions and privacy, to anonymize the majority of quotations shared here. Relevant sectoral or contextual information is provided where appropriate. Wherever an individual is named in a quotation, that statement was either already in the public domain or came from an interview where they agreed to allow their named to be used. Any and all errors, omissions, or inadvertent mischaracterizations are my own and bear no reflection on any of the individuals or institutions that participated in this research project.

This book would not have been possible without the encouragement of Paul Joskow and my colleagues at the Alfred P. Sloan Foundation. I have written this book fully in my personal capacity, and the views expressed here are wholly my own and do not in any way reflect the views of the Alfred P. Sloan Foundation or any of its grantees.

Content from the first three chapters of this study was presented at the 2011 Dupont Summit on Science, Technology, and Environmental Policy in Washington, DC. A previous version of Chapter 4 was presented at a May 2012 workshop titled "Ethics, Plausibility and Innovation" in Ispra, Italy and at the Doctoral Colloquium of the Robert F. Wagner School of Public Service at New York University in December 2012. Some material from this study was previously published as "'The Train Has Left the Station': The Project on Emerging Nanotechnologies and the Shaping of Nanotechnology Policy in the United States" in *Review of Policy Research*, volume 30, issue 5, pages 464–487, September 2013. Many thanks to the publisher John Wiley & Sons for their permission to excerpt and republish this material. Thank you as well to Inderscience for their permission to produce a reworked version of material contained in Chapter 4, which was originally published as "'Getting There Early': Strategies for Seeking Policy Influence and Anticipating Nano-technology's Alternative Futures" in *International Journal of Foresight and Innovation Policy*, volume 9, numbers 2/3/4, pages 188–212, 2013.

I owe a great debt to the fantastic teachers I had throughout my education, including Joe Borlo and Doc Bartol from Newark Academy, Janet Cooper-Nelson from Brown University, Nicholas Vonortas from The George Washington University, and many others along the way. I also want to thank my friends and family who have always been sources of inspiration and motivation, including Scott Saloway and Rich Farias, David and Laura Flink, David and Jaime Hyman, Jason and Millie Rauch, and Tami and Chris Danison. My grandfather, Harold Berlin, was a true inspiration, and Addie Berlin has been a wonderful supporter all these years. Erwin and Eunice Michelson, and Edith Glikin showed me the meaning of tradition. Thanks as well go to Randy and Jeremy Michelson; Leslie, Beth, and Laura Michelson; Ian, Julia, and little Tanner Richter; and Wendy Berlin, Lauren Sokol, and the Karlavage family (Danna, Marty, Ben, and Vivian) for their unending encouragement. Haila and David Kimball, and Daniel and Marion Kimball, are the best in-laws one can imagine. I am so thankful for my sister, Heather Michelson, who has been with me every step of the way, has an open and loving heart, and is one of my biggest champions. My mother, Lolly Michelson, has made it all possible from the very beginning. I love you and can't tell you enough how much I appreciate all you do.

Finally, none of this would have happened without my incomparable, marvelous, and spectacular wife Ilysa. I love you beyond words, and I thank you for seeing more in me than I see in myself. Finally, Mira and Seth bring sheer happiness, fulfillment, and beauty to our lives. May you both follow your dreams, see wonder in the universe, and always strive to make the world a better place.

1 Shaping policy for emerging technologies in the United States

Setting the stage

In the weeks leading up to the 2008 United States (US) presidential election, *Science* magazine published a list of the ten most important science and technology policy priorities facing the new Administration. The brief article highlighted a range of topics, including regulating carbon dioxide emissions, expanding space exploration, combating bioterrorism, managing the nation's nuclear weapon stockpile, and investing in next-generation medical interventions. This list represents well-known, often controversial policy issues. However, more conspicuously unusual among them was the third-listed critical priority: nanotechnology.

The description accompanying the article highlights the range of broader societal issues raised by nanotechnology: "long touted as the next 'big thing,' nanotechnology is already moving from research to market … But safety concerns continue to dog the emerging field" to the extent that "the next president must decide if the country needs to revise its nano safety strategy to strengthen protections for the public" (Science, 2008).

A few months before the publication of this editorial in *Science*, a real-world example illuminated the interconnected technological, regulatory, and societal puzzles posed by nanotechnology and other emerging technologies. In March 2008, the United States Environmental Protection Agency (EPA) fined IOGEAR, a California-based company, for "selling unregistered pesticides and making unproven claims about their effectiveness" (Environmental Protection Agency, 2008). Unlike more familiar pesticides, the "pesticide" in question here was a coating of nanotechnology-engineered silver applied to consumer computer equipment, such as keyboard and other related accessories, claiming that it would "eliminate pathogens and kill bacteria." Due to its antimicrobial and antibacterial properties, EPA has considered that nanosilver could be considered a pesticide for regulatory purposes. A range of products using this substance—which have included washing machines and, more recently, air purifiers—are now subject to oversight and registration under EPA's Federal Insecticide, Fungicide, and Rodenticide Act (FIFRA) (Environmental Protection Agency, 2015a).

In the years since the IOGEAR ruling, EPA has faced questions about the regulation of nanomaterials under its pesticide law. The agency ruled in August 2010 that it would apply pesticide regulation on a case-by-case basis to some nanosilver products, and, in December 2011, conditionally approved the registration of an anti-microbial nanosilver textile coating, known as HeiQ AGS-20, under pesticide law (HeiQ Materials AG, 2011). Over the course of 2012, this and other EPA rulings led to legal action by environmental organizations to try and block registration of the nanosilver coating under pesticide law (Sass and Wu, 2013). These disputes were tied-up in extended legal proceedings (Bergeson, 2012; Graham, 2013). This issue remains current today. In 2015, the EPA finally responded to a petition it received seven years ago from a group of non-governmental organizations (NGO) regarding the approval of nanosilver products (Environmental Protection Agency, 2015b), and it received another lawsuit from many of these same institutions regarding the EPA's more recent approval of another nanosilver product earlier in the year (Center for Food Safety, 2015). Moreover, beyond the minutiae of regulatory interpretation, broader questions about the role of regulation and commercialization remain. In fact, in the week leading up to the 2012 US Presidential election, another article in *Science* claimed that, "one especially thorny issue is how to regulate the minuscule products of nanotechnology without hobbling commercialization of that nascent field" (Science, 2012).

This story is relevant because it touches on not just debates about the long-term future of nanotechnology, but on what is potentially forthcoming for other emerging technologies, such as synthetic biology and geoengineering. It is not just that nanotechnology had sustained visible prominence in a prestigious journal across multiple elections, nor that the EPA was struggling to oversee a novel technology using existing legal structures that were not designed for this purpose. Rather, these and countless other examples that have emerged in recent years signal that nanotechnology, synthetic biology, and other emerging fields of science and technology have fast become principal policy issues, involving complex social, economic, and political considerations. Additionally, many view these associated challenges as harbingers of other issues to come and indicative of the increasingly inseparable nature of "converging" technological developments (Anton, Silberglitt, and Schneider, 2001; Bainbridge and Roco, 2006; Roco, 2008; National Research Council, 2009a; Roco et al., 2013; Bainbridge and Roco, 2015).

The emergence of these different technological advancements have raised a host of questions. How do different stakeholders operate within a novel science and technology policy system? How might institutions attempt to shape policy outcomes? What approaches can be put into practice to anticipate potential societal implications arising from these technological developments? Scholarship on the relevant theoretical dimensions of these questions has grown, guided by the conceptual construct of anticipatory governance (Barben et al., 2008; Guston, 2011, 2014). However, few extended, in-depth treatments address how this idea has been, and can be, implemented and institutionalized in practice, in a real-world, high-profile context.

This book fills this gap. It presents novel findings focused on examining the impact of some of the most prominent civil society institutions in this area to exist over the past decade, paying particularly close attention to the Project on Emerging Nanotechnologies (PEN), an entity deliberately established to anticipate the societal implications of nanotechnology. This book provides a granular assessment of how this and other organizations operated. It draws out comparisons with other institutions and explores how the strategies that PEN and these other organizations utilized can be further extended with respect to other emerging technologies, such as synthetic biology. By identifying specific, empirically grounded actions that other organizations can adopt to advance foresight, operate in a boundary-spanning manner, and engage lay audiences, it unpacks the process by which the future of novel technologies becomes framed, debated, and contested in public and in policy arenas. In an era when much consideration goes into thinking about how emerging technologies are impacting people's lives, combining a macro- and micro-level perspective about how anticipatory governance unfolds in action is critical to both getting prepared and staying ahead of developments in science and technology.

Brief technological overview

Although a full description of nanotechnology's and synthetic biology's emergence is not possible here, basic definitions of both technologies are needed in order to provide sufficient contextual background for the ensuing analysis. Of course, much debate surrounds these definitions and histories. With respect to nanotechnology, numerous studies have traced the technology's lineage, document disagreements and disputes, and take account of how terminologies and definitions have evolved (Johnson, 2004; Mody, 2004; McCray, 2005; Choi and Mody, 2009; McCray, 2009; Mody and McCray, 2009). Although in a somewhat earlier stage of development, the same is true for synthetic biology. Different aspects of its diverse history and trajectory are already being chronicled by natural and social scientists (Yeh and Lim, 2007; Haseloff and Ajioka, 2009; Vinson and Pennisi, 2011; Cameron, Bashor, and Collins, 2014).

While multiple definitions of nanotechnology exist at varying levels of technical specificity, the National Nanotechnology Initiative (NNI)—the US government program established to coordinate nanotechnology research and development—provides one of the most commonly used definitions. According to the NNI, "nanotechnology is the understanding and control of matter at dimensions between approximately 1 and 100 nanometers, where unique phenomena enable novel applications" (National Nanotechnology Initiative, n.d.). Embedded in this definition are three key characteristics of nano-technology: size, unique phenomena, and novel applications.

Nanotechnology is primarily concerned with atoms and molecules at the nanoscale, where a nanometer is defined as one billionth of a meter, with the prefix "nano" derived from the Greek word meaning "dwarf." The size range of 1–100 nanometers is pertinent for many natural and human-made materials. For instance, a strand of DNA is approximately 2.5 nanometers wide, while a water molecule is approximately 0.25 nanometers in size, and a gold atom is approximately 0.14 nanometers in diameter. Similarly, human-made objects, such as carbon nanotubes (a collection of carbon atoms that are arranged into a cylinder-like shape) and structures known as buckminsterfullerenes or "buckyballs" (a collection of carbon atoms arranged in a roughly spherical pattern) are on the order of 1.3 nanometers and 1 nanometer in diameter, respectively.

Developing an adequate definition of synthetic biology is similarly difficult, with multiple attempts having been made to clearly define what this technology entails. As with nanotechnology, many definitions of synthetic biology are procedural, relating to the applicability of engineering techniques to biological systems in order to create novel functions and capabilities (Andrianantoandro et al., 2006; Heinemann and Panke, 2006). For example, The Royal Society (2015) in the United Kingdom defines synthetic biology as "the design and construction of novel artificial biological pathways, organisms and devices or the redesign of existing natural biological systems." In a similar vein, Cameron et al. (2014) emphasize the procedural-driven aspects of synthetic biology, describing the field as the ability to "use . . . molecular biology tools and techniques to forward-engineer cellular behavior." Finally, the Presidential Commission for the Study of Bioethical Issues (2010) defines synthetic biology as the ability to "apply standardized engineering techniques to biology and thereby create organisms or biological systems with novel or specified functions." As with nanotechnology, synthetic biology boasts both "top-down" and "bottom-up" aspects, consisting of "systematically tuning or rearranging" (Cameron, Bashor, and Collins, 2014) existing biology systems (top-down) or building novel biological functions or entities by utilizing standardized biological "parts" (bottom-up). Some view synthetic biology as more of an extension of previously developed genetic engineering techniques (Erickson, Singh, and Winters, 2011). On the other hand, many suggest that these developments represent truly novel advancements and are discontinuous from past practices, providing the ability to create new life forms from scratch and blurring the notion between what is "natural" and what is manmade (Schwille, 2011; Zhang, Marris, and Rose, 2011; Redford, Adams and Mace, 2013).

While these definitions seem to imply the two fields developed wholly independently from one another, it is not necessarily the case. For example, the standard narrative of nanotechnology's historical development is that the idea was first popularized by physicist Richard Feynman in a 1959 talk at the American Physical Society titled, "There's Plenty of Room at the Bottom," where Feynman discusses "the problem of manipulating and controlling things on a small scale" (Feynman, 1960: 22). However, whether Feynman's talk actually influenced nanotechnology's development in the early years remains unclear (Toumey, 2008). Japanese scientist Norio Taniguchi subsequently coined the term nanotechnology in 1974. In subsequent years, the development of precision instruments, such as the invention of the scanning tunneling microscope (Mody, 2011), allowed researchers to manipulate individual atoms. These advancements led to the discovery that materials demonstrate different properties when engineered at the nanoscale. However, this canonical view often belies the manifestation of multiple and not-necessarily consistent descriptions of nanotechnology's historical development. Kim (2008) offers the view that nanotechnology did not only arise from mechanical engineering, but that it emerged from multiple originating disciplines, including biotechnology. Kim (2008) presents an alternative "hidden history" of nanotechnology's evolution from the perspective of protein engineering and molecular biotechnology. Critical nano-biotechnology research began to take place in the 1960s, with the advent of protein replication techniques. The combination of nanotechnology and biotechnology has led to the ever-more sophisticated ability to replicate RNA and other biological materials by advanced means, spurred on by the advent of high-throughput screening techniques in the 1980s and 1990s. Kim (2008) describes the resulting body of research as "molecular biomimetics," which has "blurred the boundaries" of research on inorganic nanomaterials and biomaterials. This alternative to the canonical view shows how the portrayal of the history of different emerging technologies is often a contested matter, with different claims made about the origins of the technology.

Both nanotechnology and synthetic biology also benefited from high-profile spokespersons who championed development in their respective fields early-on in their histories. For instance, Eric Drexler, in his book *Engines of Creation*, popularized a view of nanotechnology centering on the potential to create replicating molecular machines at the nanoscale, which have also been known as molecular assembler or more colloquially as "nanobots" (Drexler, 1986). However, Nobel Prize winning scientist Richard Smalley, epitomized in a popular science article written for *Scientific American*, took a rather less radical stance. His position was that nanotechnology should be viewed as the next phase in the evolution of chemistry, focusing more on the potential applications of materials such as buckyballs and carbon nanotubes (Smalley, 2001). An exchange series of "point-counterpoint" articles in 2003 published in *Chemical and Engineering News* encapsulated the fundamental disagreement between Drexler and Smalley (Kaplan and Radin, 2011). The respective stances taken by Drexler and Smalley led to a bifurcation on how nanotechnology's future was envisioned (Bueno, 2004). The increasingly marginalized Drexlerian view supported the notion that nanotechnology would eventually lead to the creation of self-replicating molecular assemblers, with the perspective espoused by Smalley focusing more on the novel physical and chemical properties that would arise from the advent of new materials.

Synthetic biology also has its high-profile supporters. Although its earliest roots date back to the 1960s and 1970s, synthetic biology truly started coming to prominence in the first decade of the twenty-first century. The eventual sequencing of the complete human genome led to further advancements in biotechnology capabilities, with prominent scientist J. Craig Venter announcing in 2010 the creation of "synthetic" bacterial life through the combination of standardized biological building blocks (Gibson et al., 2010). Researchers such as George Church, in his book *Regenesis* (2012), have talked about using synthetic biology techniques to recreate long-extinct species. While this last development is unequivocally far-off, new "gene drive" technologies that provide the ability to precisely edit the genomes of species by inserting genetic instructions that are inheritable through reproduction—especially among those that are fast-breeding—have been gaining attention as of late (Doudna and Charpentier, 2014; Esvelt et al., 2014). For instance, progress is well under way toward the creation of transgenic mosquitoes capable of breeding with wild populations that could help reduce, if not eradicate, the incidence of diseases such as malaria or dengue fever. Even more prodding are experiments that have taken place to attempt to alter inheritable traits in the human genome, also known as germline modification. These kinds of developments raise a range of policy, ethical, and regulatory concerns about the potential widespread use and implementation of this technology (Oye et al., 2014). These uncertainties spurred the leading scientific societies from around the world to hold a summit in December 2015—reminiscent of the famed Asilomar conference in 1975 that focused on recombinant bioengineering—to consider how best to address these rapidly emerging governance and ethical challenges. Discussion at this international meeting raised the prospects of scientists voluntarily placing a moratorium on this kind of research (Wade, 2015), although debates remain as to whether such a pause or cessation of research activity is possible or even desirable (Church, 2015).

Despite these similarities, a key difference between nanotechnology and synthetic biology, however, is the evolution of their funding and innovation systems, especially in the United States. Estimates of federal funding for synthetic biology research in the United States are less than $1 billion during the span of 2008–2014 (Synthetic Biology Project, 2015d). While still substantive, these amounts pale in comparison with nanotechnology, which has exceeded $1 billion annually in federal funding for the past decade. Additionally, no multi-agency equivalent of the NNI for synthetic biology currently exists—a gap that some leading scientists are trying to rectify (Keasling, 2014). This lack of an overarching institutional structure leads to less coordination on the federal level in terms of identifying research priorities and in making research spending decisions. The private sector innovation system for synthetic biology is also different from nanotechnology, with synthetic biology research conducted in smaller, start-up companies. The community of synthetic biology researchers is also often characterized as operating through more informal collaborations that arise from a prevailing do-it-yourself (DIY), open source mentality. The more modular infrastructure needed to make advancements in synthetic biology creates lower barriers to entry, especially when compared with the physically larger and relatively more expensive tools required for nanotechnology research. This more agile, informal innovation ecosystem in synthetic biology is particularly evident in the growth among student and amateur participants in the annual synthetic biology innovation competitions sponsored by the International Genetically Engineered Machine (iGEM) Foundation (iGEM Foundation, n.d.).

On the other hand, the funding system for nanotechnology has become more formalized. The NNI was initially created in 2000, with the legal authority formally establishing it passed on December 3, 2003 as part of the 21st Century Nanotechnology Research and Development Act (United States Congress, 2003). This inter-agency model adopted by the NNI was based on institutional arrangements developed for other science and technology issues, such as the Networking and Information Technology Research and Development program (National Science and Technology Council, 2012), which was implemented to promote collaboration on advanced information and communications technologies.

The NNI helps to coordinate, plan, and manage research and funding across the federal government (Lane and Kalil, 2005; Roco, 2007; National Science and Technology Council, 2011b). The federal budget for nanotechnology research in the United States was nearly $1.5 billion in fiscal year 2015, with a similar amount planned for fiscal year 2016, bringing the total federal funding for nanotechnology to over $22 billion since the NNI's inception (National Science and Technology Council, 2015). While the original funds for nano-technology research consisted of new money going toward nanotechnology, current funding practices typically allocated existing resources based on recommendations for how federal agencies should spend their research budgets. A number of developed and developing countries, especially the United Kingdom, China, India, Russia and Brazil, have created similar national nanotechnology programs since the establishment of the NNI (Maclurcan, 2005; Suttmeier, Cao, and Simon, 2006; Liu et al., 2009). There remain high expectations that nanotechnology will foster national economic competitiveness (Alencar, Porter, and Antunes, 2007; Shapira, Youtie, and Kay, 2011), spur job creation (Invernizzi, 2011), and promote regional economic growth (Shapira and Youtie, 2008).

Why are these countries and businesses investing heavily in nanotechnology? The NNI definition indicates that other factors—beyond just the small scale of the materials—make nanotechnology of interest to a broad set of countries and companies across sectors. Youtie, Iacopetta, and Graham (2008) have explored whether nanotechnology is a "general purpose technology" capable of spurring advancements in a wide array of other areas of technological development. The United Kingdom's Royal Society and Royal Academy of Engineering landmark report on the topic, *Nanoscience and Nanotechnologies: Opportunities and Uncertainties*, describes how the technology could lead to advancements in other sectors by allowing a variety of materials to be engineered in such a way that they are stronger, lighter, and more flexible

(The Royal Society, 2004). The engineering, manipulation, and control of materials—such as carbon, silver, and gold, among others—at this scale provides these substances with novel physical, chemical, and other properties. A 2012 Congressional Research Service briefing on nanotechnology summarizes that, "at this size, the properties of matter can differ in fundamental and potentially useful ways from the properties of individual atoms and molecules and of bulk matter" (Sargent Jr., 2012: i). For instance, carbon nanotubes can be created that have significantly higher strength-to-weight ratios than other forms of carbon, such as graphite or diamond. Similarly, changes at the nanoscale can transform the chemical reactivity properties of gold so that the substance becomes highly reactive instead of being inert, as is the case in gold's natural state. As noted earlier, the antimicrobial and antibacterial properties of silver can be significantly enhanced when compared with naturally occurring forms of silver.

This increased ability to engineer nanomaterials with unique properties at a small scale has led to a range of projected novel applications in fields as diverse as healthcare, energy storage, agriculture, water purification, computing, and security. While synthetic biology applications are still being proven, nanotechnology has raised substantial expectations for improvements in a number of sectors. The development of novel technological applications to address the needs of poorer populations globally has also received substantial attention (Invernizzi and Foladori, 2005; Salamanca-Buentello et al., 2005; Singer, Salamanca-Buentello, and Daar, 2005; Cozzens and Wetmore, 2011; Parker and Appelbaum, 2012; Street et al., 2014).

However, the very novelty of these nanomaterials also creates concerns from a policy perspective. These worries have predominantly focused on questions pertaining to nanotechnology's long-term effects due to a range of potential environmental, health, and safety (EHS) risks (Hett, 2004; National Science and Technology Council, 2011a; Youtie et al., 2011; Valsami-Jones and Lynch, 2015), such as novel toxicity behaviors (Oberdorster, Oberdorster, and Oberdorster, 2005; Oberdorster, Stone, and Donaldson, 2007; Lewinski, Colvin, and Drezek, 2008; Hirano, 2009; Shatkin et al., 2010; Canady, 2010; Shatkin and North, 2010) and the need for different approaches to risk characterization (Wiesner et al., 2006; Williams et al., 2010).

Research in this area has mostly focused on exploring an array of potential health impacts (Yildirimer et al., 2011; Bonner et al., 2013; Xia et al., 2013), with some of the most worrisome being the biological effects of inhaling or ingesting nanomaterials, a discovery found in at least one high profile study to lead to harm to workers handling nanomaterials (Song, Li, and Du, 2009). Two strands of EHS risk research indicate that some nanomaterials might cause a biological response similar to asbestos fibers (Poland et al., 2008; Takagi et al., 2008) or Alzheimer's disease (Linse et al., 2007). Additionally, certain populations, such as laboratory workers, may be particularly at risk of such health effects due to the frequency with which they handle nanomaterials

(Center for Nanotechnology in Society, University of California, Santa Barbara, 2007; Conti et al., 2008). Some nanomaterials—especially nano-based forms of silver—could also have long-term environmental impacts if they are released into groundwater or into the air as waste (Benn and Westerhoff, 2008; Blaser et al., 2008; Wardak et al., 2008; Hicks et al., 2015). These kinds of releases could lead to persistence in the environment and perhaps result in take-up within the food chain (MacCormack and Goss, 2008; Khanna, Bakshi, and Lee, 2008).

Valsami-Jones and Lynch (2015: 389) write that, "Nanosafety research has reached a crossroads, with opportunities still compromised by uncertainties, but with great potential for answers to emerge from application of state-of-the-art approaches." Advances in toxicity research have been made possible by new high-throughput screening techniques and the use of more sophisticated computational models. Until the adoption of these novel toxicity analysis tools becomes more widespread, however, little progress will be made on improving the risk assessment paradigms developed for the larger, bulk structures of materials that may not be valid for nanoscale versions of the same material. For these reasons, many review panels have called into question the overall adequacy of the existing EHS risk research strategy, raising the possibility that not enough is being done to ensure the regulatory system's ability to handle such novel technological risks (Choi, Ramachandran, and Kandlikar, 2009; National Research Council, 2009b; National Research Council, 2012).

Beyond potential EHS risks to workers and the general public, many questions linger about the broader societal implications of nanotechnology and synthetic biology as well. Questions have emerged related to responsible risk management, better oversight and governance, increased attention to public engagement, and ethical concerns about unequal distribution of potential benefits and risks (Bennett and Sarewitz, 2006; Fisher and Mahajan, 2006; Sandler and Kay, 2006; Morris, 2012; Bosso, 2013; Shapira, Youtie, and Li, 2015). These debates are not just taking place in the United States (Fischhoff, 2015), but they are occurring internationally as well (Marchant and Sylvester, 2006; Morris et al., 2011). These considerations will gain further significance as the functionality of nanomaterials advances and accelerates, moving from what Renn and Roco (2006a) term the first generation of "passive nanostructures" used in products and manufacturing processes to subsequent generations that involve "active nanostructures," "systems of nanosystems," and potentially "molecular nanosystems" as fourth-generation applications. Governance issues will become even more pressing when considering the intertwined characteristics with a range of technologies (Khushf, 2004; Roco, 2008; Bosso, 2010; Roco et al., 2011; Marchant, Allenby, and Herkert, 2011; Marchant, Abbott, and Allenby, 2013). Hodge, Bowman, and Maynard (2010: 4) contend that "the challenge of regulating nanotechnologies is yet another 'wicked' public policy problem facing governments, including climate change and other emerging technologies such as synthetic biology."

Two pathways forward: which model for the twenty-first century?

A growing challenge for the American policymaking system is to respond effectively to a wide range of interconnected, complex, long-term science and technology advancements. Furthermore, current approaches and institutions of governance are ill-suited to address these multidimensional, interconnected developments that are arising. The general decline in the ability of the American federal government to analyze and address the longer-term societal impacts of these new technologies is due, in part, to the closure of the Office of Technology Assessment (OTA) in 1995 (Kunkle, 1995; Knezo, 2005). OTA was established to provide scientific and technical advice to Congress and was shut down due to budget cuts as a result of political disputes among Democrats and Republicans (Bimber, 1996; Morgan and Peha, 2003).

This is not the only contributing factor. The resources available to federal agencies tasked with ensuring public safety, anticipating challenges, and managing emerging risks have also been severely weakened over the past decade. Agencies such as the Food and Drug Administration (FDA), the Consumer Product Safety Commission (CPSA), and the EPA have lost financial and human resources consistently over recent decades. And, as the example of the EPA's efforts to regulate the use of nanosilver in consumer products indicates, agencies are also constrained in their ability to apply rules and regulations that were not designed to respond to the potential challenges stemming from the emergence of new technologies (Davies, 2009). This mismatch highlights the widening gap within the American governance system between the *need* and the *ability* to take a comprehensive, forward-looking view on the ways in which nanotechnology, synthetic biology, and other new technologies might impact the policymaking system over the short-, medium-, and long-term.

In short, the next generation of innovations in science and technology is arriving at an accelerating rate, and the governance system is lagging behind. This realization leads to the vital, overarching research question guiding this investigation: *What practices and strategies are influential in anticipating the longer-term societal implications of emerging technologies, and how can they become better institutionalized in the policymaking process?*

Two solutions exist to address this question. One is a government-based model. A more promising approach, however, is a networked pathway of anticipatory governance that has recently demonstrated its viability. The first option proposed is to recreate OTA in some fashion. Writing a few years after OTA was defunded, Morgan and Peha (2003: 17) note that while "there is considerable disagreement both about how successful OTA was and why it was defunded," strong agreement remains "that Congress and the nation would be better served through the creation of one or more new institutions designed to perform balanced nonpartisan analysis and synthesis for Congress on topics involving complex issues of science and technology." Reflecting on this persistent gap in institutional capacity to provide Congress with nonpartisan advice on science and technology issues, then-Representative Rush Holt penned a 2009 op-ed in *Wired* magazine, claiming, "in the years since the demise of the OTA, no group or combination of groups has been able to assume OTA's place as the provider of scientific and technical assessment and advice to Congress" (Holt, 2009). Reaffirming this view in a blog post that same year, science policy expert Gerald Epstein writes pithily, "Congress pushed OTA's 'Pause' key in 1995. It's time to press 'Play' once again" (Epstein, 2009). This argument to recreate OTA was reprised in a more recent 2012 article in *The Atlantic*, titled "The Much-Needed and Sane Congressional Office That Gingrich Killed Off and We Need Back," which makes the case that even in an age of information saturation, a body such as the non-partisan OTA is still needed and would be relevant in government (Sadowski, 2012).

A report by Richard Sclove (2010) on the societal implications of emerging technologies, *Reinventing Technology Assessment: A 21st Century Model*, dubs recreating OTA the "Congressional option." Sclove cautions that while re-establishing OTA "would automatically confer public stature and a measure of influence upon the practice of TA [technology assessment] at the national level," the practicality of doing so in the current fractured political climate is unlikely (Sclove, 2010: x). Moreover, the specter of the previous organization's downfall would likely make any new instantiation "highly cautious and risk-averse. This could make it difficult to implement the experimentation, trial-and-error learning and innovation necessary to begin redressing weaknesses of the original OTA" (Sclove, 2010: x).

The government entity that currently comes closest to replicating OTA's function is the Center for Science, Technology, and Engineering within the Government Accountability Office (GAO) (Government Accountability Office, n.d.). This unit within GAO has produced "technology assessments" reports on a pilot basis from 2002–2006, and then in a more permanent capacity starting in fiscal year 2008 following Senate appropriations (Barkakati and Persons, 2013). Since beginning this technology assessment function, GAO technology assessment reports have spanned a range of emerging technology topics that not only include nanotechnology (Government Accountability Office, 2014) and geoengineering (Government Accountability Office, 2011a), but also on topics as diverse as additive manufacturing (Government Account-ability Office, 2015c), nuclear reactor design (Government Accountability Office, 2015a), water use in the energy sector (Government Accountability Office, 2015b), radiation and explosive detection for national security purposes (Government Accountability Office, 2011b; Government Accountability Office, 2010), wildland fire management (Government Accountability Office, 2005), and cyber-security (Government Accountability Office, 2004). However, although this technology assessment function within GAO is a valuable small-step in the direction of providing nonpartisan policy advice to Congress, it operates on a much smaller basis than OTA. However, GAO's modest set of technology assessment reports produced over a decade still fall short of the hundreds of assessment reports, briefings, summaries, meetings, and events that OTA organized over the course of its history (Barkakati and Persons, 2013).

A second option takes a different approach. Instead of formally recreating OTA, a more decentralized, loose network of non-governmental, academic, and other types of organizations would be engaged in a more participatory, experimental approach to anticipating the societal implications of emerging technologies. Sclove (2010) calls this the "institutional network option," involving a diverse collection of interlinked academic research centers and NGOs. Sclove's report even outlines the structure for one such network, called the Expert and Citizen Assessment of Science and Technology (ECAST) network, which was formed in the wake of this report (Expert and Citizen Assessment of Science and Technology, n.d.; Worthington et al., 2012). The idea behind such networks is that participating entities could produce forward-looking insights about emerging technologies for a broad range of interested parties, both within and outside of government. This pathway could allow different organizations to independently or collaboratively "select and frame topics more creatively, pro-actively or participatively" than a government-based entity (Sclove, 2010: x). It would also encourage flexibility in the use of various methodologies, as well as more substantially provide increased public and stakeholder engagement. Sclove (2010: 1) provides the underlying rationale for advancing this alternative, noting:

> A new national TA institution can be more decentralized, agile, collaborative, participatory—and thus effective—than was previously conceivable. These improvements can enable the practice of TA to better support government policy-makers and the American public in grappling with the complex but all-important links between technological developments, on the one hand, and social values, concerns and hopes on the other.

Table 1.1 indicates that when comparing these two different models, a strong rationale emerges for further exploring the non-governmental approach. First, unlike the government-based approach, interest in the institutional network option continues to increase as the benefits of an expansive, participatory, and forward-looking approach become more apparent. Second, the practical prospects for reviving OTA are diminishing in an era of economic austerity and budget constraints. Third, recent scholarship indicates a promising conceptual platform underlying this non-governmental approach. This includes the development of a host of new ideas related to anticipatory governance, participatory technology assessment, and responsible innovation. Fourth, lessons learned from this non-governmental approach are more likely transferable among the many different institutions as well as across different technologies.

The case study approach

In fact, in recent years, the number and prominence of NGOs working as think tanks and producing voluminous information on a range of policy issues

Table 1.1 Alternative approaches to anticipating the societal implications of emerging technologies

Rationale for investigation	Government model	Non-governmental model
Interest in the field	*Decreasing*, as the likelihood of recreating OTA diminishes	*Increasing*, with intensified attention from 2010 onward
Conceptual relevance	*Low*, as the concept of technology assessment is being superseded by other frameworks	*High*, with opportunities to examine new theoretical frameworks, such as anticipatory governance
Transferrable lessons	*Weak*, as individual instances are one-off and nationally specific	*Strong*, with learning relevant across institutional arrangements and from one emerging technology to another
Relevant examples for analysis in the United States	*Few*, since no formal replacement exists for OTA in the US federal government	*Increasing*, with some organizations adopting forward-looking and participatory methodologies

has increased substantially (Rich, 2004). By one measure, over 6,000 think tanks are in operation globally, with nearly 2,000 located in the United States—a quarter of which are in Washington, DC—with the number of think tanks in the United States doubling since 1980 (McGann, 2015). The attendant increase in specialization of these NGOs has led to a rise in the number of organizations that have focused on analyzing the long-term benefits and risks of new technologies, including nanotechnology. These organizations are comprised of academic-based research institutions (such as the International Council on Nanotechnology (ICON)); independent research centers (such as the Center for Policy on Emerging Technologies, the Information Technology and Innovation Foundation, and the International Risk Governance Council); existing environmental, health, and consumer NGOs (such as Environmental Defense Fund (EDF), Friends of the Earth, and Consumers Union); and industry associations (such as Lux Research, American Chemistry Council, and the Nano Business Alliance) (Bosso and Rodrigues, 2006).

In addition to this increase in the number of organizations exploring the societal implications of emerging technologies, the expanded interest and conceptual relevance of the non-governmental option for technology assessment warrants further investigation. Much is already known about the government option, as OTA was well chronicled during its life and studied perhaps even more since its untimely shuttering. While these networked, non-governmental alternatives are beginning to show great promise as a pathway forward, little is known about how such entities function, especially when compared to the government-based option. More can be learned about the efficiency and effectiveness of these institutions, how they have changed over time, and the relevant lessons that are applicable to other organizations. Less research has taken place about the role these organizations play within specific science and technology policy systems, such as within the nanotechnology policy community. In short, even though many enthusiastic claims are being made for this non-governmental model, what does this model actually look like functionally, on-the-ground?

Since these non-governmental approaches are in the early stages of development, a qualitative case study approach is a useful, if not vital, foundational undertaking and theory-enhancing effort. This approach allows for a close examination of critical operational strategies and a nuanced inquiry into the different points of view related to the topic. This book presents a detailed, high-profile case study analysis of this non-governmental pathway, with discussions of a handful of additional organizations provided for context and comparison. One of the most prominent and actualized early adopters of this model in recent years was the Project on Emerging Nanotechnologies (PEN). The predominant interest here is to gain deeper insight into how PEN sought to understand and shape the longer-term societal implications of nanotechnology and how similar practices have been, and could be, used to address the societal implications of other emerging technologies, such as synthetic biology.

PEN was selected as the primary critical and theoretically relevant case because the institution had characteristics that were "particularly suitable for illuminating and extending relationships and logic among constructs," in the words of Eisenhardt and Graebner (2007). Additionally, Flyvbjerg (2006) writes well-chosen case studies retain substantial power to inform the illumination of key concepts of interest. PEN was founded in April 2005 with an initial $3 million, two-year grant from the Philadelphia-based institution The Pew Charitable Trusts, which had previously supported similar projects focused on the policy implications of agricultural biotechnology and climate change (The Pew Charitable Trusts, n.d.; Pew Center on Global Climate Change, 2013; Project on Emerging Nanotechnologies, 2005d). PEN's institutional home was at the Woodrow Wilson International Center for Scholars in Washington, DC. The Wilson Center is a quasi-governmental institution serving as a "living memorial" to President Wilson, most closely resembling a non-governmental think tank in terms of its operating structure, outputs, and organizational goals (Woodrow Wilson International Center for Scholars, n.d.).

PEN's mission statement notes that the organization was "dedicated to helping ensure that as nanotechnologies advance, possible risks are minimized, public and consumer engagement remains strong, and the potential benefits of these new technologies are realized" (Project on Emerging Nanotechnologies, n.d.). In addition to its staff, PEN drew on the expertise of a small group of external advisors, along with a wide range of subject matter experts and other researchers that it supported or contracted with to prepare various analyses related to nanotechnology policy. Most of PEN's substantive work was completed by the end of 2010, having received a second round of funding from Pew in early 2008, bringing its total budget to approximately $6 million over a six-year time period.

Using its freedom to act largely independently within the Wilson Center, PEN produced a substantive body of material that contributed to its overall mission of "helping business, government and the public anticipate and manage the possible health and environmental implications of nanotechnology" (Project on Emerging Nanotechnologies, n.d.). PEN's extended mission statement further emphasized:

> Our goal is to inform the debate and to create an active public and policy dialogue. It is not an advocate either for, or against, particular nano-technologies. We seek to ensure that as these technologies are developed, potential human health and environmental risks are anticipated, properly understood, and effectively managed.
>
> (Project on Emerging Nanotechnologies, n.d.)

PEN's explicit goal was not to take a particular policy position, have a specific law enacted, or advance a rule interpretation. Instead, PEN's principal goal was broader and more diffuse: as they state, "to inform the debate and to create an active public and policy dialogue." While the impact of this type of outcome is harder to measure and track, it does speak to the underlying driver animating PEN's work of the need to create a strong evidence base for nanotechnology policymaking and to foster a more robust discussion around complex technology, policy, and societal issues.

Of course, PEN was not the only organization involved with these issues during that period of time. Another prominent organization operating at the time was ICON, an offshoot of the Center for Biological and Environmental Nanotechnology (CBEN) based at Rice University in Houston, Texas. CBEN was one manifestation of Smalley's desire to advance the potentially beneficial aspects of nanotechnology, striving to make scientific progress on the positive applications of nanotechnology. Alternatively, ICON was devoted to examining the scientific dimensions of nanotechnology's potential negative implications. Led by Executive Director Vicki Colvin and Director Kristen Kulinowski, ICON was founded in 2004, with most of its work taking place during a period similar to PEN, through 2010. ICON's activities started to wind down some time afterwards, with its website becoming a static record of its efforts as of 2014. ICON's mission statement explicitly noted the organization's focus on addressing the potential risks that could arise with respect to nanotechnology. The statement reads that ICON, as a multi-stakeholder organization, had the purpose "to develop and communicate information regarding potential environmental and health risks of nanotechnology, thereby fostering risk reduction while maximizing societal benefit" (International Council on Nanotechnology, 2009).

However, a number of central governance differences made ICON different from PEN. First, unlike PEN, ICON was a membership organization, with companies and other NGOs paying to formally join and help steer the institution. Second, in addition to its Executive Committee, ICON's efforts were formally overseen by its Advisory Board, which consisted of balanced membership from its four participating stakeholder groups: government, academia, industry, and NGOs. A number of interviews pointed out that the Advisory Board mostly worked through a consensus process, thereby requiring formal approval and buy-in by all of the organization's key stakeholders for any of the projects ICON undertook. Finally, as ICON was primarily focused on the scientific dimensions of nanotechnology risk assessment, it had less of an explicit public outreach role than PEN did, which led to some divergence as to how the two institutions operated.

Additionally, unlike PEN, when ICON closed down it did not transition its focus to other emerging technologies. After PEN closed in 2010, an expansion of topical focus took place at the Wilson Center to examine a broader array of science and technology issues. This led to the creation of the Science and Technology Innovation Program (STIP), which was designed to serve as an umbrella organizational structure, housing a wide range of activities associated with emerging issues in science and technology policy. STIP's mission became to focus "on emerging technologies and the critical choices innovation presents to public policy" and "to explore the scientific and technological frontier, stimulating discovery and bringing new tools to bear on public policy challenges that emerge as science advances" (Science and Technology Innovation Program, n.d.). The Sclove report (2010) cited earlier was published under the auspices of STIP, and STIP was one of the five founding institutional members of the ECAST network mentioned earlier. Since its formation, STIP has produced analysis that looks across the science and technology policy landscape, such as examining the long-term policy issues associated with geoengineering (Olson, 2011), challenges associated with overseeing the "deep web" on the Internet (Sui, Caverlee, and Rudesill, 2015), and how to improve public engagement on complex policy issues (Rejeski, Chaplin, and Olsonet, 2015).

Under the auspices of STIP a project called the Commons Lab was created to explore the policy implications of emerging social media and information and communications technology issues. The Commons Lab is based on the premise that "rapidly evolving communications, sensing, and mapping technologies have placed the extraordinary power of mass data collection and analysis into the hands of citizens, communities, governments, and businesses" and looks to ensure "that as these technologies are developed and deployed, the benefits are maximized and the potential ethical, legal, and social impacts are anticipated, properly understood, and effectively managed" (Commons Lab, n.d.). For example, reports from the Commons Lab project have addressed issues such as cybersecurity and crowdsourcing (Goolsby, 2013), the digital privacy of missing persons in disaster situations (Reidenberg et al., 2013), the reform of federal information technology policy (Bastian, 2012), and the increased technical ability to predict earthquake occurrences (Young et al., 2013).

One key element of this expanded programmatic focus under STIP was a project examining the potential societal implications of synthetic biology that emerged as a follow-on institutional analogue to PEN. Known as the Synthetic Biology Project, this subsequent effort drew on and applied many of the approaches that PEN had utilized. The mission statement of the Synthetic Biology Project echoes much of what is reflected in PEN's, noting that the project "aims to foster informed public and policy discourse concerning the advancement of synthetic biology" through the production of "independent, rigorous analysis that can inform critical decisions affecting the research, commercialization and use of synthetic biology . . . to help ensure that, as synthetic biology moves forward, possible risks are minimized and benefits maximized" (Synthetic Biology Project, n.d.). The Synthetic Biology Project was primarily supported through funding provided by the Alfred P. Sloan Foundation (Alfred P. Sloan Foundation, 2008), although in its later years it began to receive additional, activity-specific support from the National Science Foundation (NSF). Much like PEN, the Synthetic Biology Project created a host of publications and online inventories, and held multiple public events on a range of topics related to that emerging technology.

This book explores *how* PEN and these other organizations went about trying to develop a long-term perspective regarding emerging technologies in the United States. By illuminating these strategies, the intention is to help inform other similar efforts that may arise in the future. To summarize the in-depth analysis that is provided in subsequent chapters, Table 1.2 identifies the key strategies that emerge from this analysis. The efforts of these institutions are best organized using variations on the three main dimensions of the anticipatory

Table 1.2 Strategies for institutionalizing anticipatory governance

Foresight	Boundary-spanning	Communications and public engagement
• Bringing the future into the present • Regularly updating knowledge through repetition • Ensuring timeliness and capitalizing on the first mover advantage • Placing forward-looking information at the center and the periphery	• Leveraging expert credibility • Brokering partnerships and facilitating dialogue • Creating boundary objects	• Framing a clear message • Saturating the media landscape • Building a brand, institutionally and for key individuals • Combining scientific credibility with metaphorical language • Creating a "coherent design philosophy" • Experimenting with direct deliberation

governance framework: foresight, boundary-spanning, and a combination of communications and public engagement.

Book structure

Following this introductory chapter, Chapter 2 will provide additional background information on PEN and the other organizations examined, along with more details on the contextual environment within which these organizations functioned. This chapter also provides an overview of the empirical qualitative methodologies used in this research. Chapter 3 then discusses the conceptual framework of anticipatory governance in more detail, indicating how this idea has evolved in the literature and the relevance of the concept to other theories related to the policymaking process.

The next three chapters, in turn, explore the three constituent dimensions of anticipatory governance and how they are played out by PEN and the other entities studied in this book. Chapter 4 explores the foresight dimension, showing how PEN and others deployed a range of relevant strategies, such as finding ways of bringing views of nanotechnology's future into the present. Chapter 5 examines the role of boundary-spanning, indicating how institutions can position themselves to engage stakeholders from multiple perspectives by such tactics as leveraging expert credibility effectively and brokering partnerships. Chapter 6 discusses an expansive view of public engagement that spans activities ranging from communications to direct citizen deliberation. It also explores how PEN's media outreach efforts compare with those adopted by other institutions in the field. Each of these chapters situates the relevant dimension of anticipatory governance within the social science literature and integrates a diverse assortment of evidence from different source material.

The final chapter concludes by synthesizing the findings and identifies additional research questions that warrant further exploration. This chapter also highlights a set of overarching and cross-cutting operational, conceptual, and societal lessons that can be gleaned from this research. These lessons include the importance of providing a protected space for individual and institutional experimentation, highlighting the value of taking a systems-based approach to policy analysis, and the realization that attempting to replicate or evaluate the success of any organization can be confounded by a number of factors. A subsequent methodological appendix provides further detail on the qualitative research approaches utilized throughout the book.

In sum, this book attempts to advance contemporaneous debates in science and technology policy in a number of dimensions. First, it helps build connections between theory and practice by demonstrating how the conceptual framework of anticipatory governance can be applied and institutionalized in practice. In doing so, it aims to provide a deeper understanding of the strategies utilized by high profile NGOs in the field. Second, following a long tradition in science and technology policy scholarship using case study methodologies of key institutional actors, it documents and provides a detailed account of the efforts undertaken by these organizations working to shape and influence how emerging technologies are conceptualized in the United States. This is particularly germane, given that many of the entities discussed here have closed down or are in the final phases of their research activities. Finally, this book is intended to inform future efforts to anticipate the societal implications of emerging technologies, a contribution that is particularly essential given the expected rapid acceleration of new areas of technological development in the coming years.

Bibliography

Alencar, M., Porter, A., and Antunes, A. (2007). Nanopatenting Patterns in Relation to Product Life Cycle. *Technological Forecasting and Social Change*, 74(9), 1661–1680.

Alfred P. Sloan Foundation. (2008, December 18). *Alfred P. Sloan Foundation Funds New Synthetic Biology Initiative to Examine Societal Issues*. Retrieved November 16, 2015, from Alfred P. Sloan Foundation: www.sloan.org/fileadmin/media/files/press/alfred_p_sloan_foundation_funds_new_synthetic_biology_initiative_to_examine_societal_issues.pdf

Andrianantoandro, E., Basu, S., Karig, D. K., and Weiss, R. (2006). Synthetic Biology: New Engineering Rules for an Emerging Discipline. *Molecular Systems Biology*, 2(1), 1–14.

Anton, P. S., Silberglitt, R., and Schneider, J. (2001). *The Global Technology Revolution: Bio/Nano/Materials Trends and Their Synergies with Information Technology by 2015*. Santa Monica, CA: RAND.

Bainbridge, W. S., and Roco, M. C. (Eds.). (2006). *Managing Nano-Bio-Info-Cogno Innovations: Converging Technologies in Society*. Dordrecht, The Netherlands: Springer.

Bainbridge, W. S., and Roco, M. C. (Eds.). (2015). *Handbook of Science and Technology Convergence*. Dordrecht, The Netherlands: Springer.

Barben, D., Fisher, E., Selin, C., and Guston, D. H. (2008). Anticipatory Governance of Nanotechnology: Foresight, Engagement, Integration. In E. J. Hackett, O. Amsterdamska, M. Lynch, J. Wajcman (Eds.), *The Handbook of Science and Technology Studies*, (3rd ed.). (pp. 979–1000). Cambridge, MA: The MIT Press.

Barkakati, N., and Persons, T. M. (2013, May). Technology Assessment for the United States Congress: The Government Accountability Office's Center for Science, Technology, and Engineering. *Technikfolgenabschatzung—Theorie und Praxis*, 1(22), 94–96.

Bastian, Z. (2012). *Too Big to Succeed: The Need for Federal IT Reform*. Washington, DC: Woodrow Wilson International Center for Scholars.

Benn, T., and Westerhoff, P. (2008). Nanoparticle Silver Released into Water from Commercially Available Sock Fabrics. *Environmental Science and Technology*, 42(11), 4133–4139.

Bennett, I., and Sarewitz, D. (2006, December). Too Little, Too Late? Research Policies on the Societal Implications of Nanotechnology in the United States. *Science as Culture*, 15(4), 309–325.

Bergeson, L. L. (2012, June 23). *Recent Developments in NRDC's Case Concerning Conditional Registration of Nanosilver*. Retrieved November 10, 2015, from Nano and Other Emerging Chemical Technologies Blog: http://nanotech.lawbc.com/2012/06/recent-developments-in-nrdcs-case-concerning-epas-conditional-registration-of-nanosilver/

Bimber, B. (1996). *The Politics of Expertise in Congress: The Rise and Fall of the Office of Technology Assessment*. Albany, NY: State University of New York Press.

Blaser, S. A., Scheringer, M., MacLeod, M., and Hungerbuhler, K. (2008, February 15). Estimation of Cumulative Aquatic Exposure and Risk Due to Silver: Contribution of Nano-Functionalized Plastics and Textiles. *Science of The Total Environment, 390*(2–3), 396–409.

Bonner, J. C., Silva, R. M., Taylor, A. J., Brown, J. M., Hilderbrand, S. C., Castranova, V., Porter, D., Elder, A., Oberdorster, G., Harkema, J. R., Bramble, L. A., Kavanagh, T. J., Botta, D., Nel, A., Pinkerton, K. E. (2013, May 6). Interlaboratory Evaluation of Rodent Pulmonary Responses to Engineered Nanomaterials: The NIEHS NanoGo Consortium. *Environmental Health Perspectives, 121*(6), 676–682.

Bosso, C. J. (Ed.). (2010). Governing Uncertainty: Environmental Regulation in the Age of Nanotechnology. Washington, DC: Routledge.

Bosso, C. J. (2013, June). The Enduring Embrace: The Regulatory Ancien Regimer and Governance of Nanomaterials in the U.S. Nanotechnology Law and Business, 9(4), 381–392.

Bosso, C., and Rodrigues, R. (2006). Organizing around Emerging Issues: Interest Groups and the Making of Nanotechnology Policy. In A. Cigler, and B. Loomis (Eds.), *Interest Group Politics*, (7th ed.). (pp. 366–388). Washington, DC: CQ Press.

Bueno, O. (2004). The Drexler-Smalley Debate on Nanotechnology: Incommensurability at Work? *HYLE—International Journal for Philosophy of Chemistry, 10*(2), 83–98.

Cameron, D. E., Bashor, C. J., and Collins, J. J. (2014, May). A Brief History of Synthetic Biology. *Nature Review Microbiology, 12*(5), 381–390.

Canady, R. A. (2010). The Uncertainty of Nanotoxicology: Report of a Society for Risk Analysis Workshop. *Risk Analysis, 30*(11), 1663–1670.

Center for Food Safety. (2015, July 27). *Groups Sue EPA over Faulty Approval of Nanotechnology Pesticide*. Retrieved October 29, 2015, from Center for Food Safety: www.centerforfoodsafety.org/press-releases/3995/groups-sue-epa-over-faulty-approval-of-nanotechnology-pesticide#

Center for Nanotechnology in Society, University of California, Santa Barbara. (2007, November 16). *Nanotechnology and Occupational Health and Safety Conference*. Retrieved November 10, 2015, from University of California, Santa Barbara: www.cns.ucsb.edu/nano-and-occupational-health-and-safety-conference-nov-2007-ucsb/program

Choi, H., and Mody, C. H. (2009, February). The Long History of Molecular Electronics: Microelectronics Origins of Nanotechnology. *Social Studies of Science, 39*(1), 11–50.

Choi, J.-Y., Ramachandran, G., and Kandlikar, M. (2009). The Impact of Toxicity Testing Costs on Nanomaterial Regulation. *Environmental Science and Technology, 43*(9), 2030–2034.

Church, G. (2015, December 3). Encourage the Innovators. *Nature, 528*(7580), S7.

Church, G., and Regis, E. (2012). *Regenesis: How Synthetic Biology Will Reinvent Nature and Ourselves*. New York, NY: Basic Books.

Commons Lab. (n.d.). *About the Commons Lab*. Retrieved November 10, 2015, from Commons Lab: www.wilsoncommonslab.org/about

Conti, J. A., Killpack, K., Gerritzen, G., Huang, L., Mircheva, M., Delmas, M., Herr Harthorn, B., Appelbaum, R. P., Holden, P. A. (2008). Health and Safety Practices in the Nanomaterials Workplace: Results from an International Survey. *Environmental Science and Technology, 42*, 3155–3162.

Cozzens, S. E., and Wetmore, J. M. (Eds.). (2011). *Nanotechnology and the Challenges of Equity, Equality, and Development.* Dordrecht, The Netherlands: Springer.

Davies, J. C. (2009). *Oversight of Next Generation Nanotechnology.* Washington, DC: Project on Emerging Nanotechnologies.

Doudna, J. A., and Charpentier, E. (2014, November 28). The New Frontier of Genome Engineering with CRISPR-Cas9. *Science, 346*(6213), 1077–1087.

Drexler, K. E. (1986). *Engines of Creation: The Coming Era of Nanotechnology.* New York, NY: Anchor Books.

Eisenhardt, K. M., and Graebner, M. E. (2007). Theory Building from Cases: Opportunities and Challenges. *Academy of Management Journal, 50*(1), 25–32.

Environmental Protection Agency. (2008, March 5). *EPA Fines Technology Company $208,000 for 'Nano Coating' Pesticide on Computer Peripherals.* Retrieved November 14, 2015, from Environmental Protection Agency: http://yosemite.epa.gov/opa/admpress.nsf/0/16a190492f2f25d585257403005c2851?OpenDocument

Environmental Protection Agency. (2015a, October 8). *Antimicrobial Pesticides.* Retrieved November 16, 2015, from Environmental Protection Agency: www2.epa.gov/pesticides/antimicrobial-pesticides

Environmental Protection Agency. (2015b, March 25). *EPA Responds to Petition on Nanoscale Regulation.* Retrieved October 29, 2015, from Environmental Protection Agency: www2.epa.gov/pesticides/epa-responds-petition-nanoscale-silver-regulation

Epstein, G. L. (2009, March 31). *Restart the Congressional Office of Technology Assessment: Congress Pushed OTA's "Pause" Key in 1995. It's Time to Press "Play" Once Again.* Retrieved November 16, 2015, from Science Progress: http://scienceprogress.org/2009/03/restart-ota

Erickson, B., Singh, R., and Winters, P. (2011, September 2). Synthetic Biology: Regulating Industry Uses of New Biotechnologies. *Science, 333*(6047), 1254–1256.

Esvelt, K. M., Smidler, A. L., Catteruccia, F., and Church, G. M. (2014, July 17). Concerning RNA-guided Gene Drives for the Alteration of Wild Populations. *eLife*, 1–49.

Expert and Citizen Assessment of Science and Technology. (n.d.). *About.* Retrieved November 2015, from Expert and Citizen Assessment of Science and Technology: http://ecastnetwork.org/about/

Feynman, R. P. (1960, February). There's Plenty of Room at the Bottom: An Invitation to Enter a New Field of Physics. *Caltech Engineering and Science, 23*(5), 22–36.

Fischhoff, B. (2015, October 30). The Realities of Risk–Cost–Benefit Analysis. *Science, 350*(6260), 527.

Fisher, E., and Mahajan, R. L. (2006, February). Contradictory Intent? US Federal Legislation on Integrating Societal Concerns into Nanotechnology Research and Development. *Science and Public Policy, 33*(1), 5–16.

Flyvbjerg, B. (2006). Five Misunderstandings About Case-Study Research. *Qualitative Inquiry, 12*(2), 219–245.

Gibson, D. G., Glass, J. I., Lartigue, C., Noskov, V. N., Chuang, R.-Y., Algire, M. A., Benders, G. A., Montague, M. G., Ma, L., Moodie, M. M., Merryman, C., Vashee, S., Krishnakumar, R., Assad-Garcia, N., Andrews-Pfannkoch, C., Denisova, E. A., Young, L., Qi, Z-Q., Segall-Shapiro, T. H., Calvey, C. H., Parmar, P. P., Hutchison III, C. A., Smith, H. O., Venter, J. (2010, July 2). Creation of a Bacterial Cell Controlled by a Chemically Synthesized Genome. *Science, 329*(5987), 52–56.

Goolsby, R. (2013). *On Cybersecurity, Crowdsourcing, and Social Cyber-Attack.* Washington, DC: Science and Technology Innovation Program, Woodrow Wilson International Center for Scholars.

Government Accountability Office. (2004). *Cybersecurity for Critical Infrastructure Protection.* Washington, DC: Government Accountability Office.

Government Accountability Office. (2005). *Protecting Structures and Improving Communications during Wildland Fires.* Washington, DC: Government Accountability Office.

Government Accountability Office. (2010). *Explosives Detection Technologies to Protect Passenger Rail.* Washington, DC: Government Accountability Office.

Government Accountability Office. (2011a). *Climate Engineering: Technical Status, Future Directions, and Potential Responses.* Washington, DC: Government Accountability Office.

Government Accountability Office. (2011b). *Neutron Detection: Alternatives to Using Helium-3.* Washington, DC: Governmental Accountability Office.

Government Accountability Office. (2014). *Nanomanufacturing: Emergence and Implications for U.S. Competitiveness, the Environment, and Human Health.* Washington, DC: Government Accountability Office.

Government Accountability Office. (2015a). *Nuclear Reactors: Status and Challenges in Development and Deployment of New Commercial Concepts.* Washington, DC: Government Accountability Office.

Government Accountability Office. (2015b). *Water in the Energy Sector: Reducing Freshwater Use in Hydraulic Fracturing and Thermoelectric Power Plant Cooling.* Washington, DC: Government Accountability Office.

Government Accountability Office. (2015c). *3D Printing: Opportunities, Challenges, and Policy Implications of Additive Manufacturing.* Washington, DC: Government Accountability Office.

Government Accountability Office. (n.d.). *Technology Assessment.* Retrieved November 15, 2015, from www.gao.gov/technology_assessment/key_reports#t=2

Graham, S. (2013, January 16). *Circuit Chews Over EPA Approval of Fabric Pesticide.* Retrieved November 14, 2015, from The Recorder: www.therecorder.com/id=1202584762250?slreturn=20151016142138

Guston, D. H. (2011). Anticipatory Governance: A Strategic Vision for Building Reflexivity into Emerging Technologies. *Presentation at Resilience 2011.* Tempe, AZ.

Guston, D. H. (2014). Understanding "Anticipatory Governance." *Social Studies of Science, 44*(2), 218–242.

Haseloff, J., and Ajioka, J. (2009, August 6). Synthetic Biology: History, Challenges, and Prospects. *Interface: Journal of The Royal Society, 6*(S4), S389–S391.

Heinemann, M., and Panke, S. (2006). Synthetic Biology—Putting Engineering into Biology. *Bioinformatics, 22*(22), 2790–2799.

HeiQ Materials AG. (2011, December 1). *US EPA Approves Registration of Effective New HeiQ AGS-20 Antimicrobial.* Retrieved November 15, 2015, from HeiQ: http://heiq.com/news/news-menu/us-epa-approves-registration-of-effective-new-heiq-ags-20-antimicrobial/?selmenuid=2199

Hett, A. (2004). *Nanotechnology: Small Matter, Many Unknowns.* Zurich, Switzerland: Swiss Reinsurance Company.

Hicks, A. L., Gilbertson, L. M., Yamani, J. S., Theis, T. L., and Zimmerman, J. B. (2015). Life Cycle Payback Estimates of Nanosilver Enabled Textiles under Different Silver Loading, Release, and Laundering Scenarios Informed by Literature Review. *Environmental Science and Technology, 49*(13), 7529–7542.

Hirano, S. (2009, July). A Current Overview of Health Effect Research on Nanoparticles. *Environmental Health and Preventive Medicine, 14*(4), 223–225.

Hodge, G. A., Bowman, D. M., and Maynard, A. D. (2010). Introduction: The Regulatory Challenges for Nanotechnologies. In G. A. Hodge, D. M. Bowman, and A. D. Maynard (Eds.), *International Handbook on Regulating Nanotechnologies* (pp. 3–24). Cheltenham, UK: Edward Elgar Publishing Limited.

Holt, R. (2009, April 29). *Op-Ed: Reversing the Congressional Science Lobotomy.* Retrieved November 16, 2015, from Wired: www.wired.com/2009/04/fromthefields-holt/

iGEM Foundation. (n.d.). *About: Giant Jamboree.* Retrieved October 29,2015, from iGEM Foundation: http://2015.igem.org/Giant_Jamboree/About

International Council on Nanotechnology. (2009a, October). *ICON Fact Sheet.* Retrieved September 17, 2015, from International Council on Nanotechnology: http://cohesion.rice.edu/centersandinst/icon/emplibrary/ICON%20Fact%20Sheet_102609.pdf

Invernizzi, N. (2011, June). Nanotechnology Between the Lab and the Shop Floor: What are the Effects on Labor? *Journal of Nanoparticle Research, 13*(6), 2249–2268.

Invernizzi, N., and Foladori, G. (2005). Nanotechnology and the Developing World: Will Nanotechnology Overcome Poverty or Widen Disparities? *Nanotechnology Law and Business, 2*(3), 294–303.

Johnson, A. (2004). The End of Pure Science: Science Policy from Bayh-Dole to the NNI. In D. Baird, A. Nordmann, and J. Schummer (Eds.), *Discovering the Nanoscale* (pp. 217–230). Amsterdam, The Netherlands: IOS Press.

Kaplan, S., and Radin, J. (2011, August). Bounding an Emerging Technology: Para-Scientific Media and the Drexler-Smalley Debate about Nanotechnology. *Social Studies of Science, 41*(4), 457–485.

Keasling, J. D. (2014, July 17). Testimony on: "Policies to Spur Innovative Medical Breakthroughs from Laboratories to Patients." Washington, DC: United States House of Representatives, Committee on Science, Space, and Technology, Subcommittee on Research and Technology.

Khanna, V., Bakshi, B. R., and Lee, L. J. (2008). Carbon Nanofiber Production: Life Cycle Energy Consumption and Environmental Impact. *Journal of Industrial Ecology, 12*(3), 394–410.

Khushf, G. (2004). A Hierarchical Architecture for Nano-scale Science and Technology: Taking Stock of the Claims About Science Made By Advocates of NBIC Convergence. In D. Baird, A. Nordmann, and J. Schummer (Eds.), *Discovering the Nanoscale* (pp. 21–33). Amsterdam, The Netherlands: IOS Press.

Kim, E.-S. (2008). Directed Evolution: A Historical Exploration into an Evolutionary Experimental System of Nanobiotechnology, 1965–2006. *Minerva, 46*, 463–484.

Knezo, G. J. (2005). *Technology Assessment in Congress: History and Legislative Options.* RS21586. Washington, DC: Congressional Research Service.

Kunkle, G. C. (1995). New Challenge or the Past Revisited: The Office of Technology Assessment in Historical Context. *Technology in Society, 17*(2), 175–196.

Lane, N., and Kalil, T. (2005, Summer). The National Nanotechnology Initiative: Present at the Creation. *Issues in Science and Technology, XXI*(4), 49–54.

Lewinski, N., Colvin, V., and Drezek, R. (2008, January 28). Cytotoxicity of Nanoparticles. *Small, 4*(1), 26–49.

Linse, S., Cabaleiro-Lago, C., Xue, W.-F., Lynch, I., Lindman, S., Thulin, E., Radford, S. E., Dawson, K. A. (2007). Nucleation of Protein Fibrillation by Nanoparticles. *PNAS, 104*(21), 8691–8696.

Liu, X., Zhang, P., Li, X., Chen, H., Dang, Y., Larson, C., Roco, M. C., Wang, X. (2009). Trends for Nanotechnology Development in China, Russia, and India. *Journal of Nanoparticle Research, 11*(8), 1845–1866.

MacCormack, T. J., and Goss, G. G. (2008). Identifying and Predicting Biological Risks Associated with Manufactured Nanoparticles in Aquatic Ecosystems. *Journal of Industrial Ecology, 12*(3), 286–296.

McCray, P. (2005). Will Small Be Beautiful? Making Policies for Our Nanotech Future. *History and Technology, 21*(2), 177–203.

McCray, P. (2009). From Lab to iPod: A Story of Discovery and Commercialization in the Post-Cold War Era. *Technology and Culture, 50*(1), 58–81.

McGann, J. G. (2015). *2014 Global Go To Think Tank Index Report.* Philadelphia, PA: University of Pennsylvania.

Maclurcan, D. C. (2005, October 19). *Nanotechnology and Developing Countries—Part 2: What Realities?* Retrieved November 17, 2015, from AZojono—Journal of Nanotechnology Online: www.azonano.com/article.aspx?ArticleID=1429

Marchant, G. E., and Sylvester, D. J. (2006). Transnational Models for Regulation of Nanotechnology. *Journal of Law, Medicine, and Ethics, 34*(4), 714–725.

Marchant, G. E., Abbott, K. W., and Allenby, B. (Eds.). (2013). *Innovative Governance Models for Emerging Technologies.* Cheltenham, UK: Edward Elgar Publishing Limited.

Marchant, G. E., Allenby, B. R., and Herkert, J. R. (Eds.). (2011). *The Growing Gap: Between Emerging Technologies and Legal-Ethical Oversight, The Pacing Problem.* Dordrecht, The Netherlands: Springer.

Mody, C. (2004). Small, but Determined: Technological Determinism in Nanoscience. *HYLE—International Journal for Philosophy of Chemistry, 10*, 101–130.

Mody, C. (2011). *Instrumental Community, Probe Microscopy, and the Path to Nanotechnology.* Cambridge, MA: The MIT Press.

Mody, C., and McCray, W. P. (2009, April 6). *Big Whig History and Nano Narratives: Effective Innovation Policy Needs the Historical Dimension.* Retrieved November 17, 2015, from Science Progress: http://scienceprogress.org/2009/04/big-whig-history-and-nano-narratives

Morgan, M. G., and Peha, J. M. (Eds.). (2003). *Science and Technology Advice for Congress.* Washington, DC: Resources for the Future Press.

Morris, J. T. (2012). *Risk, Language, and Power: The Nanotechnology Environmental Policy Case.* Lanham, MA: Lexington Books.

Morris, J. T., Willis, J., De Martinis, D., Hansen, B., Laursen, H., Sintes, J. R., Kearns, P., Gonzalez, M. (2011). Science Policy Considerations for Responsible Nanotechnology Decisions. *Nature Nanotechnology, 6*(2), 73–77.

National Nanotechnology Initiative. (n.d.). *Nanotechnology 101: What Is It and How It Works.* Retrieved November 17, 2015, from www.nano.gov/nanotech-101/what

National Research Council. (2009a). *Persistent Forecasting of Disruptive Technologies.* Washington, DC: National Academies Press.

National Research Council. (2009b). *Review of the Federal Strategy for Nanotechnology-Related Environmental Health and Safety Research.* Washington, DC: National Academies Press.

National Research Council. (2012). *A Research Strategy for Environmental, Health, and Safety Aspects of Engineered Nanomaterials.* Washington, DC: The National Academies Press.

National Science and Technology Council. (2011a). *National Nanotechnology Initiative Environmental, Health, and Safety Research Strategy.* Washington, DC: Office of Science and Technology Policy.

National Science and Technology Council. (2011b). *National Nanotechnology Initiative Strategic Plan*. Washington, DC: Office of Science and Technology Policy.

National Science and Technology Council. (2012). *The Networking and Information Technology Research and Development (NITRD) Program 2012 Strategic Plan*. Washington, DC: Office of Science and Technology Policy.

National Science and Technology Council. (2015). *The National Nanotechnology Initiative: Supplement to the President's 2016 Budget*. Washington, DC: Office of Science and Technology Policy.

Oberdorster, G., Oberdorster, E., and Oberdorster, J. (2005). Nanotoxicology: An Emerging Discipline Evolving from Studies of Ultrafine Particles. *Environmental Health Perspectives, 113*(7), 823–839.

Oberdorster, G., Stone, V., and Donaldson, K. (2007). Toxicology of Nanoparticles: A Historical Perspective. *Nanotoxicology, 1*(1), 2–25.

Olson, R. L. (2011). *Geoengineering for Decision Makers*. Washington, DC: Science and Technology Innovation Program, Woodrow Wilson International Center for Scholars.

Oye, K. A., Esvelt, K., Appleton, E., Catteruccia, F., Church, G., Kuiken, T., Lightfoot, S. B-Y., McNamara, J., Smidler, A., Collins, J. P. (2014, August 8). Regulating Gene Drives. *Science, 345*(6197), 626–628.

Parker, R. A., and Appelbaum, R. P. (Eds.). (2012). *Can Emerging Technologies Make a Difference in Development?* New York, NY: Routledge.

Pew Center on Global Climate Change. (2013). *Pew Center on Global Climate Change*. Retrieved February 28, 2013, from www.pewclimate.org

Poland, C. A., Duffin, R., Kinloch, I., Maynard, A., Wallace, W. A., Seaton, A., Stone, V., Brown, S., MacNee, W., Donaldson, K. (2008). Carbon Nanotubes Introduced into the Abdominal Cavity of Mice Show Asbestos-like Pathogenicity in a Pilot Study. *Nature Nanotechnology, 3*(7), 423–428.

Presidential Commission for the Study of Bioethical Issues. (2010). *New Directions: The Ethics of Synthetic Biology and Emerging Technologies*. Washington, DC: Presidential Commission for the Study of Bioethical Issues.

Project on Emerging Nanotechnologies. (2005d, April 27). *Pew Charitable Trusts, Wilson Center Launch Project on Emerging Nanotechnologies*. Retrieved November 15, 2015, from Project on Emerging Nanotechnologies: www.nanotechproject.org/process/assets/files/6034/042705nanotechnology_project.pdf

Project on Emerging Nanotechnologies. (n.d.). *About the Project on Emerging Nanotechnologies—Mission*. Retrieved November 17,2015, from Project on Emerging Nanotechnologies: www.nanotechproject.org/about/mission

Redford, K. H., Adams, W., and Mace, G. M. (2013, April). Synthetic Biology and Conservation of Nature: Wicked Problems and Wicked Solutions. *PLOS Biology, 11*(4), 1–4.

Reidenberg, J. R., Gellman, R., Debelak, J., Elewa, A., and Liu, N. (2013). *Privacy and Missing Persons after Nature Disasters*. New York, NY and Washington, DC: Center on Law and Information Policy, Fordham Law School and Science and Technology Innovation Program, Woodrow Wilson International Center for Scholars.

Rejeski, D., Chaplin, H., and Olson, R. (2015). *Addressing Complexity with Playable Models*. Washington, DC: Science and Technology Innovation Program.

Renn, O., and Roco, M. (2006a). *White Paper on Nanotechnology Risk Governance*. Geneva, Switzerland: International Risk Governance Council.

Rich, A. (2004). *Think Tanks, Public Policy, and the Politics of Expertise.* Cambridge, UK: Cambridge University Press.

Roco, M. C. (2007). National Nanotechnology Initiative—Past, Present, Future. In W. A. Goddard III, D. W. Brenner, S. E. Lyshevski, and G. J. Iafrate (Eds.), *Handbook of Nanoscience, Engineering, and Technology*, 2nd ed. (pp. 3–1, 3–26). London, UK: Taylor & Francis.

Roco, M. C. (2008). Possibilities for Global Governance of Converging Technologies. *Journal of Nanoparticle Research, 10*(1), 11–29.

Roco, M. C., Bainbridge, W. S., Tonn, B., and Whitesides, G. (Eds.). (2013). *Convergence of Knowledge, Technology, and Society: Beyond Convergence of Nano-Bio-Info-Cognitive Technologies.* Dordrecht, The Netherlands: Springer.

Roco, M. C., Harthorn, B., Guston, D., and Shapira, P. (2011). Innovative and Responsible Governance of Nanotechnology for Societal Development. In M. C. Roco, C. A. Mirkin, and M. C. Hersam (Eds.), *Nanotechnology Research Directions for Societal Needs in 2020: Retrospective and Outlook* (pp. 561–618). Dordrecht, The Netherlands: Springer.

Sadowski, J. (2012, October 26). *The Much-Needed and Sane Congressional Office That Gingrich Killed Off and We Need Back.* Retrieved November 16, 2015, from The Atlantic: www.theatlantic.com/technology/archive/2012/10/the-much-needed-and-sane-congressional-office-that-gingrich-killed-off-and-we-need-back/264160/#.UI7c7hygl_A.wordpress

Salamanca-Buentello, F., Persad, D. L., Court, E. B., Martin, D. K., Daar, A. S., and Singer, P. A. (2005, May). Nanotechnology and the Developing World. *PLoS Medicine, 2*(5), 383–386.

Sandler, R., and Kay, W. (2006, Winter). The National Nanotechnology Initiative and the Social Good. *Journal of Law, Medicine and Ethics, 34*(4), 675–681.

Sargent Jr., J. F. (2012). *Nanotechnology: A Policy Primer.* Washington, DC: Congressional Research Service.

Sass, J., and Wu, M. (2013). *Superficial Safeguards: Most Pesticides Are Approved by Flawed EPA Process.* Washington, DC: National Resources Defense Council.

Schwille, P. (2011, September 2). Bottom-Up Synthetic Biology: Engineering in a Tinker's World. *Science, 333*(6047), 1252–1254.

Science. (2008). Science and the 2008 Campaign: A Full Serving of Science Awaits the Next President. *Science, 322*(5901), 520–521.

Science. (2012, October 26). Congratulations! Now Get to Work. *Science, 338*(6106), 456–461.

Science and Technology Innovation Program. (n.d.). *About the Science and Technology Innovation Program.* Retrieved November 18, 2015, from Science and Technology Innovation Program: www.wilsoncenter.org/about-stip

Sclove, R. (2010). *Reinventing Technology Assessment: A 21st Century Model.* Washington, DC: Woodrow Wilson International Center for Scholars.

Shapira, P., and Youtie, J. (2008). Emergence of Nanodistricts in the United States: Path Dependency or New Opportunities? *Economic Development Quarterly, 22*(3), 187–199.

Shapira, P., Youtie, J., and Kay, L. (2011, December). National Innovation Systems and the Globalization of Nanotechnology Innovation. *Journal of Technology Transfer, 36*(6), 587–604.

Shapira, P., Youtie, J., and Li, Y. (2015). Social Science Contributions Compared in Synthetic Biology and Nanotechnology. *Journal of Responsible Innovation, 2*(1), 143–148.

Shatkin, J. A., and North, W. (2010). Perspectives on Risks of Nanomaterials and Nanotechnologies: Advancing the Science. *Risk Analysis, 30*(11), 1627–1633.

Shatkin, J. A., Abbott, L. C., Bradley, A. E., Canady, R. A., Guidotti, T., Kulinowski, K. M., Lofstedt, R. E., Louis, G., MacDonald, M., Maynard, A. D. (2010). Nano Risk Analysis: Advancing the Science for Nanomaterials Risk Management. *Risk Analysis, 30*(11), 1680–1687.

Singer, P., Salamanca-Buentello, F., and Daar, A. (2005, Summer). Harnessing Nanotechnology to Improve Global Equity. *Issues in Science and Technology, 21*(4), 57–58.

Smalley, R. E. (2001, September). Of Chemistry, Love and Nanobots. *Scientific American, 285*(3), 76–77.

Song, Y., Li, X., and Du, X. (2009). Exposure to Nanoparticles is related to Pleural Effusion, Pulmonary Fibrosis, and Granuloma. *European Respiratory Journal, 34*(3), 559–567.

Street, A., Sustich, R., Duncan, J., and Savage, N. (2014). *Nanotechnology Applications for Clean Water: Solutions for Improving Water Quality*, (2nd ed.). Oxford, UK: William Andrew.

Sui, D., Caverlee, J., and Rudesill, D. (2015). *The Deep Web and the Darknet: A Look Inside the Internet's Massive Black Box*. Washington, DC: Science and Technology Innovation Program.

Suttmeier, R. P., Cao, C., and Simon, D. F. (2006). "Knowledge Innovation" and the Chinese Academy of Sciences. *Science, 312*(5970), 58–59.

Synthetic Biology Project. (2015d). *U.S. Trends in Synthetic Biology Research Funding*. Washington, DC: Synthetic Biology Project, Woodrow Wilson International Center for Scholars.

Synthetic Biology Project. (n.d.). *About the Synthetic Biology Project*. Retrieved September 17, 2015, from Synthetic Biology Project: www.synbioproject.org/about/

Takagi, A., Hirose, A., Nishimura, T., Fukumori, N., Ogata, N., Ohashi, N., Kitajima, S., Kanno, J. (2008, February). Induction of Mesothelioma in p53+/-Mouse by Intraperitoneal Application of Multi-Wall Carbon Nanotube. *Journal of Toxicological Sciences, 33*(1), 105–116.

The Pew Charitable Trusts. (n.d.). *Agricultural Biotechnology*. Retrieved November 18, 2015, from The Pew Charitable Trusts: www.pewtrusts.org/en/archived-projects/agricultural-biotechnology

The Royal Society. (2004). *Nanoscience and Nanotechnologies: Opportunities and Uncertainties*. London, UK: The Royal Society.

The Royal Society. (2015). Synthetic Biology. Retrieved September 16, 2015, from The Royal Society: https://royalsociety.org/topics-policy/projects/synthetic-biology/

Toumey, C. (2008). Reading Feynman into Nanotechnology: A Text for a New Science. *Techne, 13*(3), 133–168.

United States Congress. (2003, December 3). *21st Century Nanotechnology Research and Development Act*. Retrieved November 19, 2015, from Government Printing Office: www.gpo.gov/fdsys/pkg/PLAW-108publ153/html/PLAW-108publ153.htm

Valsami-Jones, E., and Lynch, I. (2015, October 23). How Safe Are Nanomaterials? *Science, 350*(6259), 388–389.

Vinson, V., and Pennisi, E. (2011, September 2). The Allure of Synthetic Biology. *Science, 333*(6047), 1235.

Wade, N. (2015, December 4). Scientists Call for Moratorium on Editing of Human Genome. *The New York Times*, p. A1.

Wardak, A., Gorman, M. E., Swami, N., and Deshpande, S. (2008). Identification of Risks in the Life Cycle of Nanotechnology-Based Products. *Journal of Industrial Ecology, 12*(3), 435–448.

Wiesner, M. R., Lowry, G. V., Alvarez, P., Dionysiou, D., and Biswas, P. (2006, July 15). Assessing the Risks of Manufactured Nanomaterials. *Environmental Science and Technology, 40*(14), 4336–4345.

Williams, R. A., Kulinowski, K. M., White, R., and Louis, G. (2010). Risk Characterization of Nanotechnology. *Risk Analysis, 30*(11), 1671–1679.

Woodrow Wilson International Center for Scholars. (n.d.). *About the Wilson Center.* Retrieved November 18, 2015, from Woodrow Wilson International Center for Scholars: www.wilsoncenter.org/about-the-wilson-center

Worthington, R., Cavalier, D., Farooque, M., Gano, G., Geddes, H., Sander, S., Sittenfeld, D., Tomblin, D. (2012). *Technology Assessment and Public Participation: From TA to pTA.* Tempe, AZ: Expert and Citizen Assessment of Science and Technology (ECAST).

Xia, T., Hamilton, R. F., Bonner, J. C., Crandall, E. D., Elder, A., Fazlollahi, F., Girtsman, T. A., Kim, K., Mitra, S., Ntim, S. A., Orr, G., Tagmount, M., Taylor, A. J., Telesca, D., Tolic, A., Vulpe, C. D., Walker, A. J., Wang, X., Witzmann, F. A., Wu, N., Xie, Y., Zink, J. I., Nel, A., Holian, A. (2013, May 6). Interlaboratory Evaluation of in Vitro Cytotoxicity and Inflammatory Responses to Engineered Nanomaterials: The NIEHS NanoGo Consortium. *Environmental Health Perspectives, 121*(6), 683–690.

Yeh, B. J., and Lim, W. A. (2007, September). Synthetic Biology: Lessons from the History of Synthetic Organic Chemistry. *Nature Chemical Biology, 3*(9), 521–525.

Yildirimer, L., Thanh, N. T., Loizidou, M., and Seifalian, A. M. (2011, December). Toxicology and Clinical Potential of Nanoparticles. *Nanotoday, 6*(6), 585–607.

Young, J. C., Wald, D. J., Earle, P. S., and Shanley, L. A. (2013). *Transforming Earthquake Detection and Science Through Citizen Seismology.* Washington, DC: Science and Technology Innovation Program.

Youtie, J., Iacopetta, M., and Graham, S. (2008). Assessing the Nature of Nanotechnology: Can We Uncover an Emerging General Purpose Technology? *Journal of Technology Transfer, 33*(3), 315–329.

Youtie, J., Porter, A., Shapira, P., Tang, L., and Benn, T. (2011). The Use of Environmental, Health and Safety Research in Nanotechnology Research. *Journal of Nanoscience and Nanotechnology, 11*(8), 158–166.

Zhang, J. Y., Marris, C., and Rose, N. (2011). *The Transnational Governance of Synthetic Biology: Scientific Uncertainty, Cross-Borderness, and the "Art" of Governance.* London, UK: Center for the Study of Bioscience, Biomedicine, Biotechnology and Society, London School of Economics and Political Science.

2 The institutional context and research overview

Background on PEN, ICON, and the Synthetic Biology Project

Understanding the background, purpose, and contextual environment of these institutions is imperative before exploring the strategies that they deployed. As described in the previous chapter, PEN began its operations in 2005 with a $3 million grant from The Pew Charitable Trusts, which had previously funded a wide range of activities in public health, the environment, and social science research (Project on Emerging Nanotechnologies, 2005d). The Pew Charitable Trusts granted PEN a second tranche of $3 million in 2008, and PEN was the recipient of a smaller supplementary grant from the European Commission that same year to work on international nanotechnology policy issues as part of a larger research consortium. The majority of PEN's work ended in the middle of 2009, with all of the organization's formal activities winding down by the end of 2010. This six-year, over $6 million project had nine full-time staff members at its height, supported by more than a dozen part-time, temporary interns and expert consultants who authored most of PEN's formal reports. The Pew Charitable Trusts decided to fund PEN following a series of initial, informal discussions that led to the production of a series of issue-related white papers laying out the primary topics such an entity would address. This then led to a formal grant application and, as is typical for such grants in the philanthropic sector, eventual approval of this funding at the level of their board of trustees.

PEN's mission of linking foresight to policy in the area of nanotechnology is apparent in the first set of internal memos that were prepared to scope the potential project in late 2004. These memos pronounced nanotechnology as entering a period of "rapid change," with "guaranteed surprise" on the horizon. The rationale for establishing PEN was to "maintain a comprehensive upstream view of new research results, emerging products, [and] media coverage" and to "develop and implement strategies and policies to deal explicitly with novelty" (Rejeski, 2004a). These themes became embedded in the standard organizational description that PEN included with many of its outputs:

> Both the Wilson Center and The Pew Charitable Trusts believe there is a tremendous opportunity with nanotechnology to "get it right." Societies

have missed this chance with other new technologies and, by doing so, forfeited significant social, economic, and environmental benefits.

(Rejeski, 2006)

This theme of linking foresight with policy and research to "get it right" would carry through all of PEN's existence. It eventually became the unifying structure that the organization used to report back to The Pew Charitable Trusts about the progress of its work and activities, as PEN employed a tripartite categorization in its quarterly reports under the titles of "Better Oversight," "Better Foresight," and "Strategic Research."

Three senior staff members set the direction for the organization as a whole. David Rejeski, PEN's Director and later Director of the Synthetic Biology Project, had previous foresight and policy experience at the EPA, the Office of Science and Technology Policy (OSTP), and the Council on Environmental Quality. The Deputy Director was Julia Moore, who had previously worked in communications at the NSF. Andrew Maynard was the Chief Science Advisor, bringing experience as a scientist from the National Institute for Occupational Safety and Health (NIOSH). PEN also engaged a number of senior external authors to produce its substantive reports on policy and scientific issues; included among them were J. Clarence (Terry) Davies, who authored the original Toxic Substances Control Act (TSCA) while at the EPA, and Michael Taylor, who had government experience at FDA and the United States Department of Agriculture. Together, Davies and Taylor wrote six of the 19 major PEN reports and provided ongoing input and conceptual guidance for PEN's work.

In terms of its organizational structure, instead of being created as a stand-alone institution, PEN was based at the Woodrow Wilson International Center for Scholars in Washington, DC. The relationship between The Pew Charitable Trusts and the Wilson Center was consistently described as a "partnership" between the two organizations. Like many other projects that The Pew Charitable Trusts funded, PEN was housed at a larger institution for both the practical reason of providing more streamlined overhead and administrative services and for substantive reasons of conferring legitimacy on PEN's work—a benefit enhanced by the Wilson Center's reputation as a non-partisan institution.

Unlike most other Washington-based think tanks and research centers, the Wilson Center is a quasi-governmental, public–private institution. Established by Congress in 1968, it has a charter from the United States government to serve as the national memorial to President Woodrow Wilson. The Wilson Center receives an annual appropriation from Congress that amounts to roughly one-third of its total operating activities, with just over $10 million requested from Congress for fiscal year 2016 (Woodrow Wilson International Center for Scholars, 2015). The remaining funding comes from philanthropic and individual donors that are used to support the Wilson Center's many research programs and institutes (Woodrow Wilson International Center for Scholars, 2012).

All of this is to say that while the Center undertakes research like other independent think tanks—staffing the organization with experts on the topics it covers, producing substantive research, holding conferences and events—this quasi-governmental status requires that the Wilson Center research be non-partisan and ensures that the scholarship it undertakes is deliberately focused on informing policymaking. The Wilson Center is required to articulate its non-partisan approach annually during the budget cycle. This role is well known throughout government, from Capitol Hill to the federal agencies, and therefore, analysis from the Wilson Center is often treated with a degree of deference that is not always bestowed on to other NGO research organizations.

That is not to say that other think tanks are unable to achieve a reputation for impartiality, nor that the types of outputs from the Wilson Center differ greatly from these traditional non-governmental research organizations. Institutions such as the Brookings Institution, RAND Corporation, Council on Foreign Relations, and Center for Strategic and International Studies are all known for their ability to produce rigorous evidence and analysis that touch on a host of policy problems. The Wilson Center is often viewed similarly to these esteemed organizations, consistently ranking among the top think tanks globally. A survey of over 3,500 experts in 2014 placed the Wilson Center as the tenth top think tank globally and the fifth best think tank in the United States (McGann, 2015). Beyond fundraising and the requirement for producing non-partisan analysis, a large part of the difference between other think tanks and the Wilson Center comes down to the Center's narrative. With a national charter and unique standing as a national monument, the Wilson Center is able to express itself as reflecting President Wilson's ideals of bridging the academic–policy divide, with Woodrow Wilson having been the only American President to have earned a doctoral degree (Woodrow Wilson International Center for Scholars, n.d.). This unusual narrative, coupled with typical activities of a think tank, provides programs at the Wilson Center with multiple elements that they can highlight depending on different contexts. For instance, when providing expert testimony before Congress, a program representative can describe how research at the Wilson Center is truly being undertaken in the national interests. In scholarly forums, the Wilson Center can be framed as providing the highest quality subject matter expertise. Of course, these narratives are not mutually exclusive and are often interwoven to provide a multifaceted depiction of the Center's purpose.

To provide a visual of PEN's work over its lifecycle at the Wilson Center, Figure 2.1 presents a timeline of select key milestones, including releases of major reports, Congressional testimonies, and updates of the Consumer Products Inventory (CPI) that PEN released online. Note that as PEN was winding down, the focus of its work had already begun to shift from sole attention on nanotechnology to synthetic biology. This timeline shows three distinct clusters of major activity took place during PEN's period of operation. An early cluster of activity took place near the end of 2005 through early 2006, just a few months after the organization was formed. This period saw the launch of two of PEN's major public online inventories, the CPI and an inventory tracking funding of EHS risk research, along with its first set of Congressional testimonies and the launch of the first report that Terry Davies produced for PEN.

The second cluster of activity took place in the second and third quarters of 2007, a period encompassing the renewal of the grant from The Pew Charitable Trusts and multiple, high-profile, public updates of the CPI. The final cluster of significant activity took place over the first few months of 2008, with the redesign of PEN's website, production of multiple Congressional testimonies by Maynard and Rejeski, receipt of a European Commission grant, and the co-authoring by Maynard of an article in *Nature Nanotechnology* (Poland et al., 2008) that suggested certain forms of nanomaterials could have asbestos-like health effects if inhaled. While this timeline highlights major milestones in PEN's history, it does not reflect the sheer quantity of activity and production of information that took place over PEN's six-year active lifetime. Numerous reports, events, meetings, press releases, and other activities constitute PEN's voluminous output, and since many of these materials are available in the public domain, they were ripe for investigation.

ICON's prime period of activity was during this period, although it generally produced fewer materials overall than PEN did. ICON's main outputs included a set of substantive reports on various EHS issues. In 2006, ICON published the results of two phases of survey research studying the implementation of EHS best practices in the workplace (Gerritzen et al., 2006a, 2006b). In 2008 and 2010, respectively, it released workshop findings that identified steps toward making progress on predicting the interactions between nanomaterials and biological systems (International Council on Nanotechnology, 2008) and ways of designing and disposing of engineered nanomaterials more responsibly (International Council on Nanotechnology, 2010). In 2007 and 2008, ICON also produced a series of short "backgrounder" papers that provided context and commentary on some of the higher-profile EHS scientific studies related to nanotechnology's potential to cause amyloid diseases (such as Alzheimer's) (Kulinowski and Colvin, 2007), mesothelioma (the disease caused by asbestos) (Kulinowski, 2008a), and negative environmental impacts due to the dispersion of nanosilver (Kulinowski, 2008b). ICON staff also published in leading academic venues, and much like PEN, ICON created a searchable database of peer-reviewed scientific articles related to nanotechnology EHS implications. These articles were packaged together into what ICON called a Virtual Journal of Nanotechnology Environment, Health and Safety that interested readers could sign-up to receive electronically on a regular basis (International Council on Nanotechnology, 2014).

In regards to PEN, even though their materials were generally produced between 2005 and 2010, activity related to nanotechnology at the Wilson Center actually preceded the formation of PEN and continued even after PEN closed down. In other words, PEN enjoyed both a running start at its outset, and had a long tail of output in the years following the transition of its staff

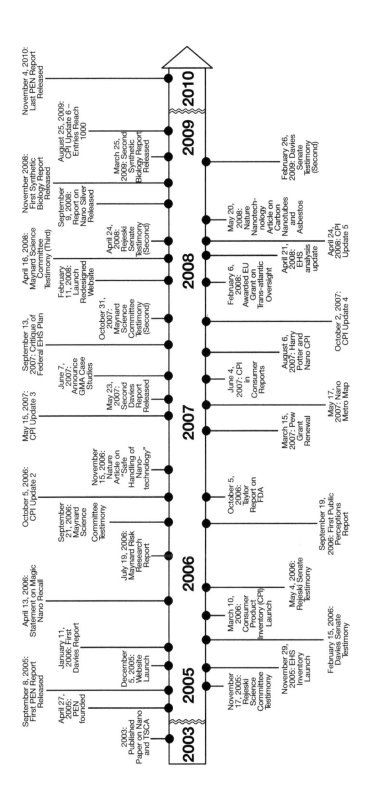

Figure 2.1 Timeline of key PEN dates and milestones

Source: Author analysis

to other topics. For instance, before PEN was formalized, Rejeski ran another project at the Wilson Center, called the Foresight and Governance Project that ran in parallel with PEN for some period of time. This project was the progenitor of PEN, and in 2003, it produced one of the first papers to focus on nanotechnology's potential impact on the TSCA law, two years before PEN was formalized (Wardak, 2003). In fact, even after PEN closed down, the PEN website remained intermittently active and updated as needed. Additionally, subsequent research with a focus on synthetic biology has also periodically tracked changes in public perceptions of nanotechnology alongside public perceptions of synthetic biology (Hart Research Associates, 2013), helping to keep nanotechnology at least mildly visible even in the midst of activities conducted by the Synthetic Biology Project.

Some of the first seeds of PEN's transition to investigating synthetic biology took place during its work on nanotechnology, before funding from The Pew Charitable Trusts ended. Specifically, Rejeski and other staff affiliated with PEN began investigating the societal implications of synthetic biology by the middle of 2008, when Rejeski started the Synthetic Biology Project. Soon afterwards, PEN began including questions about public awareness and perception of synthetic biology as part of the annual polling surveys it undertook with Hart Research Associates. The first report of the Synthetic Biology Project was released in November 2008 and tracked American and European press coverage of synthetic biology over the previous five years (Pauwels and Ifrim, 2008), which was quickly followed in 2009 by its first published report examining the regulatory system for synthetic biology (Rodemeyer, 2009).

As of September 2015, the Synthetic Biology Project had conducted at least six public perception surveys and focus groups related to measuring public opinion of different dimensions of synthetic biology. In addition to exploring general public views on synthetic biology (Hart Research Associates, 2010), these assessments also examined how the public perceives specific issues in the field, such as developments in neural engineering (Hart Research Associates, 2014) and genome editing technology (Hart Research Associates, 2015). The Synthetic Biology Project has also published a number of reports examining an array of relevant policy, oversight, and research issues, such as tracing the development of the DIY synthetic biology community (Grushkin, Kuiken, and Millet, 2013), examining potential ecological (Drinkwater et al., 2014) and biodiversity (Bagley and Rai, 2013) implications, identifying effective public communications strategies for synthetic biology (Mazerik and Rejeski, 2014), and exploring trends related to synthetic biology research and development funding (Synthetic Biology Project, 2015d). Although fewer in number, the Synthetic Biology project also launched and updated three digital inventories with a focus on identifying the products and applications arising from synthetic biology (Synthetic Biology Project, 2015a), mapping the location of key synthetic biology institutions (Synthetic Biology Project, 2013a), and tracking the implementation of synthetic biology policy recommendations (Synthetic Biology Project, 2012a). Finally, much like PEN, the Synthetic Biology

Project held a number of public events and discussion sessions at the Wilson Center and published a selection of articles in peer reviewed academic journals.

Finally, the parallels between PEN and the Synthetic Biology Project were evident to many of the individuals interviewed. In fact, one academic researcher commented:

> Almost everything that they did in synthetic biology is a reflection of what they did in nano. The way they conceptualized the problems, I think you will find that there are parallels in everything. If you were to say, "Well, they did this in nano," I could probably say, "Well, they did the same sort of thing in biology."

Comparing PEN with other projects funded by The Pew Charitable Trusts

PEN was only one of many projects related to emerging areas of science and technology that were funded by The Pew Charitable Trusts. In addition to PEN, at least three other science and technology policy projects received funding from The Pew Charitable Trusts over the past 15 years, respectively focusing on agricultural biotechnology, climate change, and genetics. Table 2.1 compares the key organizational design elements characterizing these four Pew-funded science and technology policy efforts: PEN, the Pew Initiative on Food and Biotechnology (PIFB), the Pew Center on Global Climate Change (PCGCC), and the Genetics and Public Policy Center. Information about the PIFB (DeWitt and Massey, 2007) and PCGCC (McCabe and DeWitt, 2002) are drawn from internal evaluations of these projects graciously shared by The Pew Charitable Trusts, and information about the Genetics and Public Policy Center is drawn from publicly available materials that were accessible online as of June 2013 (Genetics and Public Policy Center, 2008).

A comparison of these four projects shows a number of key similarities. First, three of these four projects were strategically positioned in and around Washington, DC—with the fourth based just a few hours' drive away from Washington. Presumably, this geographic clustering was geared toward facilitating close connections with the Washington-based policy ecosystem. Second, three of these four projects were embedded in larger academic or research-focused institutions. This design feature probably not only allowed for more efficient administration of their grants, but also ensured that the projects could draw on the intellectual integrity and authority of these host organizations. Third, many of these projects were funded by The Pew Charitable Trusts for a similar period of time, from roughly 5–10 years in length, with only the PCGCC extending much beyond this time frame. This funding cycle duration is generally consistent across the science and technology field and within the philanthropic community in general. Donor organizations increasingly look to fund an issue catalytically, generally for up to a decade or so, before moving on to other topics (Kramer, 2009; Porter and Kramer, 1999).

Table 2.1 Snapshot comparison of science and technology policy projects supported by The Pew Charitable Trusts

Domain	Project on Emerging Nanotechnologies	Pew Initiative on Food and Biotechnology	Genetics and Public Policy Center	Pew Center on Global Climate Change
Estimated funding	$6 million	$17.4 million	$13.75 million	$49 million
Timeframe of support (Start and end years included in timeframe)	6 years (2005 to 2010)	7 years (2001 to 2007)	9 years (2002 to 2010, estimate)	14 years (1998 to 2011); Transitioned to successor organization in 2011
Institution location	Washington, DC	Richmond, VA	Washington, DC	Arlington, VA
Type of host institution	Think tank (Woodrow Wilson Center)	University (University of Richmond)	University (Johns Hopkins University)	Independent organization
Number of formal reports produced	19	Over 20	15	Over 100
Issue area maturity	Unformed	Formed	Unformed	Semi-Formed

Finally, the types of public outputs produced by each project were quite similar, and they represent the standard type of deliverables associated with these kinds of institutions: research reports, Congressional testimony, public events, and broad dissemination and distribution of findings.

However, important differences distinguish these four science and technology policy projects. First and foremost, the capacities of these efforts differed greatly. PCGCC dwarfed the other projects in terms of size, duration, funding, and volume of output. Even the Genetics and Public Policy Center and PIFB had budgets two to three times the size of PEN, providing them with far larger resources to provide materials, hire staff, and undertake projects. PEN received by far the least amount of funding among these organizations and had the shortest duration. Second, PCGCC was also the only project to operate as an independent entity, requiring a larger financial investment to establish the necessary institutional infrastructure. To some degree, the other organizations were able to draw on their host institutions for administrative and other types of project support services.

Third, while the outputs from each institution were similar, each placed a different emphasis on the various kinds of materials they produced. PEN published fewer peer-reviewed papers than the other projects, but it hosted a number of unique, easily accessible online informational inventories that the others did not. On the other hand, PIFB regularly tracked legislation related to food and agriculture biotechnology, and meticulously analyzed the federal oversight system governing agricultural biotechnology, known as the Coordinated Framework for the Regulation of Biotechnology (Office of Science and Technology Policy, 1986). PCGCC even undertook and collaborated on original scientific research related to climate change, while the Genetics and Public Policy Center focused more on the production of academic publications related to the issues it studied.

Fourth, these projects also had rather different fates once funding from The Pew Charitable Trusts ceased. Both PEN and PIFB effectively disbanded and closed their doors, with staff dispersing either to new projects within their host organization or to different organizations altogether. The Genetics and Public Policy Center continued even as funding from The Pew Charitable Trusts declined, receiving grants from federal agencies such as the National Human Genome Institute and other offices within the Department of Health and Human Services. PCGCC was the only one of the four projects to formally become re-established and fully transitioned to a new successor organization once funding concluded. In 2011, supported by a diverse consortium of philanthropic, corporate, and individual donors, PCGCC was re-launched under the new name of the Center for Climate and Energy Solutions and shifted its focus to the issue of promoting clean and affordable energy (Center for Climate and Energy Solutions, n.d.).

Finally, a vital difference among these four projects was that the issue areas they were addressing existed at various stages of maturity when the project was initiated. While determining issue area "maturity" is based on judgment, it does appear that differences in the degree of issue area formation were present at the outset of each of these projects. For instance, PIFB entered agricultural biotechnology later in the debate, when the issue had become rather formed or mature. PIFB began when the Coordinated Framework was over a decade old and when stakeholder policy positions were already well formulated, if not deeply entrenched. Moving along this spectrum, PCGCC started working on climate change when the issue was in a semi-formed state, starting just after the establishment of the Kyoto Protocol and before positions of key stakeholders were fully established. While climate change has since become a more mature issue area, with stakeholder positions considerably hardened, at least the early phases of PCGCC took place in a more flexible context. Lastly, given the novelty of both genetic engineering and nanotechnology when the projects were started, both PEN and the Genetics and Public Policy Center engaged on issues that were relatively unformed, where positions of key actors were not yet fully staked out. Operating in these different contexts can bring challenges as well as advantages. For instance, effectively engaging disparate points of view can be difficult with more formed issues, while added effort is needed to start tackling previously unanswered questions for those issues on the frontier.

However, one could probably make the argument that PEN was established in the most anticipatory manner of the four, at the earliest stage of the issue's emergence among the four institutions. In many ways, the establishment of PEN was itself a response to broader lessons learned by its funder. Arguably, one reason why The Pew Charitable Trusts decided to establish PEN rather early in nanotechnology's trajectory was due to the challenging operational environment experienced by groups such as PIFB. The hope was that PEN would "get in early" and operate more upstream, as David Rejeski mentioned in an interview. The intention was to avoid the pitfalls of different stakeholders being entrenched in their positions before responsible governance mechanisms could be tried and implemented with respect to nanotechnology. One respondent with knowledge of PEN's early days noted as much, arguing that, "the debate about agricultural biotechnology has come to be seen as . . . the example against which nanotechnology, and now synthetic biology [want to avoid]."

The implicit intention in forming PEN was to outline a pathway forward for organizations involved with other emerging technologies, and this purpose was often reflected by external stakeholders as well. One illustrative indicator made apparent the link between PEN's work on nanotechnology to other emerging technologies: a slight error that sporadically but consistently appeared in media coverage of PEN. Once in a while, PEN's correct name (the Project on Emerging Nanotechnologies) was mistakenly referred to as the "Project on Emerging Technologies," with the "nano" prefix missing. For instance, a 2007 blog post from *The New York Times* written by science journalist Barnaby Feder described Andrew Maynard as being the "Chief scientific advisor at the Project on Emerging Technologies, a policy group at the Woodrow Wilson Center in Washington" (Feder, 2007). Multiple blog posts by Dexter Johnson (2007, 2009) made similar mistakes when mentioning PEN's real name, and PEN's name was even referred to incorrectly in the summary of a 2005 Congressional hearing at which Rejeski testified (United States House of Representatives, Committee on Science, 2005). These telling mistakes illustrate a tendency for external commentators to conflate the nanotechnology focus of PEN's work with a general focus on the societal implications of emerging technologies. These slip-ups suggest that it was easy for outsiders to sometimes look at PEN's nanotechnology-oriented efforts more broadly as indicative of how to consider the risks, benefits, and societal implications of other emerging technologies.

Data collection and research relationships

"What can't be counted, counts." Thus declare former Presidential Science Advisor Neal Lane and his co-author Raul Rekhi, who borrow from Albert Einstein's famous dictum, "Everything that can be counted does not necessarily count; everything that counts cannot necessarily be counted" (Rekhi and Lane, 2012: 21). Rekhi and Lane apply this aphorism to support a pluralistic methodological perspective in science and technology policy research—spanning both quantitative and qualitative approaches—to gain a better understanding of contemporary science and technology policy issues. While the bulk of science and technology policy research has recently taken a distinctive quantitative turn (Marburger III, 2005; Fealing et al., 2011), qualitative research continues to have much to offer the field, as well as to the broader disciplines of public administration, political science, and public policy (Lincoln and Guba, 1985; Yanow, 1996, 2000; Yanow and Schwartz-Shea, 2006).

Qualitative methods deserve a more esteemed place in the suite of tools to investigate pressing questions of importance in science and technology policy (Mitcham, 2007). These approaches can take many forms, ranging from on-the-ground, observation-based research to more conceptual, theoretically oriented methods (Creswell, 2007). Qualitative methods often include targeted *in situ* ethnographic research (Emerson, Fretz, and Shaw, 1995), rhetorical and narrative analysis (Feldman et al., 2004; Jones and McBeth, 2010; Shanahan, Jones, and McBeth, 2011), and abstract phenomenological analysis (Giorgi, 1997), with many combinations and permutations bringing together elements of different schools of thought. Stake (2010) emphasizes that a chief commonality across these qualitative approaches is that the individual researcher is the primary "instrument" of data collection and analysis. The researcher provides an interpretation of the information gleaned through multiple data collection efforts to strengthen and triangulate findings and then uses various communication tactics—such as contextual scene-setting, reliance on verbatim quotations, and effective story-telling—to report key insights.

The use of qualitative methods in science and technology policy can illuminate dimensions of interest to policymakers and researchers. Among the possible methodological options, one of the most often used—and one that is particularly well suited to achieve the goals of this research—is case study analysis (Maxwell, 2005; Bennett and Elman, 2006). Yin (2003: 13) defines the case study as a form of "empirical inquiry that investigates contemporary phenomenon in depth and within its real-life context," relying on "multiple sources of evidence, with data needing to converge in a triangulating fashion" and benefiting from "the prior development of theoretical propositions to guide data collection and analysis" (2003: 14). Additionally, Maxwell (2005) notes that the interpretive case study approach is particularly flexible and adaptable, being designed to unearth the underlying meaning of particular situations, events, and experiences; to illuminate the complex environments within which organizations operate and the systems within which their activities take place; to highlight critical processes and strategies; and to build and explore conceptual frameworks and constructs. Creswell (2007) argues that the case study frame-work creates a "bounded system" within which a particular set of phenomena can be explored, where multiple sources and forms of data are used to confirm, challenge, or enhance the findings. Finally, Stake (2006; 8) describes how, at their most powerful, case studies can consider both "the particular and the general" simultaneously, with the "study of the particular . . . serving grand explanation not so much in a statistical sense as in a conceptual sense." Flyvbjerg (2006) makes clear that well-chosen case studies retain substantial power to inform the advancement of key concepts of interest, and Yin (2003), Eisenhardt (1989), and Eisenhardt and Graebner (2007) all note that case studies are most effective when focusing on a "theoretically relevant" case. The organizations discussed here are especially relevant to enhancing theory, as they allow for an exploration of how key elements of the anticipatory governance conceptual framework can be applied in practice.

In fact, a rich tradition of using interpretive case studies and qualitative research methodologies exists in the science and technology studies and policy literature in general (Latour and Woolgar, 1986; Traweek, 1992)—and in nanotechnology and synthetic biology social science literature in particular (Rabinow, 1996; Rabinow and Dan-Cohen, 2005; Kelty, 2009; Macnaghten, Davies, and Kearnes, 2015)—to gain a deeper appreciation and awareness of organizational practices. For example, McCarthy and Kelty (2010) conducted a case study investigating the formation and early days of CBEN at Rice University. Kaiser (2010) used this methodology to understand how one British science policy think tank, Demos, approached the creation of delibera-tions focused on the future societal implications of emerging technologies. In terms of adopting specific qualitative research methodologies, Berne (2006) utilized semi-structured interviews to document researchers' perceptions and opinions about nanotechnology's potential long-term risks and benefits.

Document analysis has also been utilized to parse controversies regarding nanotechnology's potential societal implications (Kaplan and Radin, 2011). Similarly, Losch (2010) conducted an analysis of public information brochures produced by the German Federal Ministry of Education and Research to assess how nanotechnology's potential future is depicted in official government materials. Document analysis has also become a central methodological component of a research program called Public Value Mapping (PVM) (Bozeman, 2003, 2007; Bozeman and Sarewitz, 2005, 2011), a process developed to glean the intended public values espoused as justifications of government-funded research. At the heart of the PVM approach is the examination of statements of public value contained in government strategy documents and mission statements. This document-oriented research methodology has identified underlying public values and rationales espoused in diverse areas of science and technology policy, with particular attention paid to nanotechnology policy formation in the United States (Fisher et al., 2010; Slade, 2011; Anderson and Slade, 2013).

Multiple sources of qualitative data were examined to arrive at the conclusions presented here. The three main empirical data collection methodologies used here include an in-depth analysis of the internal and external documents produced, mostly by and about PEN; semi-structured interviews with a range of experts in the field; and a multifaceted analysis of media coverage related to nanotechnology issues. The primary research period spanned the initial data collection of documents in August 2011, followed by main interview period in the early and middle parts of 2012, through to the final consolidation of codes and research findings in May 2013. A supplementary research period then took place in the second half of 2015 to add further content. More detail on the research process is provided in the methodological appendix at the end of the book.

First, the primary phase of research included a qualitative analysis of a wide array of publicly available and internal documents produced about PEN, ICON, and the Synthetic Biology Project – documents reports, Congressional testimonies, strategic planning memos, agency submissions, and online inventories. All of these documents were analyzed to help identify the strategies, discussed in subsequent chapters, these organizations used to inform debates about emerging technologies in the United States. Second, I undertook over 50 semi-structured interviews with a range of key stakeholders who have substantive knowledge of the organizations studied here, including current and former staff, members of their advisory networks, non-governmental representatives, former and current government officials at federal and local levels in the United States, academic scholars, private sector actors, print journalists and web-based reporters, non-US based individuals, and other leading foresight experts. All of the audio interviews were transcribed and analyzed alongside the document analysis component of the research. Third, I conducted a multifaceted media analysis to understand the public engagement and communication strategies adopted by these institutions. The media analysis draws on many information sources, including data from a leading academic database that tracks coverage of PEN and other NGOs involved in nanotechnology policy and an analysis of the tone and themes of all of the press releases PEN produced during its active period.

I served as the primary instrument of qualitative data collection, analysis, and synthesis, a role that takes on increased responsibility given my former affiliation with PEN. In many ways, having worked at PEN is an asset. This relationship with PEN also facilitated access to internal documentation that other researchers might not have had the opportunity to review. Since I left PEN over eight years ago, and since the organization wound down over five years ago, I believe sufficient professional and temporal distance remains that allows me to assess PEN's materials—and tease out its principal strategies, strengths, and weaknesses—honestly and openly. Additionally, I have had no professional relationships working in ICON, the Synthetic Biology Project, or any of the other NGOs mentioned here.

A fair amount of social science literature exists related to researchers studying organizations in which they have been involved (Guston, 2001; Fisher and Guston, 2012). For instance, the action research tradition generally involves individuals knowledgeable about or affiliated with an organization (Lewin, 1946; McTaggart, 1991; Kemmis and McTaggart, 2000). Ethnographic field-work and laboratory-level interventions have also become more common in nanotechnology as a way of probing the societal implications of emerging nanotechnologies with working scientists (Fisher, 2007; Viseu, 2015). Similarly, Rabinow and Bennett (2012) report on the process of designing the "human practices" thrust of activities at the Synthetic Biology Engineering Research Center while they were actively involved in implementing this strand of investigation at the organization.

I remained alert to any potential risks that this previous relationship might raise, and I am highly confident that the interviewees were not unduly swayed by this previous affiliation, nor do I believe that interviewees withheld any criticism or unflattering views of PEN due to any potential interpersonal sensitivity. In fact, I was consistently careful to acknowledge my previous relationship with PEN when engaging interview respondents, while simultaneously indicating that I was no longer affiliated with PEN and that this research was not being undertaken under the auspices of PEN, The Pew Charitable Trusts, or my current employer. Additionally, as part of the interview portion of the study, I made an explicit commitment to interview individuals with a range of perspectives on PEN, including those who I had reason to believe may have held more of a critical view of the organization. This was all done in the service of securing a well-rounded perspective. In order to ensure transparency when analyzing documents or drawing conclusions from the media analysis, I was also careful to triangulate evidence from multiple sources—often quoting directly from interviews and documents—to make evident that the findings were supported by a diverse array of documentation. In many ways, as the researcher on this project, I have served in an insider–outsider, boundary-spanning role myself, at once familiar with PEN as an organization but taking an arm's length analytic stance.

Finally, I adapted a set of quality assurance principles throughout this research in order to ensure the robustness of results (Dodge, Ospina, and Foldy, 2005;

Akkerman et al., 2008; Tracy, 2010). For instance, I demonstrated "rich rigor" by drawing on "sufficient, abundant, appropriate, and complex" data sources and methodologies (Tracy, 2010). This included utilizing "thick description," writing in "concrete detail," drawing on "triangulation" of sources, and marshaling "evocative representation" techniques such as the use of narratives, metaphors, and direct quotations from participants (Tracy, 2010).

To be sure, these criteria do not guarantee that the findings reported here are beyond dispute or disagreement. In fact, just the opposite. Throughout the research process, necessary judgments and interpretations were made, including how to apply the conceptual framework, structure the data collection approach, and present the central findings. This was done with a reflective and self-critical eye, in the service of what would be best suited to illuminating the primary dimensions of the topic at hand. By describing the rationale underlying these choices transparently, the intention is to provide the reader with sufficient context so that they can debate, challenge, provoke, suggest alternative explanations, and ultimately draw their own conclusions.

Bibliography

Akkerman, S., Admiraal, W., Brekelmans, M., and Oost, H. (2008). Auditing Quality of Research in Social Sciences. *Quality and Quantity, 42*(2), 257–274.

Anderson, D., and Slade, C. P. (2013). Agenda Setting in Emergent R&D Policy Subsystems: Examining Discourse Effects of the 21st Century Nanotechnology Research and Development Act. *Review of Policy Research, 30*(5), 447–463.

Bagley, M. A., and Rai, A. K. (2013). *The Nagoya Protocol and Synthetic Biology Research: A Look at the Potential Impacts.* Washington, DC: Synthetic Biology Project, Woodrow Wilson International Center for Scholars.

Bennett, A., and Elman, C. (2006). Qualitative Research: Recent Developments in Case Study Methods. *Annual Review of Political Science, 9*, 455–476.

Berne, R. W. (2006). *Nanotalk: Conversations with Scientists and Engineers about Ethics, Meaning, and Belief in the Development of Nanotechnology.* Mahwah, NJ: Lawrence Erlbaum Associates, Publishers.

Bozeman, B. (2003). Public Value Mapping of Science Outcomes: Theory and Method. In B. Bozeman, D. Sarewitz, S. Feinson, G. Foladori, M. Gaughan, A. Gupta, B. Sampat, G. Zachary (Eds.), *Knowledge Flows, Innovation, and Learning in Developing Countries* (pp. 3–48). Washington, DC: Center for Science, Policy, & Outcomes.

Bozeman, B. (2007). *Public Values and Public Interest: Counterbalancing Economic Individualism.* Washington, DC: Georgetown University Press.

Bozeman, B., and Sarewitz, D. (2005, April). Public Values and Public Failure in US Science Policy. *Science and Public Policy, 32*(2), 119–136.

Bozeman, B., and Sarewitz, D. (2011). Public Value Mapping and Science Policy Evaluation. *Minerva, 49*(1), 1–23.

Center for Climate and Energy Solutions. (n.d.). *History.* Retrieved November 10, 2015, from Center for Climate and Energy Solutions: www.c2es.org/about/history

Creswell, J. W. (2007). *Qualitative Inquiry and Research Design: Choosing Among Five Approaches,* 2nd ed. Thousand Oaks, CA: SAGE Publications.

DeWitt, J., and Massey, A. (2007). *An Evaluation of The Pew Initiative on Food and Biotechnology.* Philadelphia, PA: The Pew Charitable Trusts.

Dodge, J., Ospina, S. M., and Foldy, E. G. (2005, May/June). Integrating Rigor and Relevance in Public Administration Scholarship: The Contribution of Narrative Inquiry. *Public Administration Review*, *65*(3), 286–300.

Drinkwater, K., Kuiken, T., Lightfoot, S., McNamara, J., and Oye, K. (2014). *Creating a Research Agenda for the Ecological Implications of Synthetic Biology*. Washington, DC: Synthetic Biology Project, Woodrow Wilson International Center for Scholars.

Eisenhardt, K. M. (1989). Building Theories for Case Study Research. *Academy of Management Research*, *14*(4), 532–550.

Eisenhardt, K. M., and Graebner, M. E. (2007). Theory Building from Cases: Opportunities and Challenges. *Academy of Management Journal*, *50*(1), 25–32.

Emerson, R. M., Fretz, R. I., and Shaw, L. L. (1995). *Writing Ethnographic Fieldnotes*. Chicago, IL: The University of Chicago Press.

Fealing, K. H., Lane, J. I., Marburger III, J. H., and Shipp, S. S. (2011). Editors' Introduction. In K. H. Fealing, J. I. Lane, M. III, J. H., and S. S. Shipp (Eds.), *The Science of Science Policy: A Handbook* (pp. 1–7). Stanford, CA: Stanford University Press.

Feder, B. J. (2007, July 12). *EPA to Nanotech: Size Doesn't Matter*. Retrieved November 15, 2015, from Bits Blog, *New York Times*: http://bits.blogs.nytimes.com/2007/07/12/epa-to-nanotech-size-doesnt-matter/?_r=0

Feldman, M. S., Skoldberg, K., Brown, R. N., and Horner, D. (2004). Making Sense of Stories: A Rhetorical Approach to Narrative Analysis. *Journal of Public Administration Research and Theory: J-PART*, *14*(2), 147–170.

Fisher, E. (2007). Ethnographic Invention: Probing the Capacity of Laboratory Decisions. *NanoEthics*, *1*(2), 155–165.

Fisher, E., and Guston, D. H. (2012). *STIR: Socio-Technical Integration Research*. Tempe, AZ: Arizona State University.

Fisher, E., Slade, C. P., Anderson, D., and Bozeman, B. (2010). The Public Value of Nanotechnology. *Scientometrics*, *85*(1), 29–39.

Flyvbjerg, B. (2006). Five Misunderstandings About Case-Study Research. *Qualitative Inquiry*, *12*(2), 219–245.

Genetics and Public Policy Center. (2008, November). *About the Center: Funding*. Retrieved June 26, 2013, from Genetics and Public Policy Center: www.dnapolicy.org/about.funding.html

Gerritzen, G., Huang, L.-C., Killpack, K., Mircheva, M., and Conti, J. (2006a). *Review of Safety Practices in the Nanotechnology Industry; Phase One Report: Current Knowledge and Practices Regarding Environmental Health and Safety in the Nanotechnology Workplace*. Houston, TX: International Council on Nanotechnology.

Gerritzen, G., Huang, L.-C., Killpack, K., Mircheva, M., and Conti, J. (2006b). *A Review of Current Practices in the Nanotechnology Industry; Phase Two Report: Survey of Current Practices in the Nanotechnology Workplace*. Houston, TX: International Council on Nanotechnology.

Giorgi, A. (1997). The Theory, Practice, and Evaluation of the Phenomenological Method as a Qualitative Research Procedure. *Journal of Phenomenological Psychology*, *28*(2), 235–260.

Grushkin, D., Kuiken, T., and Millet, P. (2013). *Seven Myths and Realities about Do-It-Yourself Biology*. Washington, DC: Synthetic Biology Project, Woodrow Wilson International Center for Scholars.

Guston, D. H. (2001). Boundary Organizations in Environmental Policy and Science: An Introduction. *Science, Technology and Human Values*, *26*(4), 399–408.

Hart Research Associates. (2010). *Awareness and Impressions of Synthetic Biology*. Washington, DC: Synthetic Biology Project.

Hart Research Associates. (2013). *Awareness and Impressions of Synthetic Biology*. Washington, DC: Synthetic Biology Project.

Hart Research Associates. (2014). *Perceptions of Synthetic Biology and Neural Engineering*. Washington, DC: Synthetic Biology Project, Woodrow Wilson International Center for Scholars.

Hart Research Associates. (2015). *Public Attitudes Regarding New Technology from Editing DNA*. Washington, DC: Synthetic Biology Project, Woodrow Wilson International Center for Scholars.

International Council on Nanotechnology. (2008). *Towards Predicting Nano-Biointeractions: An International Assessment of Nanotechnology Environment, Health and Safety Research Needs* . Houston TX: International Council on Nanotechnology.

International Council on Nanotechnology. (2010). *Advancing the Eco-Responsible Design and Disposal of Nanomaterials*. Houston, TX: International Council on Nanotechnology.

International Council on Nanotechnology. (2014, September 30). *NanoEHS Virtual Journal*. Retrieved November 15, 2015, from The Virtual Journal of Nanotechnology Environment, Health, and Safety: http://icon.rice.edu/virtualjournal.cfm

Johnson, D. (2007, September 4). *Five Hundred Consumer Applications for Nanotech?!!* Retrieved November 15,2015, from IEEE Spectrum: http://spectrum.ieee.org/tech-talk/semiconductors/devices/five_hundred_consumer_applicat

Johnson, D. (2009, September 10). *Reconsidering The One Thousand Nanotech Consumer Product Inventory*. Retrieved November 17, 2015, from IEEE Spectrum: http://spectrum.ieee.org/nanoclast/semiconductors/nanotechnology/reconsidering-the-one-thousand-nanotech-consumer-product-inventory-

Jones, M. D., and McBeth, M. K. (2010). A Narrative Policy Framework: Clear Enough to Be Wrong? *Policy Studies Journal, 38*(2), 329–353.

Kaiser, M. (2010). Futures Assessed: How Technology Assessment, Ethics and Think Tanks Make Sense of an Unknown Future. In M. Kaiser, M. Kurath, S. Maasen, and C. Rehmann-Sutter (Eds.), *Governing Future Technologies: Nanotechnology and the Rise of an Assessment Regime* (pp. 179–198). Dordrecht, The Netherlands: Springer.

Kaplan, S., and Radin, J. (2011, August). Bounding an Emerging Technology: Para-Scientific Media and the Drexler-Smalley Debate about Nanotechnology. *Social Studies of Science, 41*(4), 457–485.

Kelty, C. M. (2009). Beyond Implications and Applications: The Story of "Safety by Design." *Nanoethics, 3*(2), 79–96.

Kemmis, S., and McTaggart, R. (2000). Participatory Action Research: Communicative Action and the Public Sphere. In N. K. Denzin, and Y. S. Lincoln (Eds.), *The Handbook of Qualitative Research*, 2nd ed. (pp. 271–329). London, UK: Sage Publications.

Kramer, M. R. (2009, Autumn). Catalytic Philanthropy. *Stanford Social Innovation Review, 7*(4), 30–35.

Kulinowski, K. M. (2008a). *Multi-walled Carbon Nanotubes and Mesothelioma: An ICON Backgrounder*. Houston, TX: International Council on Nanotechnology.

Kulinowski, K. M. (2008b). *Environmental Impacts of Nanosilver: An ICON Backgrounder*. Houston, TX: International Council on Nanotechnology.

Kulinowski, K. M., and Colvin, V. L. (2007). *Backgrounder on Nanoparticles and Amyloid Diseases*. Houston, TX: International Council on Nanotechnology.

Latour, B., and Woolgar, S. (1986). *Laboratory Life: The Construction of Scientific Facts.* Princeton, NJ: Princeton University Press.

Lewin, K. (1946). Action Research and Minority Problems. *Journal of Social Issues, 2*(4), 34–46.

Lincoln, Y. S., and Guba, E. G. (1985). *Naturalistic Inquiry.* Newbury Park, CA: SAGE Publications.

Losch, A. (2010). Visual Dynamics: The Defuturization of the Popular "Nano-Discourse" as an Effect of Increasing Economization. In M. Kaiser, M. Kurath, S. Maasen, and C. Rehmann-Sutter (Eds.), *Governing Future Technologies: Nanotechnology and the Rise of an Assessment Regime* (pp. 89–108). Dordrecht, The Netherlands: Springer.

McCabe, W. M., and DeWitt, J. (2002). *An Assessment of the Pew Center on Global Climate Change.* Philadelphia, PA: The Pew Charitable Trusts.

McCarthy, E., and Kelty, C. (2010). Responsibility and Nanotechnology. *Social Studies of Science, 40*(3), 405–432.

McGann, J. G. (2015). *2014 Global Go To Think Tank Index Report.* Philadelphia, PA: University of Pennsylvania.

Macnaghten, P., Davies, S. R., and Kearnes, M. (2015). Understanding Public Responses to Emerging Technologies: A Narrative Approach. *Journal of Environmental Policy and Planning,* 1–19.

McTaggart, R. (1991). Principles for Participatory Action Research. *Adult Education Quarterly, 41*(3), 168–187.

Marburger III, J. H. (2005, May 20). Wanted: Better Benchmarks. *Science, 308*(5725), 1087.

Maxwell, J. A. (2005). *Qualitative Research Design: An Interactive Approach,* 2nd ed. Thousand Oaks, CA: SAGE Publications.

Mazerik, J., and Rejeski, D. (2014). *A Guide for Communicating Synthetic Biology.* Washington, DC: Synthetic Biology Project, Woodrow Wilson International Center for Scholars.

Mitcham, C. (2007, December). Qualitative Science Policy. *Qualitative Health Research, 17*(10), 1434–1441.

Office of Science and Technology Policy. (1986, June 26). *Coordinated Framework for Regulation of Biotechnology.* Retrieved November 17, 2015, from www.aphis.usda. gov/brs/fedregister/coordinated_framework.pdf

Pauwels, E., and Ifrim, I. (2008). *Trends in American and European Press Coverage of Synthetic Biology: Tracking the Last Five Years of Coverage.* Washington, DC: Synthetic Biology Project.

Poland, C. A., Duffin, R., Kinloch, I., Maynard, A., Wallace, W. A., Seaton, A., Stone, V., Brown, S., MacNee, S., Donaldson, K. (2008). Carbon Nanotubes Introduced into the Abdominal Cavity of Mice Show Asbestos-like Pathogenicity in a Pilot Study. *Nature Nanotechnology, 3*(17), 423–428.

Porter, M. E., and Kramer, M. R. (1999, November-December). Philanthropy's New Agenda: Creating Value. *Harvard Business Review, 77*(6), 121–130.

Project on Emerging Nanotechnologies. (2005d, April 27). *Pew Charitable Trusts, Wilson Center Launch Project on Emerging Nanotechnologies.* Retrieved November 15, 2015, from Project on Emerging Nanotechnologies: www.nanotechproject.org/ process/assets/files/6034/042705nanotechnology_project.pdf

Rabinow, P. (1996). *Making PCR: A Story of Biotechnology.* Chicago, IL: University of Chicago Press.

Rabinow, P., and Bennett, G. (2012). *Designing Human Practices: An Experiment with Synthetic Biology*. Chicago, IL: University of Chicago Press.

Rabinow, P., and Dan-Cohen, T. (2005). *A Machine to Make A Future: Biotech Chronicles*. Princeton, NJ: Princeton University Press.

Rejeski, D. (2004a, October 11). Memo: Nanotech Initiative—General Policy Environment. Washington, DC.

Rejeski, D. (2006, May 4). Testimony on: "Promoting Economic Development Opportunities Through Nano Commercialization." Washington, DC: United States Senate, Committee on Commerce, Science and Transportation, Subcommittee on Trade, Tourism and Economic Development.

Rekhi, R., and Lane, N. (2012, Autumn). Qualitative Metrics in Science Policy: What Can't Be Counted, Counts. *Issues in Science and Technology, 29*(1), 21–24.

Rodemeyer, M. (2009). *New Life, Old Bottles: Regulating First-Generation Products of Synthetic Biology*. Washington, DC: Synthetic Biology Project.

Shanahan, E. A., Jones, M. D., and McBeth, M. K. (2011). Policy Narratives and Policy Processes. *Policy Studies Journal, 39*(3), 535–561.

Slade, C. P. (2011). Public Value Mapping of Equity in Emerging Nanotechnologies. *Minerva, 49*(1), 71–86.

Stake, R. E. (2006). *Multiple Case Study Analysis*. New York, NY: The Guilford Press.

Stake, R. E. (2010). *Qualitative Research: Studying How Things Work*. New York, NY: The Guilford Press.

Synthetic Biology Project. (2012a, July 16). *Synthetic Biology Scorecard*. Retrieved September 17, 2015, from Synthetic Biology Project: www.synbioproject.org/scorecard/

Synthetic Biology Project. (2013a). *Maps Inventory: Updated Map Tracks Global Growth of Synthetic Biology*. Retrieved September 17,2015, from Synthetic Biology Project: www.synbioproject.org/inventories/maps-inventory/

Synthetic Biology Project. (2015a). *Synthetic Biology Products and Applications Inventory*. Retrieved September 17, 2015, from Synthetic Biology Project: www.synbioproject.org/cpi/

Synthetic Biology Project. (2015d). *U.S. Trends in Synthetic Biology Research Funding*. Washington, DC: Synthetic Biology Project, Woodrow Wilson International Center for Scholars.

Tracy, S. J. (2010). Qualitative Quality: Eight "Big Tent" Criteria for Excellent Qualitative Research. *Qualitative Inquiry, 16*(10), 837–851.

Traweek, S. (1992). *Beamtimes and Lifetimes: The World of High Energy Physicists*. Cambridge, MA: Harvard University Press.

United States House of Representatives, Committee on Science. (2005, November 17). *Environmental and Safety Impacts of Nanotechnology: What Research Is Needed?* Retrieved November 16, 2015, from Government Printing Office: www.gpo.gov/fdsys/pkg/CHRG-109hhrg24464/html/CHRG-109hhrg24464.htm

Viseu, A. (2015, October). Caring for Nanotechnology? Being an Integrated Social Scientist. *Social Studies of Science, 45*(5), 642–664.

Wardak, A. (2003). *Nanotechnology and Regulation: A Case Study Using the Toxic Substances Control Act*. Washington, DC: Foresight and Governance Project, Woodrow Wilson International Center for Scholars.

Woodrow Wilson International Center for Scholars. (2012). *Your Investment at Work*. Washington, DC: Woodrow Wilson International Center for Scholars.

Woodrow Wilson International Center for Scholars. (2015, February). *Budget Justifications for the Fiscal Year 2016*. Retrieved September 17, 2015, from Woodrow Wilson International Center for Scholars: www.wilsoncenter.org/sites/default/files/FY2016_Budget_Justification.pdf

Woodrow Wilson International Center for Scholars. (n.d.). *About the Wilson Center*. Retrieved November 18, 2015, from Woodrow Wilson International Center for Scholars: www.wilsoncenter.org/about-the-wilson-center

Yanow, D. (1996). *How Does a Policy Mean? Interpreting Policy and Organizational Actions*. Washington, DC: Georgetown University Press.

Yanow, D. (2000). *Conducting Interpretive Policy Analysis*. Thousand Oaks, CA: SAGE Publications.

Yanow, D., and Schwartz-Shea, P. (2006). *Interpretation and Method: Empirical Research Methods and the Interpretive Turn*. Armonk, NY: M. E. Sharpe.

Yin, R. (2003). *Case Study Research: Design and Methods*, 3rd ed. Thousand Oaks, CA: SAGE Publications.

3 Taking the future seriously

Anticipatory governance and a new approach to policymaking

"We need a better approach to governance"

> For the commercial success of any emerging technology, we need a better approach to governance that can support strategic risk research, provide adequate oversight, and engage the broader public in our technological future . . . This situation does not surprise people who were part of the debates around agricultural biotechnology in the 1990s or watched the tortuous path of nuclear power through the 1950s and 60s. The recurrence of issues around risk assessment, oversight, and public dialogue—irrespective of the technology involved—indicates that these challenges have deeper origins that will not respond to quick fixes. The government is not organized for the tasks at hand, and the challenges we face will only grow more complex as nanotechnology and biotechnology increasingly converge and new scientific fields, such as synthetic biology, emerge.

These final lines of Congressional testimony presented by PEN and Synthetic Biology Project Director David Rejeski in 2008 encapsulate the science and technology governance challenge facing policymakers over the coming decades (Rejeski, 2008). Rejeski observes that these issues have their roots in technologies that came of age in earlier decades, such as nuclear technology in the middle of the twentieth century and biotechnology closer to the end of the twentieth century. However, he argues that the complexity of new technologies—such as nanotechnology, synthetic biology, and geoengineering—will only speed up the onset of these interconnected challenges. The societal implications of emerging technologies raise profound issues for the policy system, especially as these technologies become more interwoven. In particular, concerns about the rapid commercialization of new technologies, the need to manage potential risks effectively, and uncertainties that come with the development of new products and processes will increasingly place multiple pressures on policy systems in the future (Stern et al., 2009; Holdren, Sunstein, and Siddiqui, 2011).

Contemplating the future is becoming an ever-more critical consideration in conceptualizing how policymaking happens (Cairney, 2013). Pierson (2004:

5–6) takes this position strongly, noting that both historical and future-oriented perspectives are significantly under-represented and under-appreciated in policymaking theory. "Many of the key concepts needed to underpin analyses of temporal processes, such as path dependence, critical junctures, sequencing, events, duration, timing, and unintended consequences, have received only very fragmented and limited discussion," Pierson writes. Quite often, standard theoretical models about how the policy process works are almost exclusively present-oriented or, at best, view change as a linear progression, and do poorly in accounting for significant changes that might take place over the long term.

Policy scholars typically break down the policymaking process into discrete steps (Lasswell, 1956; DeLeon, 1999; Sabatier, 1999; Howlett, Ramesh, and Perl, 2009), examine how policy regimes (Wison, 2000; May and Jochim, 2013) and subsystems operate (Jochim and May, 2010), and look to describe how change occurs (Lindblom, 1959). Some allowance is generally made for the unpredictable nature of complex challenges. This is present in acknowledging short bursts of unexplained change—the "punctuated equilibrium" model suggested by Baumgartner and Jones (1993)—or by simply recognizing that it is not possible to explain how the solutions that arise for policy problems come to pass—the "garbage can" model of Cohen, March, and Olsen (1972). While the "multiple streams" model of Kingdon (1995) perhaps comes closest in successfully considering the future dimensions of complex policy challenges, even Kingdon fails to fully take the role of the future seriously in the policymaking process. Kingdon suggests that time is needed for the serendipitous "coupling" of three rather independent "streams": the problem stream, the policy stream, and the political stream. A policy entrepreneur must be prepared for the auspicious moment when a policy window opens and careful planning combines with unpredictable forces, such as crises and chance, to enable the emergence of a successful solution from the "policy primeval soup." Still, Kingdon does little to detail how such policy innovation emerges, failing to discuss how new policy solutions arise that have little to no historical precedent (Mintrom and Norman, 2009). He takes the view that "there is no new thing under the sun," as Kingdon's policy entrepreneurs are often described as combining pre-existing solutions that eventually find a way of latching on to one problem or another.

While efforts are being made to synthesize existing frameworks into a more integrated view of the policymaking process (Nowlin, 2011) and to consider how institutions need to adjust to complex social challenges (Ostrom, 1990, 1998; Henry and Dietz, 2011), less attention is generally paid to how to integrate a longer-term view of the future into the policymaking process. In fact, emerging areas of science and technology are natural realms for examining how the considerations about the future can be embedded in policymaking. One conceptual framework developed by scholars over the past decade, largely in response to complex technological change, does place the future solidly at the center of the policymaking process: anticipatory governance. With multiple lineages from technology assessment, public administration, and complexity theory, anticipatory governance is a strong candidate to infuse conceptual frameworks of the policymaking process with a deeper appreciation of the future. Just as Rejeski indicates in the quotation that starts this chapter—that twenty-first century technologies cannot be adequately governed by nineteenth and twentieth century institutions—so too is it true that twentieth century conceptualizations of the policymaking process are inadequate to explain the dynamic complexity of twenty-first century social and policy challenges.

The original concept of anticipatory governance features three core dimensions: foresight, integration, and engagement. Variations of these dimensions will guide the empirical research presented in subsequent chapters. Chapter 1 indicates that exploring the application of this rather new theoretical construct in a real-world setting is one of the expected primary contributions of this research. Anticipatory governance has moved out from its origins in the university, and its principles are becoming explicitly and implicitly applied in different contexts, including within government and NGOs. This chapter explores the various adjustments to anticipatory governance that can help make this conceptual framework fit better within these settings. To do so, the following section of this chapter provides a definition and description of the canonical components of anticipatory governance. The next section then presents an overview of the historical antecedents and differing disciplinary roots of the concept. The fourth section focuses on reviewing the diffusion of this concept within recent academic literature and tracks the utilization of the framework through various bibliometric analyses (Garfield, 1955; Leydesdorff, 1987). The concluding section provides further detail regarding the application of anticipatory governance and considers how this conceptual framework can be utilized to better understand the strategies that NGOs can utilize to anticipate the societal implications of emerging technologies.

Anticipatory governance: definition and description

Anticipatory governance is a concept that emerged primarily from theoretical and empirical research undertaken at the Consortium for Science, Policy and Outcomes—another founder of the ECAST network—and the Center for Nanotechnology in Society at Arizona State University (CNS-ASU). Since its 2005 launch, CNS-ASU has become a leading center for exploring the multidimensional societal implications of nanotechnology (Guston, 2010a). While the antecedents of the term will be discussed in subsequent sections of this chapter, the most common present-day usage of anticipatory governance emerged from CNS-ASU. In one of the first fully fledged articulations of the idea, Barben et al. (2008: 992–993) describe anticipatory governance as comprising "the ability of variety of lay and expert stakeholders ... to collectively imagine, critique, and thereby shape the issues presented by emerging technologies before they become reified in particular ways." The concept was developed as an alternative to the narrow view that the specific trajectories of science and technology innovation can be deterministically projected and forecasted in the future, a mentality that Pielke, Sarewitz, and Byerly (2000) term the "prediction enterprise." At the heart of the anticipatory governance concept is a deliberate focus on expanding the functional ability and capacity of individuals and institutions to become more anticipatory. Guston (2014b: 218) further describes the concept as "a broad-based capacity extended through society that can act on a variety of inputs to manage emerging knowledge-based technologies while such management is still possible."

Guston (2010b: 433) explores the root meaning of the term by noting that the "concept of anticipation strongly reflects its etymology from the Latin as 'ante-'meaning 'beforehand' and 'capere' meaning to take into possession. It is related to 'capability' and 'capacity' and denotes the ability to take something in beforehand." Guston (2014b) further emphasizes the preparation and capacity building element at the core of anticipatory governance with a metaphor. Anticipating issues raised by emerging technologies, he argues, recalls the regular regimen of physical exercise that people put themselves through to stay fit. "Lifting weights in a gym, for example, is not intended to enable individuals to overcome a specific or predicted event. Rather, it is a form of building capacity to confront physical and mental challenges that are unknown," he writes (Guston, 2014b: 226). So too with anticipatory governance, which is "more about practicing, rehearsing or exercising a capacity in a logically, spatially, or temporally prior way than it is about divining a future" (Guston, 2014b: 226).

Barben et al. (2008) articulate the three previously mentioned core dimensions of anticipatory governance: foresight, engagement, and integration. Building on Hackett et al. (2004), the authors argue that these dimensions of anticipatory governance do not work in isolation from one another. Instead, they argue these three dimensions must be taken together as an "ensemble," operating in a mutually reinforcing, intertwined effort of research and practice. These interwoven dimensions are evident in the activities of the organizations studied here, with most of their institutional efforts demonstrating elements of more than one dimension at the same time.

The foresight dimension, explored further in Chapter 4, consists of non-predictive, non-probabilistic forms of considering a wide set of alternative futures and adopting a broad range of forward-looking methodologies. Guston (2014b) further details that foresight is a "methodologically pluralist approach to plausible futures with an emphasis on those methods such as scenario development that provide more diverse and normative visions compared to other methods that seek to identify a single, most likely future." Within CNS-ASU, foresight-informed projects include developing visions for how nanotechnology may develop over the long, structured scenario-based deliberations, and collaborative team-based activities to imagine and design potential nanotechnology-based products (Selin, 2008a, 2008b, 2011; Selin and Hudson, 2010; Guston, 2010a). Many of the efforts undertaken by PEN and the

Synthetic Biology Project—from describing hypothetical nanotechnology-based food packing to using real-world and hypothetical case studies about the interaction of synthetic biology products and the regulatory system—are infused with a strong foresight perspective, even when this future-oriented view had a dual purpose of influencing near-term policy decisions.

The engagement dimension, which will be explored further in Chapter 6, is described as "encouraging the substantive exchange of ideas among lay publics and between them and those who traditionally frame and set the agenda for, as well as conduct, scientific research" (Guston, 2014b: 226). To animate this element of work, CNS-ASU has undertaken activities such as a National Citizens' Technology Forum, a series of Science Cafes, and work to expand awareness of nanotechnology through informal settings, such as museums (Guston, 2010a, 2010b; Hamlett, Cobb, and Guston, 2008). PEN, more so than ICON, placed substantial emphasis on public engagement and conceived of these efforts broadly, undertaking substantial public outreach and communications through the widespread distribution of information coupled with direct deliberation activities that included holding small-scale focus groups and conducting online dialogue.

Finally, the integration component, a variation of which will be explored in Chapter 5, involves the "creation of opportunities, in both research and training, for substantive interchange across the traditional, 'two cultures' divide that is aimed at long-term reflective capacity building" (Guston, 2014b: 226). CNS-ASU operationalized this dimension by connecting natural and social scientists to collaboratively explore the evolution of nanotechnology's emergence through multiple disciplinary lenses (Fisher, 2007, 2011; Schuurbiers and Fisher, 2009). However, it made more sense to modify this dimension in applying the anticipatory governance conceptual framework, especially given that the NGOs examined here generally operated outside a university setting. In this revised version of the dimension, integration is conceived of as a broader boundary-spanning effort that brings together individuals and organizations holding different perspectives on an issue. This boundary-spanning variation better describes the role PEN and ICON played to link together different stakeholders and institutions within the nanotechnology policy community.

Furthermore, beyond its origins in nanotechnology, anticipatory governance is also being applied in other areas of emerging technology, including synthetic biology (Wiek et al., 2012b), novel energy technologies (Davies and Selin, 2012), and personalized medicine (Ozdemir et al., 2009). Assessing the societal implications of these and other novel technological issues involves imagining multiple alternative futures, building bridges among stakeholders that have diverse perspectives, and more fully incorporating the views and values of the public into policymaking. Before diving into these issues, however, the chapter provides conceptual grounding by exploring the antecedents and origins of anticipatory governance. Knowing where it came from can help give a better sense of how the concept might be applicable in other contexts.

The antecedents and evolution of anticipatory governance

The technology assessment era

A precursor concept to anticipatory governance that held substantive weight in the field for multiple decades is the idea of technology assessment (Rip, Misa, and Schot, 1995; Schot and Rip, 1997). Rip (2001: 15512) defines technology assessment as "the early identification and assessment of eventual impacts of technological change and applications, as a service to policymaking and decision making" that involves "an element of anticipation of future developments and an element of feedback of such anticipations into relevant decision arenas." Technology assessment, however, faces the conundrum of what is known as the Collingridge dilemma: it is impossible to know the societal implications of a new technology before the technology becomes broadly disseminated, yet once a technology enters wide use, making adjustments or changing that technology's trajectory is difficult, at best, or perhaps impossible, at worst. Collingridge (1980: 11) states:

> The social consequences of a technology cannot be predicted early in the life of the technology. By the time undesirable consequences are discovered, however, the technology is often so much part of the whole economics and social fabric that its control is extremely difficult. This is the *dilemma of control*. When change is easy, the need for it cannot be foreseen; when the need for change is apparent, change has become expensive, difficult and time consuming.

These challenges have historically made technology assessment difficult to undertake. Knowledge about the future is inherently uncertain and imperfect, and long-term projections are highly sensitive to different underlying assumptions. Expectations rarely come to pass as initially planned. Unexpected developments or unforeseen knock-on effects can arise or occur all at once. The close links between many technology assessment undertakings and broader political philosophies about the role of government further enhance these complications. Technology assessment can therefore be a risky and precarious endeavor, reflected in the challenges faced in the practical implementation of technology assessment efforts in the past.

In the United States, official attempts to implement technology assessment date back to the 1950s, when federal agencies, such as the Department of Defense, and associated consulting firms, such as the RAND Corporation, began envisaging the long-term political and societal implications of new technologies. One early, influential champion of institutionalizing technology assessment at the federal level was then-House of Representatives member Emilio Daddario, who crystallized the argument in favor of public-sector technology assessment in a 1968 *Science* article titled "Academic Science and the Federal Government" (1968: 1249). Daddario (1968: 1250) emphasizes "the need of the federal government for assessment of current technologies and predictions of problems which might result from implementation of new technologies" and suggests—after dismissing the ability of the existing bureaucratic establishment to provide such a service—the need for establishing "totally new structures" to embody this function.

After a series of political struggles, OTA was born from the Technology Assessment Act of 1972. Over the course of 23 years, OTA served Congress by providing "early indications of the probable beneficial and adverse impacts of the applications of technology" through hundreds of publications that were both self-directed and generated on-demand (Office of Technology Assessment Archives, n.d.). OTA would become the model for other countries outside of the United States—such as the United Kingdom, Germany, Switzerland, Denmark, and the European Parliament—that formed similar technology assessment institutions within their respective governments (Bimber and Guston, 1997; Vig and Paschen, 2000). Recent efforts have focused on expanding technology assessment in developing countries as well (Ely, Van Zwanenberg, and Stirling, 2011). With the tradition of government-led technology assessment waning in the United States, technology assessment remains stronger in Europe today, carrying forward the ideas and practices that OTA pioneered.

Bimber (1996), Bimber and Guston (1997), and Kunkle (1995) chronicle how, once OTA was de-funded in 1995, the US government's capacity to conduct systematic, long-term analysis addressing new science and technology issues was weakened. While the GAO has attempted to fill this gap in recent years (Barkakati and Persons, 2013), the government's ability to address the societal implications of emerging technologies remains substantially diminished. A recent report on the topic by Kelly (2012: 1) emphasizes, "Congress . . . is missing adequate means for this purpose and depends on outdated and in some cases antiquated systems of information referral, sorting, communicating, and convening." To address this gap of inadequate information provision about the societal implications of emerging technologies, one suggested response is that technology assessment should be situated in non-public settings, outside of the federal government. While industry could potentially take on a publicly oriented technology assessment function to fill this gap, scholars (La Porte, 1997; Bimber and Guston, 1997) contended that the for-profit nature of these institutions would make them poor candidates to carry the torch of technology assessment forward. La Porte (1997) imagined that other institutional arrangements would be more effective at influencing policy debates. "There are a variety of possible models of non-governmentally-funded technology assessment for the public interest," writes La Porte (1997: 203). "This would be the ideal situation for objective, high quality research that can command the attention of policy makers and the public" (La Porte, 1997: 204).

Roots of the idea

Anticipatory governance arose from an effort to rethink the intersection between foresight and the policy process in a post-OTA world in the early years of the twenty-first century. In exploring the conceptual origins of anticipatory governance, both Karinen and Guston (2010) and Guston (2014b) find no exact references to the term "anticipatory governance" before 2001, and only a few even loose references to related concepts prior to that year. A similar search of the term in Google Scholar conducted in September 2013, paired with the online bibliometric citation analysis software "Publish or Perish," version 4.4.5 (Harzing, 2007), achieved similar results. A full text search for "anticipatory governance" in September 2013 returned 634 results of publications that mention the term, although a search limited to the use of the term in a publication's title returned only 39 results. Of the 634 materials referencing anticipatory governance in some respect, an analysis conducted by "Publish or Perish" indicated that more than 82 percent were published after the Barben et al. chapter in 2008.

Even given the term's relatively recent origins, however, Karinen and Guston (2010: 224) note that its emergence is "still somewhat mysterious." They point out that one significant thread of thinking on anticipatory governance started to emerge in 2001 from the science, technology, and environmental policy literature. Gupta (2001: 258) concludes her thesis on the global governance of biosafety with a section titled "The Need for Anticipatory Governance" and makes the argument that "there is dire need for institutional and governance structures to co-evolve with technological and environmental changes which have transformative potential, rather than to follow in their wake after such changes have become entrenched or irreversible." Guston (2014b) acknowledges that the CNS-ASU team drew on Gupta in developing a conceptual framework to address the long-term societal implications of nanotechnology and other emerging technologies. Guston and Sarewitz (2002) specifically mention anticipatory governance in conjunction with their notion of real-time technology assessment (RTTA). Guston and Sarewitz (2002: 98) highlight the methodological plurality underlying RTTA—a methodological plurality that would come to underlie anticipatory governance as well— emphasizing the need for both "retrospective (historical) as well as prospective (scenario)" analysis. While anticipatory governance plays a secondary role in development of the RTTA concept in Guston and Sarewitz (2002), over time anticipatory governance would become more fleshed-out as a stand-alone framework (Sarewitz, 2011).

Even as anticipatory governance was emerging from the science and technology policy literature by way of RTTA, additional schools of thought fed into the multidimensional development of the concept. One main precursor was the literature on new public management (Hammer and Champy, 1993; Wilson, 1994; Hood, 1995, 1996). In particular, Osborne and Gaebler's *Reinventing Government* (1993) explores "anticipatory government" as one of the ten types of suggested government reform. These authors make a case for the application of foresight in policymaking, stating that "some governments are not only trying to prevent problems, they are working to anticipate the future—to give themselves radar" (Osborne and Gaebler, 1993: 229). Osborne and Gaebler (1993) in turn refer to the idea of "anticipatory democracy" popularized in Alvin Toffler's *Future Shock* (1970) and further advanced by Clement Bezold's *Anticipatory Democracy* (1978). Building on Toffler, Osborne and Gaebler profile a variety of forward-looking mechanisms that have the potential to build an anticipatory mindset within government, including creating futures commissions, improving strategic planning processes, developing long-term budgeting processes, and maintaining the availability of contingency funds for unexpected budgetary challenges. Drawing heavily on the ideas in Osborne and Gaebler, Feltmate (1993: 88) recounts the history of the environmental movement and sustainable development in North America through the prism of "anticipatory government." The core of Feltmate's argument is that "anticipatory government should follow one fundamental principle: build foresight into the decision making process. Alternatively stated, a smart person solves a problem, a genius avoids it." The spirit of this aphorism—that challenges be leapfrogged, not just addressed as they arise—permeates the drive behind the formalized notion of anticipatory governance that has emerged in the subsequent two decades.

Let us note the subtle but significant change in meaning of the idea as it evolved from Toffler's anticipatory *democracy* to Osborne and Gaebler's anticipatory *government* to Barben et al.'s anticipatory *governance*. In the broader public administration literature, this shift in phrasing is indicative of the increased attention placed on examining policymaking elements that fall outside traditional characterizations of the state, such as networks, partnerships, and markets (Rhodes, 1996, 1997, 2007; Peters and Pierre, 1998). The notion of governance harkens back to Heclo (1978), who posited that complex social issues are moving away from bounded "iron triangles" to more diffuse "issue networks" that involve a broader range of institutional stakeholders. Exploring the process of democracy—in all of its messiness—and the role of government still remain central to understanding how public views are translated into representation and eventual policy. However, this "institutional turn" (Orren and Skowronek, 2004) taken by many policy scholars emphasizes the growing interest in examining how organizational structures outside of the state affect the policymaking process and at least implicitly feeds into this conceptual shift toward a focus on governance.

This perspective of examining a wide range of institutions and "governance infrastructures" (Johnston, 2010) in the policymaking process has also taken hold in the science and technology policy literature (Smith, Stirling, and Berkhout, 2005). This interest is reflected in concepts such as "post-normal science" (Funtowicz and Ravetz, 1993), the "co-production" of knowledge (Jasanoff, 2004), and "Mode 2" research at the intersection of science and society (Gibbons et al., 1994). Leach et al. (2007: 39) note that improved governance of contemporary science, technology, and environmental issues requires "recognizing the significance of multiple actors, networks, entities and spaces, formal and informal, more fixed and more transient, across different scales." These new arenas of governance consist of a "wide variety of venues—

from formal policy institutions like legislatures and regulatory agencies, to corporate and non-profit boardrooms, to classrooms and laboratories, to homes and garages—in which decisions are made" (Guston and Michelson, 2015: 92). In the nanotechnology policy literature, this perspective of exploring new governance venues underlies newly formalized practices such as "midstream modulation" (Fisher, Mahajan, and Mitcham, 2008) and "socio-technical integration research" (Fisher and Guston, 2012) that more explicitly embed deliberations about policy and social issues directly within the research laboratory.

Scattered allusions to "anticipatory governance" in the public administration literature started to appear in the early 2000s. For instance, as part of a long list of questions surrounding state governance reform in conflict situations, Baechler (2004: 292) asks, "What are some adapted ways and means to strengthen anticipatory governance in the sense of crisis prevention and violence mitigation?" In the following years, a smattering of additional references to anticipatory governance appears. In a paper on measuring good governance in the Philippines, Mendoza and Gonzalez (2002) refer to a variation of the term anticipatory governance as one of nine key elements in their framework. Similarly, in a chapter on the role of public administration in an information-rich society, Caldwell (2002: 153) reflects on the challenge that "governments and their administrators . . . characteristically focus on immediate situations and pressing problems. There are few political rewards for anticipating the long-range future."

Chi (2008) describes anticipatory governance as one of four critical strategies for transforming state policymaking. Echoing Toffler, Chi (2008: 12) defines anticipatory governance as "governing with foresight," as a way to "engage in a wide range of forward-looking activities and engage policy makers, managers, and the public on a regular basis." Chi (2008) suggests a range of "best practices in anticipatory governance" that include forming state futures commissions, undertaking policy visioning and planning exercises, adopting multi-year budgeting practices, and developing contingency plans and resources to deal with unexpected emergencies. Finally, moving closer to its canonical contemporary usage, Anderson (2007) applies the term in conjunction with the concept of "anticipatory knowledge" associated with two reports on nanotechnology produced by the United Kingdom government.

One additional thread of antecedent scholarship—one that is only tangentially referenced in Karinen and Guston (2010) but that appears to have at least implicitly influenced the development of the anticipatory governance concept—comes from the literature on complex adaptive systems. The connection between complexity theory and public administration began most famously in Rittel and Webber (1973), who single out the rise of "wicked" policy problems that have no "optimal solutions." Jervis (1998: 236) describes complex policy systems as "nonlinear relationships, outcomes [that] cannot be understood by adding together the units or their relations, and many of the results of actions are unintended." Rosen (2012) uses the concept of "anticipatory systems" as central to his explanation of how to apply complexity science to mathematics, physics, and biology. More recently, a white paper by Hartzog (2004) briefly mentions the link between anticipatory governance and complex adaptive systems. Hartzog (2004) writes, "Political order must pursue a corresponding policy shift from predictive and anticipatory governance to rapid-response networks, and must learn to act as a complex adaptive system." Finally, Swanson and Bhadwal (2009), who produced perhaps the most extensive treatment of any international development scholars on the connection between complexity theory and policymaking, reflect much of the spirit underlying anticipatory governance. They argue:

> adaptive policies anticipate the array of conditions that lie ahead through robust design using: (1) integrated and forward-looking analysis, including scenario planning; (2) multi-stakeholder deliberation to illuminate potential pitfalls and unintended consequences and (3) by monitoring key performance indicators to trigger automatic policy adjustments.
>
> (Swanson and Bhadwal, 2009: x)

While outside the scope of this book, the relationship between concepts arising from the complex adaptive systems literature—such as emergence, self-organization, tipping points, and network effects (Organisation for Economic Co-Operation and Development, 2009a)—and the anticipatory governance conceptual framework certainly warrant further investigation.

Variations on a theme

A variety of affiliated and related concepts have emerged as well, demonstrating alternatives and offshoots of the framework originally described by Barben et al. (2008). For example, Kuzma, Romanchek, and Kokotovich (2008) use the term "upstream oversight assessment" and Kuzma et al. (2008) adopt the notion of "integrated oversight assessment" as variants on anticipatory governance. Building on Guston and Sarewitz (2002), Kuzma et al. (2008: 1197) describe integrated oversight assessment as blending "historical analysis, expert elicitation, and behavioral consensus" in the service of "multidisciplinary criteria for evaluating oversight of emerging technologies." The phrase "participatory technology assessment" is also often used in discussions about how to rethink technology assessment (Sclove, 2010: vii). Participatory technology assessment emphasizes the possibilities of decentralized organizational structures to integrate citizen participation and expert analysis in discussions about the future of emerging technologies. Anticipatory governance has also been connected to the more recent idea of "responsible research and innovation" (Owen, Macnaghten, and Stilgoe, 2012: 751), a notion that has begun to gain traction predominantly in Europe (European Commission, 2011; Owen et al., 2013; Shelly-Egan and Davies, 2013; Stahl, 2013; Owen, 2014; Landeweerd et al., 2015) as a way of creating "better alignment of research and innovation with societal needs" (European Commission, 2013: 3). Responsible research and innovation has begun to receive a great deal of attention in academic and policy circles (Owen, Bessant, and Heintz, 2013; Valdivia and Guston, 2015), even spawning the creation of a new journal, *Journal of Responsible Innovation*, devoted to the concept (Guston et al., 2014). Anticipatory governance is also being used as a guiding framework for empirical research in areas such a geoengineering (Stilgoe, 2015) and synthetic biology (Brian, 2015). Finally, DeLeo (2016) developed the term "anticipatory policymaking" as a way of linking anticipatory governance to the broader literature on theories of the policy process.

Taken together, these conceptual constructs are intended to suggest the various ways in which knowledge aimed at anticipating future science and technology innovations can be utilized for policymaking purposes (Brown and Michael, 2003; Lyall and Tait, 2005; Pereira, von Schomberg, and Funtowicz, 2007). Kaiser et al. (2010) describe these various concepts as the emergence of an "assessment regime," noting, "The assessment regime is not additive to but *constitutive of* the formation of novel technologies." Anticipating future societal implications will increasingly play an integral, explicit role in the development of new technologies.

Although the idea has begun to face its share of criticism (Nordmann, 2010, 2014), anticipatory governance has continued to gain prominence in the general science and technology policy literature. One recent landscape analysis traces the various definitions of "anticipation" in fields as diverse as philosophy, biology, psychology, anthropology, resilience thinking, and futures thinking, among others (Boyd et al., 2015). Science and technology policy scholars and practitioners have adopted anticipatory governance as a way of addressing complex challenges that cut across multiple time spans, diffuse institutional boundaries, overlapping jurisdictions, and different communities of practice. The concept has helped in better understanding a diverse array of topics, including the environmental impacts of products that use carbon nanotubes (Philbrick, 2010; Wender et al., 2012), the long-term effects of climate change (Quay, 2010), novel energy technologies (Davies and Selin, 2012), urban sustainability practices (Wiek, Foley, and Guston, 2012; Wiek et al., 2013), robotics (Diep, Cabibihan, and Wolbring, 2014); and as not above, synthetic biology as well (Wiek et al., 2012; Gorman, 2012). A rather distinct subset of this literature has also applied the concept in the context of public health and biomedical research, including exploring advanced diagnostics (Fisher et al., 2012), vaccine development (Ozdemir, Faraj, and Knoppers, 2011), pharmacogenomics (Dove et al., 2012), personalized medicine (Ozdemir et al., 2009), infectious disease management (Barker, 2012), and bioethics (Ozdemir, 2009; Harvey and Salter, 2012).

Elsewhere, building on Anderson's (2007) use of the term, anticipatory governance has continued to appear in the communications literature to describe how differing narratives of the future can arise and the resulting impact on how the future is discussed and framed (Mittelstadt, Stahl, and Fairweather,

2015). For instance, research based on this conceptual framework has explored rhetoric surrounding security responses to potential terrorist threats (Aradau and van Munster, 2012) and to unpack descriptions of the travel disruption caused by the 2010 Iceland volcano eruption (Adey and Anderson, 2011). The term has also begun to appear in the complexity literature (Poli, 2012) to articulate the importance of preparing for unexpected events. Even farther afield, Engelbrecht (2012) developed the concept of "anticipatory corporate governance" in an examination of the role of the private sector in South Africa, showing how the phrase can be applied to understand behavior in the private sector. However, despite these disparate uses, few previous applications of the anticipatory governance framework are geared toward understanding the operational strategies adopted by NGOs.

To get a better handle on how the anticipatory governance idea has evolved in the academic literature, a bibliometric analysis was conducted to track the evolving use of the term within the science and technology policy literature. Through September 2013, citations of the term were tracked using a Google Scholar search and the bibliometric analysis software "Publish or Perish," version 4.4.5 (Harzing, 2007). A more detailed analysis of bibliometric coupling and co-citation counts of cited references was also undertaken through September 2013, using a set of journal articles identified through a search on the Web of Science database (Thomson Reuters, n.d.). The visualization package called VOSviewer, a standard software program designed for this purpose, was used to map the results (van Eck and Waltman, n.d.; Cobo et al., 2011).

Many of these uses of the term anticipatory governance do ultimately refer back to the Barben et al. (2008) publication or the Guston and Sarewitz (2002) article. The "Publish or Perish" software analyzing the full search results from Google Scholar indicates that the Guston and Sarewitz (2002) article, with 337 citations, is by far the most often cited source for the term. The Barben et al. (2008) chapter follows closely, three places later, with 157 citations. Using the Web of Science database, a search for the term "anticipatory governance" in article titles, abstracts, or keywords was conducted in the Web of Science database, returning 50 results as of September 2013. This substantially smaller number of results from the Web of Science search as compared to the Google Scholar is as expected: Web of Science only contains peer-reviewed articles published in academic journals listed in that database, and searching that database is restricted to title, abstract, and keyword fields. A search of Google Scholar covers a broader range of publication types, not just academic journals, and searches for keywords throughout a document's text, not just in the headline fields. The Web of Science results were then manually reviewed for relevancy, resulting in 33 articles that were extracted for analysis using the VOSviewer software.

The analyses performed on the resulting set of articles from the Web of Science search found that the contemporary use of anticipatory governance has started to cluster around distinct themes such as nanotechnology, synthetic biology, health and biomedical issues, and urban sustainability. Figure 3.1 shows a map of co-citations of cited references among the set of 33 articles. Figure 3.1 is a bibliographic coupling map, which clusters articles based upon how frequently they reference similar citations in their bibliographies. To ensure that only the most often-cited references are called-out clearly, a minimum threshold of four co-citations among cited references was used. This means that a reference was cited a minimum of four times among the set of 33 articles included in the analysis. This resulted in ten references meeting this threshold out of the 1,956 total references cited in the bibliographies of all of these articles combined. The threshold of four co-citations is shown here to emphasize the most relevant and frequently cited references among the 33 articles. The size of the node within the figure indicates the frequency of citation among these references. The lines between the cited references indicates those references that are cited together among the 33 articles (Small, 1973). This graph confirms the findings from the Google Scholar search and the "Publish or Perish" analysis. Barben et al. (2008) and Guston and Sarewitz (2002) are among the two most frequently cited references at nine times each. Guston (2008) is also cited nine times, with Macnaghten, Kearnes, and Wynne (2005) following with eight citations. Ulrich Beck's classic book *Risk Society* (1992) has seven citations, with the other frequently cited articles (Collingridge, 1980; Wilsdon and Willis, 2004; Renn and Roco, 2006b; Selin, 2007, 2008c) declining in citation counts from there. These analyses highlight how a few key source documents have influenced the spread of the anticipatory governance concept over the past few years.

Finally, the connection between the anticipatory governance concept and the broader policy studies literature, as constituted by the likes of Kingdon

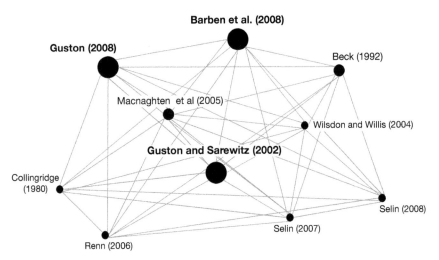

Figure 3.1 Co-citations of cited references map, minimum of four citations

Source: Author analysis

(1995) and Baumgartner and Jones (1993), is not yet well integrated. One particularly fruitful area to explore is what anticipatory governance suggests in terms of alterations or alternatives for the traditional stages model of policy development, as described in books such as Howlett, Ramesh, and Perl (2009). In their rubric, policies are developed in a five-step process that moves from agenda setting and problem definition to policy formulation to decision making to implementation to evaluation. While this is a useful heuristic, anticipatory governance offers an opportunity to rethink some of these stages and offer potential improvements. For instance, anticipatory governance suggests that the problem definition stage could be more usefully viewed as one of problem *imagination*, where long-term challenges are envisioned through foresight modalities such as scenario planning or trend monitoring. Similarly, the implementation and evaluation stages could better integrate *real-time feedback* and flesh out a strong public engagement component. Taking the future seriously requires integrating anticipatory thinking into all aspects of the policymaking process.

Expansion beyond the university

Beyond the multitude of recent scholarly applications of anticipatory governance, the application of the concept has also broadened beyond the academic sphere (Padukone, 2008; Fuerth and Faber, 2013; Miller, 2014). Fuerth (2012: 1) applies the notion of anticipatory governance as a way of improving the functioning of the United States executive branch in his call for "upgrading our legacy systems of management to meet today's unique brand of accelerating and complex challenges." This usage evolved from Fuerth's earlier focus on "forward engagement" (Fuerth, 2006; Fuerth, 2009), which applied "systematic foresight" to the federal policymaking process, addressing "challenges that are 'complex,' rather than just 'complicated'" (Fuerth, 2012: iv).

Fuerth (2012: 7) further describes anticipatory governance as "a systems-based approach for enabling governance to cope with accelerating, complex forms of change," closely recalling the framework developed by Barben et al. (2008). In his version of the concept, Fuerth (2012: 1) describes three constitutive elements as "*foresight* fused to policy analysis; *networked governance* for mission-based management and budgeting; and *feedback* to monitor and adjust policy relative to initial expectations" (italics in original). Relatedly, Fuerth (2012: 1) offers a number of "practical upgrade" suggestions designed to be "light on resources, compatible with the existing structures and processes of government, and fully executable under customary Presidential authorities." Echoing the description of anticipatory governance from Barben et al. (2008), Fuerth (2012: 4) argues:

> [T]hese new systems should enable the U.S. Government to deal more effectively with today's class of high-stakes, high-speed, complex issues on a more systematic basis, where we typically find ourselves acting

short term, even though we are aware of the need to shape events over the long term.

Fuerth (2012: 7) characterizes foresight as a process of "monitoring prospective oncoming events, analyzing potential implications, simulating alternative courses of action, asking unasked questions, and issuing timely warning to avert a risk or seize an opportunity." Here, the resemblance with the academic description of the theory is evident, covering issues such as the adoption of long-term thinking and ways to establish and constantly refresh a functional foresight system in government. The section on networked governance roughly corresponds to the Barben el al. (2008) notion of integration, in the sense of developing new ways to link actors within an organization more fluidly, across organizational or hierarchical boundaries. Fuerth (2012: 30) notes, "Modern policy issues erode the customary boundaries that differentiate bureaucratic concepts and the missions that are based on them." Addressing these challenges requires moving away from "vertical (stovepiped) hierarchies" toward more interdisciplinary, "lateral," and "cross-cutting" integration. Finally, Fuerth (2012) proposes that feedback be routinely integrated into the policy process through tracking policy execution, establishing explicit venues for coordinating broader input into policymaking, and through a regular diagnostic review of policy consequences that involves vigorous external auditing and stakeholder commentary.

Table 3.1 summarizes the application of the anticipatory governance concept as applied in three different settings—academia (Barben et al., 2008), government (Fuerth, 2012), and NGOs (this book)—with each variation roughly following a similar arrangement. Each includes a forward-looking dimension, a dimension related to organizational function and role, and a dimension concerned with the public. The intention and objective of each configuration,

Table 3.1 Comparison of anticipatory governance dimensions

Category	Barben et al. (2008)	Fuerth (2012)	This research
Context	University	Government	Non-governmental organizations
Forward-looking dimension	Foresight	Foresight	Foresight, coupled with strategies directed at near-term policy influence
Organizational dimension	Integration of social and natural scientists	Networked governance	Boundary-spanning
Public dimension	Engagement and direct deliberation	Feedback	Combination of communications and deliberation

however, is different. Barben et al. (2008) introduced their conceptual framework for a program of academic research and social science experimentation. Fuerth (2012), in contrast, seeks to apply the idea to a setting where collaboration across bureaucracies and government structures is of utmost concern. Here, the goal is to show how anticipatory governance can be applied in a non-governmental setting to better understand the strategies used by NGOs as they seek to influence policymaking about emerging technologies.

Key lessons arise here when taking account of these three variations in tandem. First, the notion of foresight is at the core of all three versions. While the various foresight methods championed in each form are disparate—scenario planning comes to the forefront in Barben et al. (2008), horizon scanning is mentioned more prominently in Fuerth (2008), and the use of hypotheticals and vignettes by the organizations studied here is described in subsequent chapters—all three versions portray a non-predictive, non-probabilistic view of foresight and emphasize the centrality of taking a long-term view on the issue at hand. Second, all three versions of anticipatory governance contain an element focused on engaging the public. This is a core consideration in Barben et al. (2008) and, as this research will show, PEN in particular adopted an expansive view of public engagement, one that encompassed a spectrum of activities that ranged from external communications to direct deliberation. The role of the public does emerge somewhat less strongly in the description provided in Fuerth (2012), as more attention is paid toward implementing a process of regular policy iteration and review than in gaining widespread input across audiences.

The organizational dimension is perhaps the most varied across the three iterations of the concept, the one requiring the most substantive adjustments. This is due, in part, because this dimension is most closely tied to the different kinds of institutions under consideration. For Fuerth (2012), the integration of the social sciences with the natural sciences is not as pertinent or relevant an issue as in the academic context. Instead, Fuerth (2008) describes networking and feedback as the prescription for reorganizing government functions. This research emphasizes more of the boundary-spanning role played by groups such as PEN and ICON within the nanotechnology policy community. In making these modifications, the intention is to show how anticipatory governance can be applied to a broad array of organizational types beyond the university.

Organizations such as PEN did not necessarily describe their work as taking place under the rubric of anticipatory governance: the exact term or its cognates are not used in any of PEN's documents or on its website. However, PEN did operate with a strong anticipatory approach, made evident through the organization's mission statement and ideas presented in its planning documents. The notion of anticipation was in every self-description that PEN included in its public reports, affirming that PEN "is dedicated to helping business, governments, and the public *anticipate* and manage the possible human and environmental implications of nanotechnology" (italics added) (Project on Emerging Nanotechnologies, n.d.).

The distinct elements of the theory are still present, however, especially in PEN's early strategic planning documents. Foresight was mentioned explicitly as one of PEN's primary focal points. In one of the four pre-project planning documents produced in 2004 describing potential "key characteristics of an initiative on nanotechnology," PEN's role was emphasized as being to "address surprise" and "stay strategic" by keeping a long-term view of nanotechnology at the forefront of consideration (Rejeski, 2004a: 7). Substantial emphasis in this planning document is devoted to articulating need to "develop mechanisms to deal with the novelty factor and potential surprises that are bound to be a continuing part of nanotechnology development into the future" and on "track potential long-term developments that could pose new and unique risks and proactively position research and oversight or regulatory mechanisms to address these" (Rejeski, 2004a: 7). Once the organization was formally established, PEN further emphasized its focus as exploring nanotechnology's potential future benefits and risks. Its mission statement alluded to this points, noting that, "from new cancer therapies to pollution-eating compounds, from more durable consumer products to detectors for biohazards like anthrax, from novel foods to more efficient solar cells, nanotechnologies are changing the way people think about the future" (Project on Emerging Nanotechnologies, n.d.). Additionally, in each quarterly report, "Better Foresight" was included as one of the three main groups of topics that PEN used to describe its work to its funder.

Foresight is less explicitly mentioned as an underlying rationale for ICON's activities. A search for the term "foresight" in two publicly available documents representing ICON's governance structure and operational plan returned no results (International Council on Nanotechnology, 2007; International Council on Nanotechnology, 2009b). This should not be surprising, nor does it imply that foresight considerations were wholly outside the scope of ICON's work. Instead, because ICON has a predominant focus on advancing scientific research on potential EHS implications, this likely explains this lack of mention of foresight as an explicit motivating factor for the organization's activities.

In terms of boundary-spanning, PEN, ICON, and the Synthetic Biology Project made this dimension explicit in their mission statements. In many ways, this boundary-spanning role was embedded in ICON's governance structure, with representatives from different sectors taking on decision-making authority to direct the activities the organization undertook. The focus on boundary-spanning by PEN and the Synthetic Biology Project is made explicit in their mission statement, although not formally embodied in their organizational structure, as was the case with ICON. For example, boundary-spanning is made explicit in PEN's mission statement by noting that the organization "collaborates with researchers, government, industry, NGOs, policymakers, and others to look long term, to identify gaps in knowledge and regulatory processes, and to develop strategies for closing them" (Project on Emerging Nanotechnologies, n.d.). The mission statement of the Synthetic Biology Project uses also verbatim language as well. In PEN's quarterly reports, the other two categories that PEN used to describe and structure its efforts in addition to "Better Foresight"—"Strategic Research" and "Better Oversight"— explicitly set out a boundary-spanning component. One of the 2004 planning documents articulated this approach early on in PEN's history. This memo noted that the project would "leverage the system" by focusing on "building and leveraging networks, not just individual entities. The number of players (sectors, scientific disciplines, agencies, businesses, etc.) involved in nanotechnology results in high value added from improved coordination and knowledge transfer" (Rejeski, 2004a: 8).

Finally, PEN's broad take on public engagement included efforts that tried to both build public understanding through communications while also directly soliciting the views of individuals about their perceptions on the risks and benefits of nanotechnology. This theme was first articulated in one of the pre-project planning documents, which lays out that PEN would "conduct a focus group to look more deeply at public attitudes towards specific regulatory agencies with large roles to play in nanotech" (Rejeski, 2004b). The dual communications and direct engagement components were also articulated clearly in PEN's mission statement: "All research results, reports, and the outcomes of our meetings and programs are made widely available through publications and over the web. We include a wide variety of stakeholders, both domestically and internationally, in our work" (Project on Emerging Nanotechnologies, n.d.). Much of this phrasing was also used in describing the dissemination strategy of the Synthetic Biology Project as well.

PEN ended up devoting substantial attention to public information dissemination and direct deliberation activities, with the former receiving more attention than the latter. The Synthetic Biology Project disseminated its work as PEN did but did not achieve PEN's level of prominence and notoriety in terms of communications and engagement. For instance, many of PEN's quarterly reports presented reams of pages dedicated to the organization's press coverage, including reprints of key articles and reports the organization published. These internal reports also included statistics tracking the usage levels of PEN's website and other multimedia content. Furthermore, one interviewee with knowledge of PEN's formation described how developing a detailed communications strategy and, to some extent direct deliberation activities, were both important underlying reasons as to why The Pew Charitable Trusts decided to support PEN in the first place. These dimensions of PEN's work were deliberately "written into the overall architecture of the grant," said the interviewee.

Notions related to anticipatory governance also are included in PEN's substantive analyses. Ideas suggestive of anticipatory governance were present in many conclusions included in the reports PEN published, even if the phrase "anticipatory governance" itself was not referred to explicitly in these materials. For instance, PEN advisor and report author Terry Davies articulated various elements of the anticipatory governance conceptual framework in two of the reports he wrote for PEN. In *Oversight of Next-Generation Nanotechnology*, Davies

(2009: 31) made the case for improved foresight capabilities: "What is needed is a capability to consider the overall impacts of major new technologies and to do so while there is still time to deal with the impacts." In *Nanotechnology Oversight: An Agenda for the New Administration*, Davies (2008: 19) also argued that expanding public engagement in decision making processes was critical:

> Many of the policies for dealing with new technologies entail questions of ethics and values. The experts on these subjects are members of the general public, so it is important to obtain their views . . . and to give the public an opportunity to express opinions and to be heard.

In both reports, Davies hits on the key themes embedded in anticipatory governance: the need for new capabilities to respond to rapidly advancing technologies, an institutionalized ability to think about long-term effects and unintended consequences, and enhanced efforts to integrate the public's views into the policymaking process.

Interviews also indicated that senior PEN staff and advisors, in particular, were very familiar with themes related to anticipatory governance and technology assessment, having worked at OSTP and NSF and being knowledgeable about OTA. One interviewee with knowledge of PEN's connection with The Pew Charitable Trusts said, "A lot of these guys came out of the same general school in the policy world, and many of them had close connections with OTA," noting that this imbued senior PEN staff with "a different way of thinking about issues across fields."

Finally, given their closely aligned interests, PEN did collaborate with scholars at CNS-ASU over the course of their history. The two institutions held a joint event at the Wilson Center in 2009 focused on nanotechnology's role in building a future innovation economy (Project on Emerging Nano-technologies, 2009b). They also co-organized a briefing for the United States Congressional Nanotechnology Caucus that same year, bringing together scholars from both institutions to brief Congressional staff and federal policy-makers on public understanding, views, and opinions toward nanotechnology risks and benefits (Nanotechnology Now, 2009).

The following chapters show that the three dimensions of anticipatory governance do not exist or operate independently. Considering them as an ensemble and exploring their mutually reinforcing connections is particularly vital on two levels. Practically, NGOs are unlikely to operationalize these dimensions separately from one another; they will draw on elements of each when developing their programming and plans of action. Conceptually, an integrated view helps to show how alternative considerations of the long-term future can combine with other strategies and be marshaled to influence the policymaking process.

In summary, a signal theoretical contribution of this research is exploring the evolution of anticipatory governance and how it can be applied in different sectoral contexts. These adjustments to the main dimensions of the original academic conceptualization—particularly with respect to the notion of integration—can add versatility to the conceptual framework and facilitate its application to institutions in the public and non-governmental realms. The increasingly long-term and complex nature of contemporary scientific and technology policy challenges suggests that theories of the policy process must do more to explicitly take account of the future. Anticipatory governance represents an especially promising conceptual and practical approach to better account for this future-centered orientation. Adopting this variation on the original conceptual framework can help build understanding and structure insights about how the organizations studied here operated and shed light on the strategies they used to assess the societal implications of emerging technologies. Examining each of the adjusted dimensions of anticipatory governance—foresight, boundary-spanning, and a combination of communications and direct engagement—and discussing how these dimensions are interwoven with one another will be the subject of the following three chapters.

Bibliography

Adey, P., and Anderson, B. (2011, February). Anticipation, Materiality, Event: The Icelandic Ash Cloud Disruption and the Security of Mobility. *Mobilities*, *6*(1), 11–20.

Anderson, B. (2007). Hope for Nanotechnology: Anticipatory Knowledge and the Governance of Affect. *Area*, *39*(2), 156–165.

Aradau, C., and van Munster, R. (2012). The Time/Space of Preparedness: Anticipating the "Next Terrorist Attack." *Space and Culture*, *15*(2), 98–109.

Baechler, G. (2004). Conflict Transformation through State Reform. In A. Austin, M. Fischer, and N. Ropers (Eds.), *Berghof Handbook for Conflict Transformation* (pp. 273–294. Wiesbaden, Germany: VS Verlag.

Barben, D., Fisher, E., Selin, C., and Guston, D. H. (2008). Anticipatory Governance of Nanotechnology: Foresight, Engagement, Integration. In E. J. Hackett, O. Amsterdamska, M. Lynch, and J. Wajcman (Eds.), *The Handbook of Science and Technology Studies*, (3rd ed.). (pp. 979–1000). Cambridge, MA: The MIT Press.

Barkakati, N., and Persons, T. M. (2013, May). Technology Assessment for the United States Congress: The Government Accountability Office's Center for Science, Technology, and Engineering. *Technikfolgenabschatzung—Theorie und Praxis*, *1*(22), 94–96.

Barker, K. (2012). Influenza Preparedness and the Bureaucratic Reflex: Anticipating and Generating the 2009 H1N1 Event. *Health and Place*, *18*(4), 701–709.

Baumgartner, F., and Jones, B. (1993). *Agendas and Instability in American Politics*. Chicago, IL: The University of Chicago Press.

Beck, U. (1992). *Risk Society: Towards a New Modernity*. London, United Kingdom: SAGE Publications.

Bezold, C. (Ed.). (1978). *Anticipatory Democracy: People in the Politics of the Future*. New York, NY: Random House.

Bimber, B. (1996). *The Politics of Expertise in Congress: The Rise and Fall of the Office of Technology Assessment*. Albany, NY: State University of New York Press.

Bimber, B., and Guston, D. (1997). Technology Assessment: The End of OTA. *Technological Forecasting and Social Change*, *54*(2/3), 125–308.

Boyd, E., Nykvist, B., Borgstrom, S., and Stacewicz, I. A. (2015). Anticipatory Governance for Social-Ecological Resilience. *AMBIO, 44*(S1), S149-S161.

Brian, J. D. (2015). Special Perspectives Section: Responsible Research and Innovation for Synthetic Biology. *Journal of Responsible Innovation, 2*(1), 78–80.

Brown, N., and Michael, M. (2003). A Sociology of Expectations: Retrospecting Prospects and Prospecting Retrospects. *Technology Analysis and Strategic Management, 15*(1), 3–18.

Cairney, P. (2013). Standing on the Shoulders of Giants: How Do We Combine the Insights of Multiple Theories in Public Policy Studies? *Policy Studies Journal, 41*(1), 1–21.

Caldwell, L. (2002). Public Administration, The New Generation: Management in High Information Level Society. In E. Vigoda (Ed.), *Public Administration: An Interdisciplinary Critical Analysis* (pp. 133–155). New York, NY: Marcel Dekker.

Chi, K. S. (2008). *Four Strategies to Transform State Governance.* Washington, DC: IBM Center for The Business of Government.

Cobo, M., Lopez-Herrera, A., Herrera-Viedma, E., and Herrera, F. (2011). Science Mapping Software Tools: Review, Analysis, and Cooperative Study Among Tools. *Journal of the America Society for Information Science and Technology, 62*(7), 1382–1402.

Cohen, M. D., March, J. G., and Olsen, J. P. (1972, March). A Garbage Can Model of Organizational Choice. *Administrative Science Quarterly, 17*(1), 1–25.

Collingridge, D. (1980). *The Social Control of Technology.* London, UK: Frances Pinter.

Daddario, E. Q. (1968). Science in the Federal Government. *Science, 162*(3859), 1249–1251.

Davies, J. C. (2008). *Nanotechnology Oversight: An Agenda for the Next Administration.* Washington, DC: Project on Emerging Nanotechnologies.

Davies, J. C. (2009). *Oversight of Next Generation Nanotechnology.* Washington, DC: Project on Emerging Nanotechnologies.

Davies, S. R., and Selin, C. (2012). Energy Futures: Five Dilemmas of the Practice of Anticipatory Governance. *Environmental Communication: A Journal of Nature and Culture, 6*(1), 119–136.

DeLeo, R. A. (2016). *Anticipatory Policymaking: When Government Acts to Prevent Problems and Why It Is So Hard.* New York, NY: Routledge.

DeLeon, P. (1999). The Stages Approach to the Policy Process: What Has it Done? Where is it Going? In P. A. Sabatier (Ed.), *Theories of the Policy Process* (pp. 19–32). Boulder, CO: Westview Press.

Diep, L., Cabibihan, J.-J., and Wolbring, G. (2014). Social Robotics through an Anticipatory Governance Lens. In M. Beetz, B. Johnston, and M.-A. Williams (Eds.), *Social Robotics, 6th International Conference, ICSR 2014* (pp. 115–124). Dordrecht, The Netherlands: Springer.

Dove, E. S., Faraj, S. A., Kolker, E., and Ozdemir, V. (2012). Designing a Post-Genomics Knowledge Ecosystem to Translate Pharmacogenomics into Public Health Action. *Genome Medicine, 4*(91), 1–11.

Ely, A., Van Zwanenberg, P., and Stirling, A. (2011). *New Models of Technology Assessment for Development.* Brighton, UK: STEPS Centre.

Engelbrecht, M. (2012, March). *The Art of Shapeshifting: Facilitating Strategic Foresight to Independent Non-Executive Directors—A Strategic Approach to Corporate Governance in SA.* Capetown, South Africa: Stellenbosch University.

European Commission. (2011, May 16–17). *DG Research Workshop on Responsible Research and Innovation in Europe.* Retrieved September 9, 2015, from European

Commission: http://ec.europa.eu/research/science-society/document_library/pdf_06/responsible-research-and-innovation-workshop-newsletter_en.pdf

European Commission. (2013). *Options for Strengthening Responsible Research and Innovation.* Luxembourg: European Union.

Feltmate, B. W. (1993). *Barriers to Achieving Sustainable Development in North America: Historical Naivety, Media Limitations and Non-Anticipatory Governance.* 382. Toronto, Canada: Wilfrid Laurier University, Theses and Dissertations (Comprehensive).

Fisher, E. (2007). Ethnographic Invention: Probing the Capacity of Laboratory Decisions. *NanoEthics, 1*(2), 155–165.

Fisher, E. (2011). Public Science and Technology Scholars: Engaging Whom? *Science and Engineering Ethics, 17*(4), 607–620.

Fisher, E., and Guston, D. H. (2012). *STIR: Socio-Technical Integration Research.* Tempe, AZ: Arizona State University.

Fisher, E., Boenink, M., van der Burg, S., and Woodbury, N. (2012). Responsible Healthcare Innovation: Anticipatory Governance of Nanodiagnostics for Theranostics Medicine. *Expert Review of Molecular Diagnostics, 12*(8), 857–870.

Fisher, E., Mahajan, R. L., and Mitcham, C. (2008, December). Midstream Modulation of Technology: Governance From Within . *Bulletin of Science Technology Society, 26*(6), 485–496.

Fuerth, L. (2006, Spring). Strategic Myopia: The Case for Forward Engagement. *The National Interest, 83*, 58–63.

Fuerth, L. (2009). Foresight and Anticipatory Governance. *Foresight, 11*(4), 14–32.

Fuerth, L. (2012). *Anticipatory Governance: Practical Upgrades.* Washington, DC: Project on Forward Engagement.

Fuerth, L., and Faber, E. M. (2013, July–August). Anticipatory Governance: Winning the Future. *Futurist, 47*(4), 42–49.

Funtowicz, S. O., and Ravetz, J. R. (1993, September). Science for the Post-Normal Age. *Futures, 25*(7), 739–755.

Garfield, E. (1955). Citation Indexes for Science: A New Dimension in Documentation through Association of Ideas. *Science, 122*(3159), 108–111.

Gibbons, M., Limoges, C., Nowotny, H., Schwartzman, S., Scott, P., and Trow, M. (1994). *The New Production of Knowledge: The Dynamics of Science and Research in Contemporary Societies.* London, UK: SAGE Publications.

Gorman, M. E. (2012). A Framework for Anticipatory Governance and Adaptive Management of Synthetic Biology. *International Journal of Social Ecology and Sustainable Development, 3*(2), 64–68.

Gupta, A. (2001, December). Doctoral Dissertation. *Searching for Shared Norms: Global Governance of Biosafety.* New Haven, CT: Yale University.

Guston, D. H. (2008, August 21). Innovation Policy: Not Just a Jumbo Shrimp. *Nature, 454*(7207), 940–941.

Guston, D. H. (2010a). *Societal Dimensions Research in the National Nanotechnology Initiative.* Tempe, AZ: Consortium for Science, Policy and Outcomes, Arizona State University.

Guston, D. H. (2010b). The Anticipatory Governance of Emerging Technologies. *Journal of the Korean Vacuum Society, 19*(6), 432–441.

Guston, D. H. (2011). Anticipatory Governance: A Strategic Vision for Building Reflexivity into Emerging Technologies. *Presentation at Resilience 2011.* Tempe, AZ.

Guston, D. H. (2014b). Understanding "Anticipatory Governance." *Social Studies of Science, 44*(2), 218–242.

Guston, D. H., and Michelson, E. S. (2015). Anticipatory Governance. In J. Holbrook, and C. Mitcham, *Ethics, Science, Technology, and Engineering: A Global Resource*, 2nd ed. (pp. 92–94). Farmington Hills, MI: Macmillan Reference.

Guston, D. H., and Sarewitz, D. (2002). Real-time Technology Assessment. *Technology in Society, 24*(1–2), 93–109.

Guston, D. H., Fisher, E., Gurnwald, A., Owen, R., Swierstra, T., and van der Burg, S. (2014). Responsible Innovation: Motivations for a New Journal. *Journal of Responsible Innovation, 1*(1), 1–8.

Hackett, E. J., Conz, D., Parker, J., Bashford, J., and DeLay, S. (2004, July). Tokamaks and Turbulence: Research Ensembles, Policy and Technoscientific Work. *Research Policy, 33*(5), 747–767.

Hamlett, P., Cobb, M. D., and Guston, D. H. (2008). *National Citizens' Technology Forum: Nanotechnologies and Human Enhancement.* Tempe, AZ: The Center for Nanotechnology in Society, Arizona State University.

Hammer, M., and Champy, J. (1993). *Reengineering the Corporation: A Manifesto for Business Revolution.* New York, NY: HarperBusiness.

Hartzog, P. B. (2004). *21st Century Governance as a Complex Adaptive System.* Retrieved November 14, 2015, from Panarchy: www.panarchy.org/hartzog/governance.html

Harvey, A., and Salter, B. (2012, September). Anticipatory Governance: Bioethical Expertise for Human/Animal Chimeras. *Science as Culture, 21*(3), 291–313.

Harzing, A.-W. (2007). *Publish or Perish.* Retrieved November 14, 2015, from Harzing.com: www.harzing.com/pop.htm

Heclo, H. (1978). Issue Networks and the Executive Establishment. In A. King (Ed.), *The New American Political System* (pp. 87–124). Washington, DC: American Enterprise Institute.

Henry, A. D., and Dietz, T. (2011). Information, Networks, and the Complexity of Trust in Commons Governance. *International Journal of the Commons, 5*(2), 188–212.

Holdren, J. P., Sunstein, C. R., and Siddiqui, I. A. (2011, June 9). *Policy Principles for the U.S. Decision-Making Concerning Regulation and Oversight of Applications of Nanotechnology and Nanomaterials.* Washington, DC: Office of Science and Technology Policy .

Hood, C. (1995). Contemporary Public Management: A New Global Paradigm? *Public Policy and Administration, 10*(2), 104–117.

Hood, C. (1996). Exploring Variations in Public Reform in the 1980s. In H. A. Bekke, J. L. Perry, and T. A. Toonen (Eds.), *Civil Service Systems in Comparative Perspective* (pp. 268–287). Bloomington, IN: Indiana University Press.

Howlett, M., Ramesh, M., and Perl, A. (2009). *Studying Public Policy: Policy Cycles and Policy Subsystems,* (3rd ed.). Oxford, UK: Oxford University Press.

International Council on Nanotechnology. (2007, October 25). *Governance Structure and Operational Plan.* Retrieved September 18, 2015, from International Council on Nanotechnology: http://cohesion.rice.edu/centersandinst/icon/emplibrary/ICO Nmanagementv7_4%20Full%20Text.pdf

International Council on Nanotechnology. (2009b, October 21). *Governance Structure and Operational Plan.* Retrieved September 17, 2015, from International Council on Nanotechnology: http://cohesion.rice.edu/centersandinst/icon/emplibrary/ICON managementv2009_1_Full_Text.pdf

Jasanoff, S. (Ed.). (2004). *States of Knowledge: The Co-Production of Science and Social Order.* London, UK: Routledge.

Jervis, R. (1998). Complex Systems: The Role of Interactions. In D. S. Alberts, and T. J. Czerwinski (Eds.), *Coping with the Bounds: Speculations on Nonlinearity in Military*

Affairs (pp. 235–251). Washington, DC: Department of Defense Command and Control Research Publication.

Jochim, A. E., and May, P. J. (2010, May). Beyond Subsystems: Policy Regimes and Governance. *Policy Studies Journal, 38*(2), 303–327.

Johnston, E. (2010, December). Governance Infrastructures in 2020. *Public Administration Review, 70*(S1), S122–S128.

Kaiser, M., Kurath, M., Maasen, S., and Rehmann-Sutter, C. (Eds.). (2010). *Governing Future Technologies: Nanotechnology and the Rise of the Assessment Regime*. Dordrecht, The Netherlands: Springer Science and Media.

Karinen, R., and Guston, D. H. (2010). Toward Anticipatory Governance: The Experience with Nanotechnology. In M. Kaiser, M. Kurath, S. Maasen, and Christoph Rehmann-Sutter (Eds.), *Governing Future Technologies: Nanotechnology and the Rise of an Assessment Regime* (pp. 217–232). Dordrecht, The Netherlands: Springer Science & Media.

Kelly, L. (2012). *Congress' Wicked Problem: Seeking Knowledge Inside the Information Tsunami*. Washington, DC: New America Foundation.

Kingdon, J. (1995). *Agendas, Alternatives, and Public Policies*. New York, NY: Addison-Wesley.

Kunkle, G. C. (1995). New Challenge or the Past Revisited: The Office of Technology Assessment in Historical Context. *Technology in Society, 17*(2), 175–196.

Kuzma, J., Paradise, J., Ramachandran, G., Kim, J.-A., Kokotovitch, A., and Wolf, S. M. (2008). An Integrated Approach to Oversight Assessment for Emerging Technologies. *Risk Analysis, 28*(4), 1197–1220.

Kuzma, J., Romanchek, J., and Kokotovich, A. (2008). Upstream Oversight Assessment for Agrifood Nanotechnology: A Case Studies Approach. *Risk Analysis, 28*(4), 1081–1098.

La Porte, T. M. (1997). New Opportunities for Technology Assessment in the Post-OTA World. *Technological Forecasting and Social Change, 54*(2–3), 199–214.

Landeweerd, L., Townend, D., Mesman, J., and Van Hoyweghen, I. (2015). Reflections on Different Governance Styles in Regulating Science: A Contribution to "Responsible Research and Innovation." *Life Sciences, Society and Policy, 11*(8), 1–22.

Lasswell, H. D. (1956). *The Decision Process: Seven Categories of Functional Analysis*. College Park, MD: University of Maryland Press.

Leach, M., Bloom, G., Ely, A., Nightingale, P., Scoones, I., Shah, E., and Smith, A. (2007). *Understanding Governance: Pathways to Sustainability*. Brighton, UK: STEPS Centre.

Leydesdorff, L. (1987). Various Methods for the Mapping of Science. *Scientometrics, 11*(5–6), 295–324.

Lindblom, C. E. (1959, Spring). The Science of "Muddling Through." *Public Administration Review, 19*(2), 79–88.

Lyall, C., and Tait, J. (2005). *New Modes of Governance: Developing an Integrated Policy Approach to Science, Technology, Risk and the Environment*. Aldershot, UK: Ashgate Publishing.

Macnaghten, P., Kearnes, M. B., and Wynne, B. (2005, December). Nanotechnology, Governance, and Public Deliberation: What Role for the Social Sciences? *Science Communication, 27*(2), 268–291.

May, P. J., and Jochim, A. E. (2013, August). Policy Regime Perspectives: Policies, Politics, and Governing. *Policy Studies Journal, 41*(3), 426–452.

Mendoza, M. L., and Gonzalez, E. T. (2002). *Between Good Management and Good Governance: The Cast for the Philippine Quality Award for the Public Sector.* Brisbane, Australia: Asia Pacific Conference on Governance.

Miller, R. (2014). *Networking to Improve Global/Local Anticipatory Capacities: A Scoping Exercise.* Paris, France: UNESCO.

Mintrom, M., and Norman, P. (2009). Policy Entrepreneurship and Policy Change. *Policy Studies Journal, 37*(4), 649–667.

Mittelstadt, B. D., Stahl, B. C., and Fairweather, N. B. (2015, November). How to Shape a Better Future? Epistemic Difficulties for Ethical Assessment and Anticipatory Governance of Emerging Technologies. *Ethical Theory and Moral Practice, 18*(5), 1027–1047.

Nanotechnology Now. (2009, March 5). *Briefing before the U.S. Congressional Nanotechnology Caucus.* Retrieved November 17, 2015, from Nanotechnology Now: www.nanotech-now.com/news.cgi?story_id=32349

Nordmann, A. (2010, June). A Forensics of Wishing: Technology Assessment in the Age of Technoscience. *Poiesis and Praxis, 7*(1), 5–15.

Nordmann, A. (2014). Responsible Innovation, The Art and Craft of Anticipation. *Journal of Responsible Innovation, 1*(1), 87–98.

Nowlin, M. C. (2011). Theories of the Policy Process: State of Research and Emerging Trends. *Policy Studies Journal, 39*(S1), 41–60.

Office of Technology Assessment Archives. (n.d.). *Technology Assessment Act.* Retrieved November 14, 2015, from Princeton University: www.princeton.edu/~ota/ns20/act_f.html

Organisation for Economic Co-Operation and Development. (2009a). *Applications of Complexity Science for Public Policy: New Tools for Finding Unanticipated Consequences and Unrealized Opportunities.* Paris, France: Organization for Economic Co-operation and Development, Global Science Forum.

Orren, K., and Skowronek, S. (2004). *The Search for American Political Development.* Cambridge, UK: CUP.

Osborne, D., and Gaebler, T. (1993). *Reinventing Government: How the Entrepreneurial Spirit is Transforming the Public Sector.* New York, NY: Addison-Wesley.

Ostrom, E. (1990). *Governing the Commons: The Evolution of Institutions for Collective Actions.* Oxford, UK: CUP.

Ostrom, E. (1998, March). A Behavioral Approach to the Rational Choice Theory of Collective Action: Presidential Address, American Political Science Association, 1997. *The American Political Science Review, 92*(1), 1–22.

Owen, R. (2014). The UK Engineering and Physical Sciences Research Council's Commitment to a Framework for Responsible Innovation. *Journal of Responsible Innovation, 1*(1), 113–117.

Owen, R., Macnaghten, P., and Stilgoe, J. (2012). Responsible Research and Innovation: From Science in Society to Science for Society, with Society. *Science and Public Policy, 39*(6), 751–760.

Owen, R., Bessant, J., and Heintz, M. (Eds.). (2013). *Responsible Innovation: Managing the Responsible Emergence of Science and Innovation in Society.* Chichester, UK: John Wiley & Sons.

Owen, R., Stilgoe, J., Macnaghten, P., Gorman, M., Fisher, E., and Guston, D. (2013). A Framework for Responsible Innovation. In R. Owen, J. Bessant, and M. Heintz (Eds.), *Responsible Innovation: Managing the Responsible Emergence of Science and Innovation in Society* (pp. 27–50). Chichester, United Kingdom: John Wiley & Sons.

Ozdemir, V. (2009). What To Do When the Risk Environment Is Rapidly Shifting and Heterogeneous? Anticipatory Governance and Real-Time Assessment of Social Risks in Multiply Marginalized Populations Can Prevent IRB Mission Creep, Ethical Inflation or Underestimation of Risks. *The American Journal of Bioethics, 9*(11), 65–68.

Ozdemir, V., Faraj, S. A., and Knoppers, B. M. (2011). Steering Vaccinomics Innovations with Anticipatory Governance and Participatory Foresight. *OMICS A Journal of Integrative Biology, 15*(9), 637–646.

Ozdemir, V., Husereau, D., Hyland, S., Samper, S., and Salleh, M. (2009, December). Personalized Medicine Beyond Genomics: New Technologies, Global Health Diplomacy and Anticipatory Governance. *Current Pharmacogenomics and Personalized Medicine, 7*(4), 225–230.

Padukone, N. (2008, December 10). *India's "September 12th."* Retrieved November 16, 2015, from Observer Research Foundation: www.orfonline.org/cms/sites/orfonline/modules/analysis/AnalysisDetail.html?cmaid=15513&mmacmaid=15514

Pereira, A. G., von Schomberg, R., and Funtowicz, S. (2007). Foresight Knowledge Assessment. *International Journal of Foresight and Innovation Policy, 3*(1), 53–75.

Peters, B. G., and Pierre, J. (1998, April). Governance without Government? Rethinking Public Administration. *Journal of Public Administration Research and Theory: J-PART, 8*(2), 223–243.

Philbrick, M. (2010). An Anticipatory Governance Approach to Carbon Nanotubes. *Risk Analysis, 30*(11), 1708–1722.

Pielke, J. R., Sarewitz, D., and Byerly, J. R. (2000). Decision Making and the Future of Nature: Understanding and Using Predictions. In D. Sarewitz, J. R. Pielke, and J. R. Byerly (Eds.), *Prediction: Science, Decision Making, and the Future of Nature* (pp. 361–389). Washington, DC: Island Press.

Pierson, P. (2004). *Politics in Time: History, Institutions, and Social Analysis.* Princeton, NJ: Princeton University Press.

Poli, R. (2012). Complexity, Acceleration, and Anticipation. *Emergence: Complexity and Organization, 14*(4), 124–138.

Project on Emerging Nanotechnologies. (2009b, March 23). *Nanotechnology: Will It Drive a New Innovation Economy for the U.S.?* Retrieved November 17, 2015, from Project on Emerging Nanotechnologies: www.nanotechproject.org/events/archive/shapira

Project on Emerging Nanotechnologies. (n.d.). *About the Project on Emerging Nanotechnologies—Mission.* Retrieved November 17, 2015, from Project on Emerging Nanotechnologies: www.nanotechproject.org/about/mission

Quay, R. (2010, Autumn). Anticipatory Governance: A Tool for Climate Change Adaptation. *Journal of American Planning Association, 76*(4), 496–511.

Rejeski, D. (2004a, October 11). Memo: Nanotech Initiative—General Policy Environment. Washington, DC.

Rejeski, D. (2004b, November 8). Memo: Nanotech Initiative—Regulation and Oversight. Washington, DC.

Rejeski, D. (2008, April 24). Testimony on: "National Nanotechnology Initiative: Charting the Course for Reauthorization." Washington, DC: United States Senate, Committee on Commerce, Science, and Transportation, Subcommittee on Science, Technology, and Innovation.

Renn, O., and Roco, M. C. (2006b, April). Nanotechnology and the Need for Risk Governance. *Journal of Nanoparticle Research, 8*(2), 152–191.

Rhodes, R. (1996). The New Governance: Governing without Government. *Political Studies, XLIV*, 652–667.

Rhodes, R. (1997). *Understanding Governance*. Buckingham, UK: Open University Press.

Rhodes, R. (2007). Understanding Governance: Ten Years On. *Organization Studies, 28*(8), 1243–1264.

Rip, A. (2001). Technology Assessment. In N. J. Smelser, and P. B. Baltes (Eds.), *International Encyclopedia of the Social and Behavioral Sciences* (pp. 15512–15515). Oxford, UK: Elsevier Science.

Rip, A., Misa, T. J., and Schot, J. (Eds.). (1995). *Managing Technology in Society: The Approach of Constructive Technology Assessment*. London, UK: Pinter.

Rittel, H. W., and Webber, M. M. (1973). Dilemmas in a General Theory of Planning. *Policy Sciences, 4*, 155–169.

Rosen, R. (2012). *Anticipatory Systems: Philosophical, Mathematical, and Methodological Foundations*, 2nd ed. New York, NY: Springer.

Sabatier, P. A. (Ed.). (1999). *Theories of the Policy Process*. Boulder, CO: Westview Press.

Sarewitz, D. (2011). Anticipatory Governance of Emerging Technologies. In G. E. Marchant, B. Allenby, and J. R. Herkert (Eds.), *The Growing Gap Between Emerging Technologies and Legal-Ethical Oversight* (pp. 95–105). Dordrecht, The Netherlands: Springer.

Schot, J., and Rip, A. (1997). The Past and Future of Technology Assessment. *Technological Forecasting and Social Change, 54*(2–3), 251–268.

Schuurbiers, D., and Fisher, E. (2009). Lab-scale Intervention. *EMBO Reports, 10*(5), 424–427.

Sclove, R. (2010). *Reinventing Technology Assessment: A 21st Century Model*. Washington, DC: Woodrow Wilson International Center for Scholars.

Selin, C. (2007, March). Expectations and the Emergence of Nanotechnology. *Science, Technology and Human Values, 32*(2), 196–220.

Selin, C. (2008a). *CNS Visioning Workshop: Creating Scenarios about the Future of Anticipatory Governance*. Tempe, AZ: Center for Nanotechnology in Society.

Selin, C. (2008b). *The Future of Medical Diagnostics*. Tempe, AZ: Center for Nanotechnology and Society, Arizona State University.

Selin, C. (2008c, November). The Sociology of the Future: Tracing Stories of Technology and Time. *Sociology Compass, 2*(6), 1878–1895.

Selin, C. (2011). Negotiating Plausibility: Intervening in the Future of Nanotechnology. *Science and Engineering Ethics, 17*(4), 723–737.

Selin, C., and Hudson, R. (2010). Envisioning Nanotechnology: New Media and Future-Oriented Stakeholder Dialogue. *Technology in Society, 32*(3), 173–182.

Shelly-Egan, C., and Davies, S. R. (2013). Nano-Industry Operationalizations of "Responsibility": Charting Diversity in the Enactment of Responsibility. *Review of Policy Research, 30*(5), 588–604.

Small, H. (1973, July–August). Co-citation in the Scientific Literature: A New Measure of the Relationship Between Two Documents. *Journal of the American Society for Information Science, 24*(4), 265–269.

Smith, A., Stirling, A., and Berkhout, F. (2005). The Governance of Sustainable Socio-Technical Transitions. *Research Policy, 34*(10), 1491–1510.

Stahl, B. C. (2013). Responsible Research and Innovation: The Role of Privacy in an Emerging Framework. *Science and Public Policy, 40*(6), 708–716.

Stern, P., Wilbanks, T. J., Cozzens, S., and Rosa, E. (2009). *Generic Lessons Learned about Societal Responses to Emerging Technologies Perceived as Involving Risks*. Oak Ridge, TN: Oak Ridge National Laboratory, United States Department of Energy.

Stilgoe, J. (2015). *Experiment Earth: Responsible Innovation in Geoengineering.* Oxford, UK: Routledge.

Swanson, D., and Bhadwal, S. (Eds.). (2009). *Creating Adaptive Policies: A Guide for Policy-Making in an Uncertain World.* New Delhi, India: SAGE Publications India.

Thomson Reuters. (n.d.). *Web of Science.* Retrieved November 16, 2015, from Thomson Reuters: http://thomsonreuters.com/web-of-science/#

Toffler, A. (1970). *Future Shock.* New York, NY: Random House.

Valdivia, W. D., and Guston, D. H. (2015). *Responsible Innovation: A Primer for Policymakers.* Washington, DC: Brookings Institution.

van Eck, N. J., and Waltman, L. (n.d.). *VOSviewer.* Retrieved September 16, 2015, from VOSviewer: www.vosviewer.com

Vig, N. J., and Paschen, H. (Eds.). (2000). *Parliaments and Technology: The Development of Technology Assessment in Europe.* Albany, NY: State University of New York Press.

Wender, B., Foley, R., Guston, D., Seager, T., and Wiek, A. (2012, Winter). Anticipatory Governance and Anticipatory Life Cycle Assessment of Single Wall Carbon Nanotube Anode Lithium ion Batteries. *Nanotechnology Law and Business,* *9*(3), 201–216.

Wiek, A., Foley, R. W., and Guston, D. H. (2012). Nanotechnology for Sustainability: What Does Nanotechnology Offer to Address Complex Sustainability Problems? *Journal of Nanoparticle Research,* *14*(9), 1093.

Wiek, A., Guston, D., Frow, E., and Calvert, J. (2012, April–June). Sustainability and Anticipatory Governance in Synthetic Biology. *International Journal of Social Ecology and Sustainable Development,* *3*(2), 25–38.

Wiek, A., Guston, D., van der Leeuw, S., Selin, C., and Shapira, P. (2013). Nanotechnology in the City: Sustainability Challenges and Anticipatory Governance. *Journal of Urban Technology,* *20*(2), 45–62.

Wilsdon, J., and Willis, R. (2004). *See-Through Science: Why Public Engagement Needs to Move Upstream.* London: Demos.

Wilson, J. Q. (1994). Can the Bureaucracy Be Deregulated? Lessons from Government Agencies. In J. J. Dilulio (Ed.), Deregulating the Public Service: Can the Government be Improved? (pp. 37–61). Washington, DC: Brookings Institution.

Wison, C. A. (2000, December). Policy Regimes and Policy Change. *Journal of Public Policy,* *30*(3), 247–274.

4 "Getting there early"

Anticipating alternative futures

The challenge of framing the future

The foresight and policymaking communities often find themselves at an unfortunate impasse, talking past one another and working in disconnected, siloed, parallel processes although they are generally aimed at achieving rather similar goals. Foresight practitioners generate information that is forward-looking in nature and use a range of approaches, from scenario planning to simulations to horizon scanning, that attempt to look ahead years, and even decades, in the future (Rip, Misa, and Schot, 1995; Rycroft, 2006). In many cases, the intention of these foresight exercises is to give policymakers an early sense of potential problems and to suggest a set of opportunities that might be available to address these challenges. On the other hand, policymakers are often constrained in making decisions related to present-day issues. They may not be able to act or even consider the type of perspective that the foresight community provides and can struggle to operate with the longer-term future in mind, either due to lack of political will, skepticism about its value, or simply given the pressing nature of immediate, day-to-day considerations.

Science and technology policy is one area where the application of foresight has played a role in the policymaking process and has the potential to do so even more in the future (Brown and Michael, 2003; Borup et al., 2006). However, Chapter 1 showed that the closing of OTA in the United States highlights the need for experimenting with new institutional forms that provide the capacity to link the practice of foresight with policymaking, especially given the emergence of new technologies over the past decade. The rise of nanotechnology and synthetic biology has created focal points for rethinking the connection between foresight and policy. This is particularly vital given that these technologies are emerging on the heels of highly polarized debates about agricultural biotechnology and genetically modified organisms (GMOs), in which a failure of foresight in anticipating public backlash was viewed as a contributing factor to ongoing disputes about their environmental and health effects (Tutton, 2011; Walker and Morrissey, 2012). One former Congressional staffer stated that considering nanotechnology during its early stages of development:

sort of resonated on the Hill, I think, with Members [of Congress]. They had the memory of what had happened with genetically modified plants. The fact that if you get the technology out in front of public acceptance, you ultimately end up with [a] problem.

Moreover, the close connection between nanotechnology and synthetic biology indicates that these issues are not going away (Wiek et al., 2012). This implies that how the future of these technologies plays out is significant on two fronts: as a way of demonstrating what has changed in comparison to previous technologies and as a way of anticipating the potential pathways that future oncoming technologies might follow as well.

Since foresight serves a central role in the anticipatory governance framework, this chapter focuses on the foresight activities of the three institutions analyzed in this book, with the majority of attention focused on PEN. In doing so, this chapter has two primary goals. The first is to highlight a set of approaches and tactics that other institutions can utilize to render foresight efforts actionable for policymakers. The second goal is to consider how such strategies contribute to increasing the plausibility of future-oriented information—often termed *anticipatory knowledge*—thereby deepening the conceptual understanding of plausibility as a criterion for assessing the quality of outputs produced by foresight practices. Following this introduction, the next section presents a brief overview describing the connection between foresight, emerging technologies, and the policymaking process. The subsequent section then examines the tactics that PEN in particular utilized to ensure that the anticipatory knowledge it produced was relevant to the policymaking process. The chapter concludes with a consideration about the role that social processes play in producing plausible, policy-relevant foresight and anticipatory knowledge.

Foresight and the policymaking process

The central argument in Chapter 3 is that a key tenet underlying the notion of anticipatory governance is the importance of creating a broader set of alternative futures and utilizing various foresight methodologies to prepare decision makers for the potential long-term uncertainties associated with emerging technologies. While no hard and fast definition of foresight exists, Fuerth (2012: 7) describes foresight as:

the disciplined analysis of alternative futures . . . it is a distinct process of monitoring prospective oncoming events, analyzing potential implications, simulating alternative courses of action, asking unasked questions, and issuing timely warning to avert a risk or seize an opportunity.

Elsewhere, Fuerth (2009: 17) states that "as a factor in governance, the purpose of foresight is to enhance the ability of decision-makers to engage and shape events at a longer range and, therefore, to the best advantage of the citizens they serve." Foresight activities are typically designed to look ahead into the medium- or long-term future—typically no less than ten years ahead and generally many decades in the future—and identify multiple alternative pathways along which a particular issue might follow (Loveridge, 2008).

Foresight, as properly conceived and as contrasted to predictions, consists of a broad array of efforts that consider a rich and complex set of future possibilities. Foresight practiced systemically involves adopting a wide range of methodologies that are specifically designed to explore multiple alternatives (Glenn and Gordon, 2009; Bland and Westlake, 2013; Glenn, Gordon, and Florescu, 2015). Perhaps the most common foresight method applied to in policy contexts is scenario planning, which involves identifying critical driving forces underlying an issue, considering the intersection of the top two prioritized drivers, and then creatively generating multiple narratives about the future using the identified drivers as a framework for storytelling (van der Heijden, 1996; Schwartz, 1996; Ringland, 2002, 2010; Selin, 2006; Ronis, 2010).

The practice of scenario planning emerged from multiple points of origin, most notably from war gaming activities pioneered at the RAND Corporation in the 1950s and 1960s (Kahn and Wiener, 1967) and from practices developed in the early 1970s at what is now Royal Dutch Shell to help the company prepare for unexpected developments in the global geopolitical and energy landscape (Royal Dutch Shell, 2013). Studies have discussed how the contingencies developed in their first scenario planning exercise helped Shell to weather the effects of the 1973 oil crisis, and this methodology eventually came to be widely adopted by businesses in other sectors as a way of becoming better prepared to deal with uncertainty (Wilkinson and Kupers, 2013).

In their explication of anticipatory governance, Barben et al. (2008) spotlight that in addition to scenario planning, a wide range of additional tools can be used as stand-alone foresight methodologies or in combination with one another. These methods include but are not limited to: systemic horizon scanning and trend monitoring (Amanatidou et al., 2012; Miles and Saritas, 2012; Saritas and Miles, 2012); futures implications wheels (Farrington, Henson, and Crews, 2012); expert elicitations, called Delphi and Real-Time Delphi panels (Dalal et al., 2011); quantitative modeling (Davis, Bankes, and Egner, 2007; Lempert, Popper, and Bankes, 2003); prototyping (Carleton and Cockayne, 2009); visioning (Losch, 2006); analysis of wild cards (Saritas and Smith, 2011); creating a dedicated futurist role within organizations (Hines, 2012); and, increasingly, the use of large-scale, web-based, public, participatory games and social media dialogues (Pang, 2010; Raford, 2011).

These foresight methods have been applied to a range of public policy issues in the United States and abroad (Riedy, 2009; O'Leary and Van Slyke, 2010; Schwartz, 2011; Oppenheimer, 2016). One of the most well-known applications of foresight in the social sector is the set of "Mont Fleur" scenarios, developed in South Africa following the end of apartheid. These scenarios are generally recognized for helping to ease societal tensions in a divided South

Africa by illuminating the various potential pathways forward for the country, both desirable and undesirable (Kahane, 2012). Companies and NGOs globally have since applied similar types of scenario planning efforts in various ways. Scenarios have explored the future of individual countries, such as Germany (Deutsche Bank, 2007) and the Russian Federation (World Economic Forum, 2013), along with entire geopolitical regions, such as East Africa (Society for International Development, 2010), the Mediterranean Region (World Economic Forum, 2011), and the Middle East (World Economic Forum, 2010). A small number of governments in the developed world, particularly the United Kingdom, Finland, and Singapore, have established their own government-wide foresight functions that cut across multiple agencies and are dedicated to ensuring that a view of the future is interwoven into elements of the policymaking process in those countries (Kuosa, 2012).

In the United States over the last decade and a half, the National Intelligence Council has produced scenario reports on a quadrennial basis, deliberately corresponding to the Presidential election cycle. One of its latest reports, titled *Global Trends 2030: Alternative Worlds*, focused on the United States' global role in the wake of the financial crisis, creating scenarios anticipating different potential futures, such as China's continued rise to power and future global shifts in economic inequality (National Intelligence Council, 2012). Beyond this regular scenario effort undertaken by the National Intelligence Council, a number of federal agencies in the United States have also used scenario planning activities. Agencies adopting this methodology include FDA on the topic of managing food-related emergencies (Food and Drug Administration, 2012); the Federal Emergency Management Agency to plan for crisis response and disaster resilience (Federal Emergency Management Administration, 2012); the National Aeronautics and Space Administration on the future of American leadership in aeronautics (National Research Council, 1997a); the Library of Congress on preserving digital heritage (Library of Congress, 2002); the Department of Transportation's Federal Highway Administration for regional and metropolitan urban planning (Federal Highway Administration, 2011); and the United States Coast Guard for the purpose of strategy development (United States Coast Guard, 2009).

Science fiction has also become a contributor to envisioning the future of emerging technologies in general (Bassett, Steinmueller, and Voss, 2013; Turney, 2013). Miller and Bennett (2008: 597) describe this visioning role that science fiction can play as providing "a unique approach to thinking longer term about technology: one grounded in narratives that are people-centric, future-oriented, and focused on non-linear dynamics across the interaction of multiple technologies." Technology companies such as Intel have developed in-house practices that apply narrative science fiction techniques to inspire technological innovation and even influence the prototype design (Johnson, 2011; Rushkoff et al., 2011). Science fiction authors such as Cory Doctorow and Bruce Sterling have helped to outline the contours of the potential future societal implications of emerging technologies (Institute for the Future, 2013).

Building on this long history of applying foresight approaches to science and technology (Wilkinson and Eidinow, 2008 Miles, 2010), recent efforts designed to anticipate alternative futures with respect to nanotechnology and other emerging technologies have expanded on this tradition (Schaper-Rinkel, 2013; Smadja, 2006; Robinson, 2009; Groves, 2013; Wiek, Gasser, and Siegrist, 2009; Foley and Wiek, 2014; Read et al., 2015; Fisher, Selin, and Wetmore, 2008). For example, Selin and Hudson (2010: 173) describe using a virtual public engagement platform to engage in "open-source scenario planning" based on set of scenes and visions related to nanotechnology's potential impact on human enhancement. Similarly, Selin (2008b) discusses how a prototype health application of nanotechnology was used as the focal point for a scenario exercise related to nanotechnology's long-term societal implications. Davies and Selin (2012) describe a similar scenario process related to the application of nanotechnology to the energy sector.

While much progress has been made in applying foresight to anticipate nanotechnology's potential longer-term societal implications, the expanded use of these future-oriented methods has spawned discussion about how to determine the quality of the future-oriented knowledge produced by such efforts. Pereira, von Schomberg, and Funtowicz (2007) identified the need to conduct stronger "foresight knowledge assessment" that can help to strengthen the quality of information arising from the type of foresight exercises espoused by anticipatory governance. One criterion, suggested by Selin (2011), is strengthening the plausibility of information used in foresight activities, which can be accomplished through an explicit articulation of the methodologies and processes used in generating the anticipatory knowledge. A key component of strengthening plausibility is a robust vetting of the information that is used to set the stage and contribute to scenario, visioning, or other future-oriented deliberative processes. Selin (2011: 732) acknowledges that the anticipatory knowledge generated in a robust foresight process "is not about facts, historical evidence, or presently observable phenomena. Instead, it is speculation and knowledge claims positioned in the future." This comment highlights the integrative nature of the foresight dimension with others in the anticipatory governance framework. Strengthening the plausibility of future-oriented information, therefore, requires negotiation with multiple stakeholders, from scientists and engineers to policymakers to journalists and the lay public. The centrality of multi-stakeholder and public input in generating future-oriented information demonstrates the interplay of the foresight, boundary-spanning, and engagement dimensions of anticipatory governance.

Using plausibility to seek policy influence

PEN was one of the most prominent NGOs in the field to deliberately attempt integrating foresight with the policy analysis activities it undertook, with many of the same strategies subsequently adopted by the Synthetic Biology Project. However, the evidence shows that using foresight for policy influence purposes remains a challenge. First, information about how nanotechnology—or any emerging technology—might progress is necessarily uncertain, always incomplete, and highly debatable. Adopting a future-oriented stance about unpredictable technologies requires a level of comfort in operating in a contested space of competing claims about their long-term implications. Second, since both individuals and institutions inevitably approach foresight with embedded assumptions and a set of beliefs that greatly influence how they view the future, organizations such as PEN and the Synthetic Biology Project need to find ways of being open to considering alternative, conflicting, or even contradictory possibilities about how a technology could evolve. Navigating these factors successfully requires knowledge about how to frame and present information so that intended target audiences pay attention to these issues, particularly given competing priorities. By adopting the series of strategies described in this chapter, PEN and the Synthetic Biology project produced a substantive body of anticipatory knowledge about the future of nanotechnology and synthetic biology. Other institutions can draw lessons about how to strengthen the near-term plausibility of future-oriented information related to other emerging technologies by adopting these tactics.

Bringing the future into the present

The first approach used to strengthen the plausibility of forward-looking research was finding ways to *bring the future into the present*. A challenge that any anticipatory effort faces—particularly one with the intention of influencing policy decisions—is how to demonstrate that an issue with long-term implications is actually relevant in the here-and-now. PEN articulated this strategy in its earliest planning documents, noting in one of the briefings that the organization would work to "fill short-term gaps," while at the same time "focus on emerging issues" (Rejeski, 2004a). One way to address this challenge was to create a particular focal point that could connect pressing considerations in the short term, while at the same time identify relevant issues that might have relevance farther out in the future. These types of outputs are often described as boundary objects that are flexible enough to allow different communities to come together and interact productively, providing a common reference to which each community can ascribe different meaning (Star and Griesemer, 1989; Guston, 2001). Boundary objects can, therefore, help to strengthen plausibility. Communities with an interest in the future can utilize such objects for this purpose, while communities with an interest in the present can find value in these materials as well.

One central, future-oriented device of this kind that PEN created to help make nanotechnology's future relevant in the present-day was the CPI. PEN's planning memos identified the need for getting a better handle on the nanotechnology consumer products on the market. One of these documents describes undertaking a "scanning function that will allow us to identify what products are close to commercialization" (Rejeski, 2004b: 8). When first released as an interactive online tool in March 2006, the CPI contained just over 200 entries. In the following years, the CPI was updated almost annually, either by adding new products, archiving products no longer available for purchase, or improving the functionality of the tool. The CPI contained just over 1,000 products by 2011, and as PEN began to wind down and transition to focus on other topics, the organization forged a partnership with researchers at Virginia Tech to keep the inventory current. This second iteration of the CPI, known as CPI 2.0, was brought up to date and made easier to use, resulting in a total of 1,814 products listed as of March 2015 (Vance et al., 2015). A determination as to whether to include a product in the CPI was fully based on manufacturers' claims about the product, with links provided to online retailer sites. PEN did not conduct testing or other scientific verification of those claims. Vance et al. (2015: 1771) provide the product inclusion criteria in plain language: "(1) they [products] can be readily purchased by consumers; (2) they are claimed to contain nanomaterials by the manufacturer or another source; and (3) their claim to contain nanomaterials appears reasonable to CPI curatorial staff."

When PEN updated the CPI, it often accompanied these changes with public announcements with claims about the accelerating growth of nanotechnology products entering the market. PEN then leveraged this information about the rising number of nanotechnology consumer products as evidence that nanotechnology, and its broader societal implications, should be taken seriously in the near-term. PEN stated: "the inventory is an essential resource for consumers, citizens, policymakers, and others who are interested in learning about how nanotechnology is entering the marketplace" (Project on Emerging Nanotechnologies, 2006b).

Analyzing the policy implications of nanotechnology's utilization in consumer products became one of the linchpins of PEN's policy influence strategy. The CPI helped bolster the argument that these products both demonstrated the immediacy of nanotechnology's near-term uses as well as serving as a harbinger of future applications. By identifying how consumers might come into contact with nanotechnology—whether recognized as such or not—PEN was able to introduce policymakers to a relevant, concrete issue that also gave a glimpse into some of the more sophisticated applications of nanotechnology that could emerge in the coming years. The video from the public launch event of the CPI in March 2006 demonstrated this idea. David Rejeski described how the unexpectedly large number of products available on the market implied that the government—and society as a whole—needed to respond swiftly, so that the oversight system would not fall behind fast-moving developments in nanotechnology. "Scientists like to talk about space elevators and cures for cancer and better renewable energy," he stated. However, "this [consumer products] is the face of nanotechnology that the public is seeing . . . these are the artifacts where public policy, science, and public interest are meeting right now, today." "The train has left the station," he continued. "This is obviously just the beginning. There are over

200 products now . . . and this might be the first wave of a kind of product tsunami that floods across the market landscape" (Project on Emerging Nanotechnologies, 2006a).

By creating this inventory, PEN aimed to influence debates around nanotechnology in a variety of ways. First, by cataloging these signals of what was already on the market using nanotechnology, PEN tried to debunk the argument that nanotechnology consisted only of vague promises. The aim was to show that nanotechnology was not something to be framed in a future tense. Second, PEN highlighted the stealth nature of nanotechnology's development. While much attention was placed on the grand visions of future health, environmental, and economic benefits, the CPI showed that nano-technology was already being used in existing products, potentially introducing novel uncertainties at the same time. One NGO representative observed, "PEN's greatest influence, in my opinion, was to bring the reality of nanotechnology to the fore."

This is not to say that everybody agreed with this strategy or that attempts to bring the future into the present made PEN immune to controversy. Berube et al. (2010: 152) wrote a critique of the CPI, arguing that "substantive deficiencies [exist] that call the validity of claims associated with the CPI into question." This article warns, "Individuals and organizations citing the CPI should be wary of over-claiming the reliability and validity of nanotechnology in consumer products" (2010: 152). Similarly, some interviewees argued that trying to make nanotechnology relevant in the present could lead to misrepresentation. For instance, one private sector analyst working on nanotechnology wrote to me about the CPI as part of the interview process:

> This inventory drove me bonkers for years. I think it was one case where the PEN work contributed significantly to people *mis*understanding nanotechnology and its impact, because it was so commonly cited as a complete and representative list of nanotech-enabled products on the market, which was not the case (by a rather wide margin). [use of asterisks included in the original]

The respondent continued, "I know it was not really intended to be comprehensive . . . but that nuance was almost always lost, and I do not think the promotion and explanations of it helped make that as clear as it should have been." In short, this interviewee distinguished between products where the consumer might be more directly exposed to nanomaterials, such as when they are used in beauty creams, as opposed to situations where the consumer is highly unlikely to be in contact with the nanomaterials, such as when they are embedded in the body of cars or in tennis rackets. This critique resonates with the perspective expressed in the following description, excerpted from one company's briefing on the CPI, dated March 13, 2006:

> While the Wilson Center's nanotech initiative has produced some important and useful work, like a thoughtful report on nanotech regulation

and an inventory of nanotech EHS research, this project is sloppy and poorly thought out . . . While we appreciate the Wilson Center's stance as an NGO that's willing to take a hard look at both the risks and benefits of nanotechnology, it'd be better served to focus more on constructive initiatives, like its "Green nanotechnology" program, and less on projects like this that don't do much more than attract a lot of press.

In interviews, Rejeski acknowledged this criticism, but noted that stimulating debate around how nanotechnology was entering the market was of particular importance. "Whether the agencies liked it or hated it, they actually used it," he said, referring to the CPI.

> It was helpful in a sense because it was one place where they could go and see what is out there. They did not have mechanisms to do the scanning themselves. It was an early warning system for the agencies, because they were so far behind.

In other words, Rejeski notes that the CPI was intended to produce the kind of in-depth engagement and debate that Berube et al. (2010) undertook. This point is indicated in the disclaimer provided on the CPI's homepage. "The material contained in this inventory is for informational purposes only," it says. "The Project has made this material available to stimulate discussion and comment about the emergence of nanotechnology in commerce" (Project on Emerging Nanotechnologies, 2015).

When such disputes arose, PEN always turned to the fact that the methodology used to collect the data constituting the CPI was presented transparently on its website. PEN documents also reference that consumer products were only listed if companies made claims about the use of nanotechnology and that all CPI entries were linked back to information available on the Internet to allow for traceability. The CPI website claimed:

> The information contained within this inventory is solely based on information that can be readily found on the Internet . . . By taking this approach, all entries can be validated by anyone with internet access. Products have been identified for inclusion in the inventory following systematic web-based searches.
>
> (Project on Emerging Nanotechnologies, 2015)

This methodology inevitably made the inventory less than comprehensive or ideal, leading to both false negatives (missing out on listing products that actually were nanotechnology-enabled if such claims were not made and verifiable through online sources) and the inclusion of false positives (having some products listed in the inventory that claim to use nanotechnology even if they did not).

However, the initial version of the inventory was not as sophisticated as the second iteration developed in 2011. The second version includes informational categories such as the implied functions of the nanomaterial described and, perhaps even more importantly, the location of the nanomaterial in the product. This recognition is critical. Nanomaterials that are included deep into a solid (such as in a computer) have different potential exposure and dispersion pathways than nanomaterials that sit at the surface of products (such as in clothing or textiles) or that are suspended in a liquid form (such as in sunscreens). Additionally, as nanotechnology has evolved, the inventory's impact has also shifted over time. For example, one academic interviewee highlighted, "Nanoscale materials ended up becoming . . . incorporated into pre-existing products . . . that don't have the same visibility." Another researcher echoed this idea and discussed it at length, arguing: "I think the rhetorical force of the inventory decreased substantially over time. People are less willing to just left handedly point at it and say 'There's, whatever, 1,700 products on the market.'" This interviewee continued by stating:

> [nanomaterials] are so buried in the product at this point that it's not as salient as we thought it was gonna be. We thought people were gonna paint their houses in silver paint. We thought people were gonna wear clothes which were heavily enhanced with nano particles. Those markets are not really there.

A number of other observers who were interviewed still saw value in producing even a flawed tool. One journalist said:

> In my experience of covering these topics for over 30 years, few organizations have managed to attain this level of recognition or respect. For example, the creation by PEN of the database of nanotechnology-claimed products filled a big gap that no one else showed any inclination to tackle.

This interviewee continued, "PEN's effort helped establish the need and highlighted the problems between the claims and reality of nanotechnology products, especially those originating outside of the United States and Europe." One representative from the private sector echoed this sentiment about the value of this public source of information on nanotechnology consumer products, even if incomplete. This interviewee said:

> The inventory of consumer products is a little bit of a mixed blessing, because anything and everything got into that, which probably had a distorting impact on what truly is nano. But, at least it started people thinking about, well, are nanomaterials, or the products of engineered nanomaterials in consumer products in ways that people a) should be aware of, and b) if it is real, how might they be marketed, and might there be labelling requirements? And so, again, it got everybody talking.

In this person's mind, the importance of "getting everybody talking" outweighed the "mixed blessing" that came with the CPI. In this view, providing the information at an early stage was needed to get "people thinking about" nanotechnology's societal implications.

Of course, deliberately connecting the future with the present is a strategy that is not necessarily unique to PEN. The Center for Responsible Nanotechnology, a NGO devoted to promoting the view that nanotechnology will lead to advanced atomically precise molecular manufacturing over the coming decades, created a task force to produce a set of scenarios about nanotechnology's future (Center for Responsible Nanotechnology, 2008a, 2008b). This set of eight scenarios covers a range of topics, from the application of molecular manufacturing to the military to the dissemination of molecular manufacturing machines in every American household. These scenarios provide multiple chronological narratives about how molecular manufacturing might progress between 2008 and 2018. However, these scenarios do not take the next step and offer an explicit tether to present day oversight or regulatory issues. These scenarios provide plenty of vision about nanotechnology's alternative future but offer less translation about what these visions mean for policy or technological issues today. Correspondingly, no indications are present on the website for the Center for Responsible Nanotechnology about the policy application of these scenarios.

Alternatively, the Foresight Institute—which was founded by Drexler in 1986 to advance the view of atomically precise molecular manufacturing—created a forward-looking roadmap document in 2008 that explored what technological and policy developments were needed to "get from here to there" (Battelle Memorial Institute and Foresight Nanotech Institute, 2008). Unlike the aforementioned scenarios, the roadmap connects a future vision of nanotechnology (atomically precise manufacturing) with a set of concrete, near-term recommendations for a research agenda. Such a forward-looking roadmap is a valuable tool in articulating the tangible steps that can be taken to realize a potentially radically different future. While these organizations undertook these kinds of activities primarily independent from one another, the number of foresight efforts in the field speaks to the breadth of interest in infusing a forward-looking perspective into discussions about nanotechnology's societal implications.

One of the unique features of the CPI is that it allowed PEN to try to transform the face of nanotechnology away from posited forthcoming innovations to the iconic images of everyday consumer products, including tennis rackets, pants, cosmetics, socks, cleaning sprays, and food containers. Through this perspective and the inventory's publicly searchable interface, PEN underscored nanotechnology's transition into the marketplace. A non-governmental representative highlighted the value of this kind of information, stating: "The inventory project showed real savvy with different types and kinds of information—simple, numbers based information—that grabs the attention of policymakers and the media because it makes such a great talking point." Rejeski's claim is that while space elevators and cures for cancer are possible—and would be welcome developments when they arrive someday—they are still not the kind of immediate, pressing developments that will guide policymakers' decisions. Instead, the view adopted was that the way that federal agencies approach the oversight of nanotechnology consumer products will serve as the guideposts for the types of actions that will shape and determine nanotechnology's future over the longer term.

The Synthetic Biology Project also found ways of bringing the future into the present, approaches that were previously pioneered by PEN. Much like PEN produced the CPI to provide a benchmark for the advancement of nanotechnology, so too did the Synthetic Biology Project. The Synthetic Biology Project created an online inventory to track the initial commercialization of synthetic biology applications, even though the original version of this inventory was presented less dynamically and interactively than the original CPI. The original version of the synthetic biology inventory frames the issue of that technology's advancement in ways similar to how the CPI portrayed nanotechnology. The synthetic biology applications inventory notes that, "for good or ill, new technologies are often defined by a few iconic examples that capture the public imagination. Early on, nanotechnology was defined by its application to stain-resistant clothing and sunscreens, convenient improvements but hardly transformational" (Synthetic Biology Project, 2012b). It continues, "So far, synthetic biology has been associated with a few limited applications, but this initial inventory provides a glimpse of its impact on multiple sectors ranging from energy to pharmaceuticals, chemicals, and food" (Synthetic Biology Project, 2012b).

A subsequent, more interactive version of this Synthetic Biology Products and Applications Inventory further echoes the rationale that PEN cited in producing the CPI. The first motivating factor was determining how many products are available on the market. Another intention was to show that synthetic biology is not only a far-off, futuristic technology but one becoming more tangible in the present, faster than expected or realized by decision makers. The inventory website highlights:

> It has been difficult to find out how many "synbio" products are on the market or may potentially enter the marketplace in the near future. While not comprehensive, this inventory gives the public the best available look at the many manufacturer-identified synbio-based products and the companies that produce them.
>
> (Synthetic Biology Project, 2015a)

Regularly updating knowledge through repetition

The second strategy utilized to strengthen plausibility was *regularly updating knowledge through repetition*. Although rather straightforward, one component of PEN's approach to strengthening the plausibility of anticipatory knowledge was continually updating the inventories and information it produced. For example, in association with Hart Research Associates (2006, 2007, 2008), PEN conducted a series of public perception polls to gauge public awareness and interest in nanotechnology. "We put those out like clockwork," said one former PEN staff member, emphasizing the regularity of updating the public perception information studies produced by the organization. This persistent frequency was critical to stimulating a fresh round of conversations about nanotechnology and society on a consistent basis. These polls also offered a recurring opportunity to influence the thinking of policymakers and other stakeholders. A similar approach was used in the release of reports and the discussion events PEN organized at the Wilson Center. One private sector representative stressed the continual stream of PEN outputs, stating that "the sheer volume of information released through the reports, panels, and discussions" on public perception and regulatory issues was crucial to regularly energize the conversation around distinct components of nanotechnology policy.

Nowhere are this utilization of repetition and the regularity of revisiting previous findings more evident than with the CPI. "It's the idea of constantly updating your knowledge," said Rejeski, who commented on how every major update of the CPI would be widely publicized, leading to a fresh round of attention from stakeholders interested in the latest findings about nanotechnology-based products. "The data became sticky," said Rejeski, and PEN became increasingly well known for this work throughout the nano-technology policy community. In fact, the number of products contained in this inventory became a regularly cited data point for policymakers and other interested parties in the nanotechnology policy arena who wished to demonstrate nanotechnology's advance in society.

Consider just a few examples. The use of the inventory was reflected in the opening statement kicking off a hearing of the United States House of Representatives Committee on Science and Technology on September 21, 2006. Ranking Committee Member Bart Gordon asserted, "Consumer products employing nanomaterials are now on the market. The Wilson Center's Nanotechnology Project has identified at least 200 such products, many of which are actually designed to be ingested" (United States House of Representatives, Committee on Science and Technology, 2006b). Slightly over a year later, at a follow-up Committee hearing held on October 31, 2007, Congressman Brian Baird referenced the updated number of products in the inventory, claiming that "more and more products containing engineered nanoparticles continue to enter the marketplace—the number of such products has doubled to 500 over the past year, according to surveys by the Wilson Center's Project on Emerging Nanotechnologies" (United States House of Representatives, Committee on Science and Technology, 2007). At a subsequent hearing held on April 16, 2008, Congressman Gordon, who had since become Chairman of the committee, alluded that "nanotechnology is advancing rapidly, and at least 600 products have entered commerce that contain nanoscale materials, including aerosols and cosmetics," borrowing his statistic directly from the PEN inventory that was updated a few weeks earlier on February 22, 2008 (United States House of Representatives, Committee on Science and Technology, 2008).

Information from the CPI has also been cited in a number of high-level policy documents as a way of highlighting nanotechnology's importance as both a near- and long-term science and technology policy issue. For example, the GAO explicitly referenced the CPI on the first page of a March 31, 2008 document on the federal government's risk research funding: "The Project on Emerging Nanotechnologies has identified over 500 consumer products that already are available to consumers that may contain nanoscale materials" (Government Accountability Office, 2008). Information from the CPI has also been used to frame discussions about how quickly nanotechnology has advanced out of the laboratory and into society in other reports, such as in the EPA's *Nanotechnology White Paper* (2007) and in a report from The National Academies assessing the government's risk research strategy (National Research Council, 2009b). Data from the inventory was also used for this purpose at the local level, as it helped to provide a framework for a 2008 report from the Cambridge Nanomaterials Advisory Committee to the City Manager of Cambridge, Massachusetts. This report, which recommended a series of steps to better inform the local government and the public about nanotechnology activities underway in the city, directly cites the CPI and referred to the number of nano-enabled products available on the market (Cambridge Nanomaterials Advisory Committee, 2008).

Finally, the publicity the inventory received through these regular updates led to global influence as well, spawning imitators worldwide. For example, researchers in Europe (The European Consumer's Organisation, 2010) and Japan (National Institute of Advanced Industrial Science and Technology, 2007) created similar inventories that track nanotechnology consumer products sold predominantly in those regions, complete with the explicit acknowledgment that these tools were preceded and influenced by PEN's work. The Japanese inventory was explicitly described as using a similar methodology and employing a similar structure to the CPI. While this inventory does not appear currently active and the only indication was that it was updated once, in 2008, the very fact that it and others were created as replications of the CPI is one subtle indication of the CPI's reach within the nanotechnology policy community.

Ensuring timeliness and capitalizing on the first mover advantage

The third strategy utilized was *ensuring timeliness and capitalizing on the first mover advantage*. Rejeski accentuated this notion, stating: "The main critical success factor was getting there early. If I had to pick one thing that had a huge impact it was that we were in very early." The idea, in his words, was to "fill new niches in the policy ecosystem" as soon as possible to frame the debate whenever a new nanotechnology-related issue would emerge. The strategy of "getting there early" was also one that was repeated by a number of other interviewed individuals. One person who works closely with nanotechnology companies in the private sector said that PEN's "huge influence on the field" was due directly to "an early, clear, and cogent identification of EHS issues on the implications and applications of nanotechnology." Similarly, one researcher who works on nanotechnology policy said that PEN helped nanotechnology cross "a valley of death" by sustaining the excitement, enthusiasm, and interest in the topic for an extended period of time. A particular boon was that the law establishing the NNI, which occurred just a few years before PEN opened its doors, provided a window of opportunity (Kingdon, 1995) for this kind of effort. The 21st Century Nanotechnology Research and Development Act makes explicit reference to a need for research examining the societal implications of nanotechnology, creating a mandate for the NNI to develop a related program of social science research activities. PEN was able to help maintain a spotlight on these topics and continue to press that they get addressed, given that they were one of the earlier NGOs focused on these topics. "There was no other game in town," as one former PEN staff member phrased it.

Throughout the interviews, experts from a range of perspectives reinforced the idea that this first-mover role, coupled with data that no other organization had at their disposal, was a distinct advantage for PEN, especially when considering the project in light of similar efforts. One journalist contended:

> PEN provided an informed forum for discussion of topics or issues that were sometimes ahead of the formal federal nanotechnology . . . effort. In this respect, PEN was viewed mostly as an external and neutral source of knowledge and opinion about nanotechnology.

A representative from the private sector concurred that, "A group like this is probably most needed in the early days when the issues and the dialogue are just taking shape." One policymaker said, "PEN was a little bit ahead of the curve in the rate of the development of the technology." A science policy journalist stated, "Often PEN would consider different timescales—short-term, mid-term, and long-term" that were not on the radar of federal agencies.

One expert with knowledge of both agriculture biotechnology and nano-technology said that PEN had more of an opportunity to inform conversations about nanotechnology than was possible with respect to agricultural biotechnology. This was due in large part, as the interviewee argued, because PEN entered nanotechnology policy debates at such an early stage, just as the science was being researched and the technology was being developed. "The critical difference . . . in the agricultural biotech area you had vested interests and positions that had been hardened over 25 years of debate . . . and it was hard to have people think out of the box," said the researcher.

In contrast, of course, the appeal of nanotechnology was to get in there early, to begin to shape and frame the debate and perspectives about regulatory policy before positions got hardened, in some respects having the ghosts of ag biotech as what not to do.

By entering the fray before these positions had a chance to "harden," as this expert said, PEN might have had a unique opportunity to engage a wider range of stakeholders around nanotechnology's potential societal risks and benefits.

Rejeski emphasized how being an early entrant into this space provided PEN with a wide range of options about how it could operate:

> Most of the early work was to convince Pew to invest and show that the shaping capacity is really high, that it [nanotechnology policy] is not polarized. On climate and GMO foods, there was no flexibility, since once you get into that spot where it is regulated, there are fewer degrees of freedom. I remember one of the first meetings on nanotechnology we had representatives from the ETC Group [a NGO], Intel, and trade associations, and I thought "this is going to be a disaster." But it went fine, since nobody knew what to expect.

Beyond capitalizing on the first mover advantage, one former PEN staffer also emphasized, "The timing of analysis matters." Multiple interviewees highlighted PEN's ability to produce relevant material in an exceptionally timely way, providing information that touched on a topic just as the issue was reaching the forefront of policy debates. Such timeliness is a feature that is increasingly seen as critical to the uptake of foresight efforts as policy is being made (Marchant, Allenby, and Herkert, 2011). One private sector representative placed a strong emphasis on PEN's ability to quickly and accurately time the provision of information:

> It was almost like an issue would be forming and getting a lot of attention and there would be a report out [from PEN]. The early identification of what would be the major concerns or critical issues and then coming up with an appropriate report, article, panel discussion, a contribution to a story, or a story from someone there was done very, very well.

One good example of this timeliness is apparent in PEN's efforts related to considering environmental issues surrounding nano-based silver. PEN was able to combine findings from the CPI with information from its inventory tracking federally funded EHS risk research to show that gaps existed between the materials being commercialized in products hitting the market and the relative focus of EHS risk research. PEN Chief Science Advisor Andrew Maynard highlighted this mismatch in Congressional testimony on September 21, 2006, noting that while 30 percent of consumer products listed in the CPI claimed to use nano-engineered silver, less than 9 percent of EHS risk research funding focused explicitly on silver nanotechnology (Maynard, 2006b). Since then, the environmental implications of silver nanotechnology have become an increasingly crucial area of attention (Quadros and Marr, 2011; Quadros et al., 2013). Even as EPA fined a business for selling computer peripherals coated with nano-engineered silver due to their failure to register the product under EPA's pesticide law, PEN had already begun working with an external expert on a report focused on the environmental implications of silver nanotechnology (Louma, 2008). PEN also assembled an online inventory devoted exclusively to identifying the use of silver nanotechnology in consumer products to accompany the report's release (Project on Emerging Nanotechnologies, 2008f).

This ability to respond quickly was difficult for some other organizations involved in nanotechnology policy. For instance, while the multisectoral, consensus-based decision-making approach that ICON utilized helped the organization generate sufficient buy-in from its many stakeholder groups, it did not allow for a similarly rapid production of new content as novel issues emerged. One academic interviewee described, "The whole model of ICON was one of shared governance across these different stakeholder sectors, a consensus model, [so] everybody had to be happy with everything . . . in order for it to see the light of day." Another researcher repeated that, "For ICON to do anything, they had to have full buy-in from industry partners, from small business entrepreneurial partners, from NGOs, from academics, from government agencies." Additionally, as Chapter 6 will discuss further, ICON was generally less focused on generating press coverage than PEN, which also contributed to shifting its focus away from rapid production of materials for speedy dissemination. One interviewee with knowledge of ICON professed as much, articulating:

> Because of ICON's niche in this very narrow area of environmental, health and safety research, our target audience was different than the Wilson Center's. And so, instead of trying to get coverage in major media outlets, our primary audiences were government regulators, and funding agencies, and companies.

One interviewee from outside of ICON summarized:

> The media was not a part that ICON focused on mostly. ICON did not host press conferences. It did not create work products for media consumption . . . it essentially alerted the media that ICON was there and were able to provide information on an as-needed basis.

An example of the quickness at which PEN produced foresight-oriented material is also manifest in the number of press releases and announcements circulated by the organization. PEN distributed an average of over one press release per month from the time it began in April 2005 through April 2010. At the height of its activity, from 2006 through 2008, PEN averaged nearly

2.5 press releases a month. In comparison, PEN released roughly four times as many press releases from 2005 to 2010 than ICON did during the same period. While decisive conclusions should not necessarily be drawn from this comparison—PEN's media outreach and information dissemination was a deliberately explicit component of its organizational activities, unlike ICON— these numbers are intended to offer an initial appreciation of the swiftness associated with PEN's output. The speed of PEN's information generation also helped shape the topics that eventually became viewed as primary discussion topics within the nanotechnology policy community. One interviewee with experience in the philanthropic sector commented:

> What stands out for me is the creativity, the opportunism in the best possible interpretation of that word, and part and parcel to that is the agility. There was also an incredible ability to respond quickly to what is going on, what is in the press, what other folks were interested in.

The Synthetic Biology Project also aimed to capitalize on its own first mover advantage by addressing the issue of synthetic biology oversight early in the issue's life cycle. In fact, the Synthetic Biology Project was involved in synthetic biology topics at an even earlier stage in the technology's development than PEN was with respect to nanotechnology. The Synthetic Biology Project was among one of the first organized, systemic efforts geared towards anticipating the societal implications of synthetic biology. Rejeski has written that synthetic biology is currently a "frontier" science and technology policy issue, with the present state of the synthetic biology governance system at a similar state to where nanotechnology was a decade ago (Rejeski, 2011). Many interviewees highlighted this distinction. One researcher said, "the difference with synthetic biology is that they were a lot earlier on in the development of the technology when they stepped in . . . the field is just not as mature as in nanotechnology." Another researcher upheld this view, claiming that "there are not as many players in the synthetic biology space, for sure . . . There are also very few environmental organizations that have, in essence, dedicated staff and programs for synthetic biology."

The predominance of a DIY culture and the larger number of small, start-up businesses that constitute the structure of the synthetic biology industry also necessitated a rapid response time from groups such as the Synthetic Biology Project, as the landscape of synthetic biology actors might be more fluid than for nanotechnology. One researcher linked these concepts by remarking, "I think the industry structure is a bit different . . . With nanotechnology, you had more of the chemical companies, the material sciences companies . . . With synthetic biology, you are seeing, of course, a lot more smaller start-ups." This interviewee continued by noting, "Then of course you have the DIY people as well, which puts a whole new twist on things as far as policy and governance goes." These synthetic biology start-up companies rarely have staff devoted to government affairs or with experience navigating the regulatory system, unlike the larger chemical companies involved with nanotechnology that might have entire personnel teams and divisions for this purpose. The Synthetic Biology Project recognized early on that this different industrial structure required being even more attentive to the shifting interests and priorities of the community, which led to even more hands-on forms of interaction and engagement on policy and regulatory issues.

Downsides can arise regarding this quick response strategy, as it is not necessarily foolproof. An organization faces risks in releasing a high volume of material in swift succession, particularly if the flood of output is filtered out from serious consideration by policymakers. One journalist affirmed:

> The pace of release of these reports and findings was frequent during the early years of PEN and at times risked becoming an avalanche of material that would not be read or considered because of its frequency and content. But I think that risk was reduced or overcome because the quality of PEN documents was recognized as being higher than normal, which made them worthy of reading in their entirety rather than just their executive summaries.

It can also lead to the creation of closed systems of collaboration, if the speed to produce outputs outweighs the time it takes to foster collaboration. One researcher alluded:

> I think one thing that was missing was that although PEN did develop a network that they relied upon, that network sometimes was more closed than open. They had a good network . . . as an outsider from that network, you would often just get a little peek into it once in a while.

Placing forward-looking information at the center and the periphery

The fourth strategy to pay attention to here is *placing forward-looking information at both the center and periphery*. In some cases, both PEN and the Synthetic Biology Project aimed to create and disseminate anticipatory knowledge as the primary output of their work, making the provision of foresight the explicit and almost sole focus of some efforts. In others, these institutions instead looked to interweave a foresight perspective as a complementary component throughout the materials they produced, using anticipatory knowledge in a secondary, supporting role.

For instance, PEN created an entire series called *NanoFrontiers*, which originated with a workshop of leading scientists to discuss nanotechnology's long-term potential. The follow-up report from that workshop presented different "visions for the future of nanotechnology," centered around three different metaphors describing critical research needs associated with "the nano toolshed, the nano library, and the nano workshop" (Schmidt, 2007: i). Building on this initial report, PEN then created three shorter *NanoFrontiers* newsletters focusing on potentially critical applications of nanotechnology in the future: to "solve the energy crisis, revolutionize medicine, and produce clean water." Each of these colorful newsletters provided a detailed look into how nanotechnology could revolutionize the delivery of goods and services in these areas. Finally, PEN rounded-out this longer-term visioning initiative by producing a series of downloadable podcasts that consisted of interviews with leading nanotechnology researchers, thinkers, and visionaries, including Samuel Stupp, Jim Heath, and Angela Belcher.

Karen Schmidt, a freelance science journalist who also authored the original *NanoFrontiers* report, conducted the complete series of podcast interviews. These one-on-one interviews included future-oriented and far-ranging discussions on nanotechnology's potential for making advancements in regenerative medicine, its potential to reduce the cost of water desalinization, identifying new ways of making computer chips, and exploring the connection between nanotechnology and synthetic biology that could yield the production of artificial cellular building blocks. One public relations firm representative mentioned that engaging journalists in highlighting such "whiz-bang" applications of nanotechnology was crucial to making the field seem exciting and interesting to a non-expert. Having a science journalist conduct these podcast interviews not only helped to enliven and energize these conversations, but also drew out the distinct aspects of nanotechnology's potential long-term applications.

Future-oriented regulatory and institutional mechanisms were also the topics of three of the four reports written for PEN by Terry Davies. In the first report Davies wrote for PEN, titled *Managing the Effects of Nanotechnology*, he presented a prototype of a "new law . . . to manage potential risks of nanotechnology" (Davies, 2006: 3). Davies described how such a law could work in practice, describing the gaps in the current regulatory system that the law would address and articulating why such a law is necessary. In the third report Davies wrote for PEN, titled *Nanotechnology Oversight: An Agenda for the New Administration* and published in advance of the 2008 election, Davies suggested creating a hypothetical "Nanotechnology Effects Institute," modeled on the Health Effects Institute that is jointly funded by the federal government and the automobile industry to conduct environmental impact research of automobile emissions. Davies argued that Health Effects Institute could be a model for a potential "Nanotechnology Effects Institute" since:

> the federal government and the nanotechnology industry have a joint stake in improving scientific knowledge about the effects of nanotechnology. This shared interest could be embodied in the creation of a scientific research institute devoted to understanding the effects of nanotechnology.
>
> (Davies, 2008: 8)

Although this idea fizzled without uptake, floating this hypothetical organization was indicative of how PEN used examples from the past to suggest options for the future.

Finally, the last report Davies wrote for PEN, *Oversight of Next Generation Nanotechnology* (2009), also recommended creating a "hypothetical organization, the Department of Environmental and Consumer Protection," that would incorporate and integrate oversight, research, and monitoring currently conducted by six existing federal agencies: EPA, CPSC, the United States Geological Survey, the National Oceanic and Atmosphere Administration, the Occupational Safety and Health Administration, and NIOSH. Davies suggested that such a hypothetical agency could be a new "Earth Systems Science Agency" and that it would be responsible for conducting "technology assessment, forecasting, and health and safety monitoring" (Davies, 2009: 3). In the appendix of this report, Davies continues on to outline an approximation of the funding and human resources needed in this new hypothetical agency. Whether Davies thought that such an agency could actually be created in practice remains uncertain, but the seeming intention underlying this suggestion appears to be in offering an alternative vision of how governmental structures to address these new technologies could evolve over the coming years.

Some of the analysis presented in reports released by the Synthetic Biology Project similarly attempt to bring the future into the present. For example, Michael Rodemeyer's report on the future of synthetic biology, *New Life, Old Bottles*, used scenario-based thinking when considering the potential environmental and public health risks of synthetic biology. Rodemeyer considers two scenarios about synthetic biology's potential societal implications that correspond to "an accidental release from a contained facility and an intentional release into a non-contained environment" (Rodemeyer, 2009: 8). By addressing multiple scenarios about synthetic biology's potential future course, Rodemeyer's *New Life, Old Bottles* report offers an open-ended set of alternative views as to how synthetic biology might play out in the future.

In addition to placing foresight at the center of some of its work, PEN also utilized foresight in an indirect and secondary role, thereby infusing its other reports and policy analyses with more of a forward-looking component. Consider how PEN used various scenarios and hypothetical prototype examples. In one report on the potential applications of nanotechnology in food packaging, written by Michael Taylor and produced in collaboration with the Grocery Manufacturers Association, PEN assembled a group of industry, government, civil society, and academic experts to discuss the potential regulatory implications and pathways of three hypothetical food packaging products and their characteristics (Taylor, 2008). These hypotheticals combined both scientific information and practical applications and included applications such as a "nanosanitizer that prevents contamination of the packaging film used to wrap fresh produce or meat" (2008: 57), "packaging film that detects and quantifies microbial pathogens in products as they move through the food-processing chain" (2008: 58), and "a barrier package for carbonated beverages" (Taylor, 2008: 59). Although the working groups discussing these issues, and the resulting report, were ostensibly about regulatory implications—this particular project involved a consultative process with the FDA to determine how each of these hypothetical packages might be regulated in the United States—the use of hypothetical product examples added a distinctly forward-looking component to the deliberation process.

This same type of approach was taken in a report produced by Linda Breggin and John Pendergrass on end-of-life regulation of nanotechnologies. Their report began with an extended discussion of the two major environmental laws that govern the environmental impacts of the disposal of wasted materials, the Resource Conservation and Recovery Act (RCRA) and the Comprehensive Environmental Response, Compensation, and Liability Act (CERCLA). Then, starting halfway through the report, two "hypothetical scenarios" were introduced in a sidebar box "to explore the issues relating to the application of RCRA and CERCLA to nanomaterials" (Breggin and Pendergrass, 2007). Touching again on the issue of plausibility, the report noted, "the hypothetical scenarios are not based on any specific situations, but rather attempt to link theoretical discussion to situations that are within the realm of possibility in order to illustrate how the statutes would work in practice" (Breggin and Pendergrass, 2007: 15). These hypothetical scenarios consisted of two fictitious organizations: one called CNT Inc., a start-up company producing its own carbon nanotubes at its manufacturing plant; the other called Q-Dot, an established company with its own EHS division that produces quantum nanoparticles. These fictitious companies were referred to seven times in the remainder of the report to illustrate a range of situations related to waste disposal and hazard liability for small-sized and larger corporations involved in the manufacturing of different types of nanomaterials.

Similarly, in a report produced on nanotechnology's potential ethical implications, a set of five short narrative scenarios were developed to illustrate relevant ethical dimensions that could emerge from the growth of nanotechnology (Sandler, 2009). These included short, fictitious stories about how the siting of nanotechnology production plants and waste disposal operations disproportionately takes place in low-income communities, highlighting potential social, equity, and environmental justice issues. Other stories included a scenario about the rise of nanotechnology-enabled cognitive enhancement technologies and the creation of new bacteria designed to ward-off infections for soldiers in combat, which both touched on a range of moral and religious themes. The same approach was employed in a report written by Suellen Keiner about the viability of state and local regulatory approaches to nanotechnology oversight. While the report systematically analyzed existing sub-national EHS policies, Keiner ended the report with a forward-looking discussion of four alternative mini-stories about how this issue could evolve. These scenarios ranged from a proliferation of localities adopting their own unique standards to multiple localities adopting agreed-upon international standards to states and cities banding together to creating regional oversight mechanisms (Keiner, 2008).

The Synthetic Biology Project also helped to motivate discussion about longer-term regulatory challenges through the use of forward-looking case studies that utilized foresight in a secondary role to consider how both theoretical and real-world applications of synthetic biology might impact the regulatory system. For instance, the Synthetic Biology Project report *Creating a Research Agenda for the Ecological Implications of Synthetic Biology*— produced in conjunction with researchers at the Massachusetts Institute of Technology—documents discussions held at two workshops that explored the potential regulatory impacts of synthetic biology developments such as gene drive technologies and the potential distribution of transgenic plant material (Drinkwater et al., 2014). A more recent report from the Synthetic Biology Project, titled *The DNA of the U.S. Regulatory System: Are We Getting It Right for Synthetic Biology?*, uses legal analysis of real-world and prospective cases to explore how synthetic biology applications might be regulated under various existing federal regulations in the United States (Bergeson et al., 2015). In sum, efforts such as considering hypothetical scenarios and their potential pathways through the regulatory system also allowed the Synthetic Biology Project to make explicit the real-world impact of potential synthetic biology products by using foresight modalities in a peripheral and secondary manner.

Even given this approach of using foresight at both the center and periphery of research, it remains a question as to whether most of PEN's and the Synthetic Biology Project's visioning and scenario-related activities were truly attuned to issues that would arise distinctly farther out in the future. One researcher wondered whether the degree to which an organization should be considered "forward-looking" must take into account its institutional context. This interviewee posited that, in regards to PEN, "taking the long-term means looking [at least] ten years out. It is a luxury in DC of looking ten years out," principally given the daily pressures and challenges of the policy environment in Washington. In this interviewee's view, other organizations actually tried to anticipate developments in nanotechnology much farther ahead when compared with PEN, looking 50 or even 100 years in the future. One private sector representative reiterated:

> I wouldn't say I would envision PEN as particularly visionary, in terms of most of the work that they did struck me as certainly very useful and very applied, but it was more about here and now and what's going to happen over the next few years.

It seems that PEN's foresight efforts were generally viewed as being directed at issues closer to today—marshaled in a secondary or peripheral way—about five to ten years out in the future. To some respondents, especially those from the foresight or futures community, this timeframe falls short of addressing the long-term future. For instance, the interviewee who said that looking ahead ten years in the nation's capital is a "luxury" further cautioned: "To DC, it [PEN] could feel long-term."

The social construction of plausible foresight

This examination of the strategies used to strengthen the plausibility of anticipatory knowledge demonstrates that organizations can take concrete and replicable action to make foresight relevant and actionable for policymakers. The example of the CPI and the synthetic biology applications inventory shows that these kinds of outputs are invaluable in stressing the immediacy of nanotechnology's and synthetic biology's emergence and can provide a basis to explore their impact on society. Additionally, PEN and its successor organization used information of the kind provided by these inventories as foundational platforms to discuss wide-ranging regulatory and oversight issues. Without the immediacy of these databases, the plausibility of claims about nanotechnology's and synthetic biology's present and future relevance as a policy issue would be weakened and potentially undermined.

The ability to transfer learning about the implementation of these strategies to other emerging technologies is indispensable. One journalist interviewed made explicit this transferability aspect, characterizing the demonstration value of PEN's foresight work as being "one of the lasting benefits of PEN and something which will also be beneficial for discussion of other emerging areas, such as synthetic biology, that could face some of the same uncertainties and regulatory challenges." However, one former PEN staff member indicated that keeping an eye on ensuring that such forward-looking information is consistently plausible is a constant challenge. "Plausibility is a tricky concept," said this interviewee. "There is a difference between saying things because they sound exciting and saying them because they are plausible."

Creating plausible foresight with respect to emerging technologies requires navigating a tension between envisioning their potential future applications and maintaining a pragmatic focus on near-term policy consideration and EHS risks. PEN, in particular, balanced this simultaneous emphasis on the present and the future by producing a wide range of informational inventories, publishing reports, and holding events that addressed multiple timeframes. It anticipated the future by highlighting the early signals of nanotechnology's commercialization and presented a vision of nanotechnology's ability to transform society in its *NanoFrontiers* series. PEN focused on the present by emphasizing the rapidly expanding number of existing products on the market and combined this information with the funding gap it identified related to EHS risk research. Both PEN and the Synthetic Biology Project created substantive bodies of work devoted to both the present and the future that could either operate on their own or in a more integrated fashion. They showed that employing different outputs flexibly is a vital factor to have policy influence.

In conclusion, this chapter shows that strengthening the plausibility of anticipatory knowledge reflects the close-coupling of many social, technical, and regulatory factors. Plausibility is not an all-or-nothing criterion but, instead, emerges in fits and starts over time, as information gets socialized, shared, and used in a community of scholars and practitioners. In some respects, especially when considering an organization seeking to influence policymaking processes, the plausibility of anticipatory knowledge can only be bestowed by external sources. In short, perceptions matter and go a long way towards determining whether organizations such as PEN, ICON, or the Synthetic Biology Project are deemed as visionary or future-oriented. This reputation-building occurs through engaging trustworthy users, the extensive citing of this information in other outlets, regulatory reporting findings, discussing these tools publicly, and ensuring such information gets attention in key forums. While these strategies do not constitute a rigid set of judgment criteria, they show how, through the socialization of foresight, plausibility can eventually arise over time.

Bibliography

Amanatidou, E., Butter, M., Carabias, V., Konnola, T., Leis, M., Saritas, O., Schaper-Rinkel, P., van Rij, V. (2012). On Concepts and Methods in Horizon Scanning: Lessons from Initiating Policy Dialogues on Emerging Issues. *Science and Public Policy*, *39*(2), 208–221.

Barben, D., Fisher, E., Selin, C., and Guston, D. H. (2008). Anticipatory Governance of Nanotechnology: Foresight, Engagement, Integration. In E. J. Hackett, O. Amsterdamska, M. Lynch, and J. Wajcman (Eds.), *The Handbook of Science and Technology Studies*, 3rd ed. (pp. 979–1000). Cambridge, MA: The MIT Press.

Bassett, C., Steinmueller, E., and Voss, G. (2013). *Better Made Up: The Mutual Influence of Science Fiction and Innovation*. London, UK: NESTA.

Battelle Memorial Institute and Foresight Nanotech Institute. (2008). *Productive Nanosystems: A Technology Roadmap*. Menlo Park, CA: Battelle Memorial Institute and Foresight Nanotech Institute.

Bergeson, L. L., Campbell, L. M., Dolan, S. L., Engler, R. E., Baron, K. F., Auerbach, B., Backstrom, T. D., Vergnes, J. S., Bultena, J. P., Auer, C. M. (2015). *The DNA of the U.S. Regulatory System: Are We Getting It Right for Synthetic Biology?* Washington, DC: Synthetic Biology Project, Woodrow Wilson International Center for Scholars.

Berube, D. M., Searson, E. M., Morton, T. S., and Cummings, C. L. (2010, Summer). Project on Emerging Nanotechnologies: Consumer Product Inventory Evaluated. *Nanotechnology Law and Business*, *7*(2), 152–163.

Bland, J., and Westlake, S. (2013). *Don't Stop Thinking about Tomorrow: A Modest Defence of Futurology*. London, UK: NESTA.

Borup, M., Brown, N., Konrad, K., and Van Lente, H. (2006, July–September). The Sociology of Expectations in Science and Technology. *Technology Analysis and Strategic Management*, *18*(3/4), 285–298.

Breggin, L. K., and Pendergrass, J. (2007). *Where Does the Nano Go? End-of-Life Regulation of Nanotechnologies*. Washington, DC: Project on Emerging Nanotechnologies.

Brown, N., and Michael, M. (2003). A Sociology of Expectations: Retrospecting Prospects and Prospecting Retrospects. *Technology Analysis and Strategic Management*, *15*(1), 3–18.

Cambridge Nanomaterials Advisory Committee. (2008). *Recommendations for a Municipal Health and Safety Policy for Nanomaterials*. Cambridge, MA: Cambridge Public Health Department.

Carleton, T., and Cockayne, W. (2009, August 24–27). The Power of Prototypes in Foresight Engineering. *International Conference on Engineering Design, ICED'09.* Stanford, CA: Stanford University.

Center for Responsible Nanotechnology. (2008a). *CRN Global Task Force on Implications and Policy.* Retrieved November 10, 2015, from http://crnano.org/CTF.htm

Center for Responsible Nanotechnology. (2008b). *CRN Task Force Scenario Project.* Retrieved November 10, 2015, from Nano Tomorrows: http://crnano.org/CTF-Scenarios.htm

Dalal, S., Khodyakov, D., Srinivasan, R., Straus, S., and Adams, J. (2011, October). ExpertLens: A System for Eliciting Opinion from a Large Pool of Non-Collocated Experts with Diverse Knowledge. *Technology Forecasting and Social Change, 78*(8), 1426–1444.

Davies, J. C. (2006). *Managing the Effects of Nanotechnology.* Washington, DC: Project on Emerging Nanotechnologies.

Davies, J. C. (2008). *Nanotechnology Oversight: An Agenda for the Next Administration.* Washington, DC: Project on Emerging Nanotechnologies.

Davies, J. C. (2009). *Oversight of Next Generation Nanotechnology.* Washington, DC: Project on Emerging Nanotechnologies.

Davies, S. R., and Selin, C. (2012). Energy Futures: Five Dilemmas of the Practice of Anticipatory Governance. *Environmental Communication: A Journal of Nature and Culture, 6*(1), 119–136.

Davis, P. K., Bankes, S. C., and Egner, M. (2007). *Enhancing Strategic Planning with Massive Scenario Generation.* Santa Monica, CA: RAND Corporation.

Deutsche Bank. (2007). *Germany 2020: New Challenges for a Land on Expedition.* Frankfurt, Germany: Deutsche Bank.

Drinkwater, K., Kuiken, T., Lightfoot, S., McNamara, J., and Oye, K. (2014). *Creating a Research Agenda for the Ecological Implications of Synthetic Biology.* Washington, DC: Synthetic Biology Project, Woodrow Wilson International Center for Scholars.

Environmental Protection Agency. (2007). *Nanotechnology White Paper.* Washington, DC: Environmental Protection Agency. Retrieved November 14, 2015, from www2.epa.gov/sites/production/files/2015–01/documents/nanotechnology_white paper.pdf

Farrington, T., Henson, K., and Crews, C. (2012, March–April). Research Foresights: The Use of Strategic Foresight Methods for Ideation and Portfolio Management. *Research-Technology Management, 55*(2), 26–33.

Federal Emergency Management Administration. (2012). *Crisis Response and Disaster Resilience 2030: Forging Strategic Action in an Age of Uncertainty.* Washington, DC: Federal Emergency Management Administration.

Federal Highway Administration. (2011). *FHWA Scenario Planning Guidebook.* Washington, DC: Department of Transportation.

Fisher, E., Selin, C., and Wetmore, J. M. (Eds.). (2008). *The Yearbook of Nanotechnology in Society—Volume 1: Presenting Futures.* Dordrecht, The Netherlands: Springer.

Foley, R. W., and Wiek, A. (2014, December). Scenarios of Nanotechnology Innovation vis-a-vis Sustainability Challenges. *Futures, 64*, 1–14.

Food and Drug Administration. (2012). *Food Related Emergency Exercise Bundle (FREE-B).* Silver Spring, MD: Food and Drug Administration.

Fuerth, L. (2009). Foresight and Anticipatory Governance. *Foresight, 11*(4), 14–32.

Fuerth, L. (2012). *Anticipatory Governance: Practical Upgrades.* Washington, DC: Project on Forward Engagement.

Glenn, J. C., and Gordon, T. (2009). *Futures Research Methodology, Version 3.0.* Washington, DC: Millennium Project.

Glenn, J. C., Gordon, T. J., and Florescu, E. (2015). *2015–16 State of the Future.* Washington, DC: Millennium Project.

Government Accountability Office. (2008). *Nanotechnology: Better Guidance Is Needed to Ensure Accurate Reporting of Federal Research Focused on Environmental, Health, and Safety Risks.* Washington, DC: Government Printing Office.

Groves, C. (2013). Four Scenarios for Nanotechnologies in the UK, 2011–2020. *Technology Analysis and Strategic Management, 25*(5), 507–526.

Guston, D. H. (2001). Boundary Organizations in Environmental Policy and Science: An Introduction. *Science, Technology and Human Values, 26*(4), 399–408.

Hart Research Associates. (2006). *Attitudes Toward Nanotechnology and Federal Regulatory Agencies.* Washington, DC: Project on Emerging Nanotechnologies.

Hart Research Associates. (2007). *Awareness of and Attitudes Toward Nanotechnology and Federal Regulatory Agencies.* Washington, DC: Project on Emerging Nanotechnologies.

Hart Research Associates. (2008). *Awareness of and Attitudes Toward Nanotechnology and Synthetic Biology.* Washington, DC: Project on Emerging Nanotechnologies.

Hines, A. (2012). *The Role of Organizational Futurist in Integrating Foresight into Organizations.* Faculty of Business and Law, Leeds Business School. Leeds, UK: Leeds Metropolitan University.

Institute for the Future. (2013). *Aura of Familiarity: Visions from the Coming Age of Networked Matter.* Palo Alto, CA: Institute for the Future.

Johnson, B. D. (2011, April). Science Fiction Prototyping: Designing the Future with Science Fiction. *Synthesis Lectures on Computer Science, 3*(1), 1–190.

Kahane, A. (2012). *Transformative Scenario Planning: Working Together to Change the Future.* San Francisco, CA: Berrett-Koehler Publishers.

Kahn, H., and Wiener, A. J. (1967). *The Year 2000: A Framework for Speculation on the Next Thirty-Three Years.* New York, NY: Collier Macmillan.

Keiner, S. (2008). *Room at the Bottom? Potential State and Local Strategies for Managing the Risks and Benefits of Nanotechnology.* Washington, DC: Project on Emerging Nanotechnologies.

Kingdon, J. (1995). *Agendas, Alternatives, and Public Policies.* New York, NY: Addison-Wesley.

Kuosa, T. (2012). *The Evolution of Strategic Foresight: Navigating Public Policy Making.* Farnham, UK: Gower Publishing.

Lempert, R. J., Popper, S. W., and Bankes, S. C. (2003). *Shaping the Next One Hundred Years: New Methods for Quantitative, Long-Term Policy Analysis.* Santa Monica, CA: RAND.

Library of Congress. (2002). *Preserving our Digital Heritage: Plan for the National Digital Information Infrastructure and Preservation Program.* Washington, DC: Library of Congress.

Losch, A. (2006). Anticipating the Futures of Nanotechnology: Visionary Images as Means of Communication. *Technology Analysis and Strategic Management, 18*(3–4), 393–409.

Louma, S. N. (2008). *Silver Nanotechnologies and the Environment: Old Problems or New Challenges?* Washington, DC: Project on Emerging Nanotechnologies.

Loveridge, D. (2008). *Foresight: The Art and Science of Anticipating the Future.* Florence, KY: Routledge.

Marchant, G. E., Allenby, B. R., and Herkert, J. R. (Eds.). (2011). *The Growing Gap: Between Emerging Technologies and Legal-Ethical Oversight, The Pacing Problem.* Dordrecht, The Netherlands: Springer.

Maynard, A. D. (2006b, September 21). Testimony on: "Research on Environmental and Safety Impacts of Nanotechnology: What are the Federal Agencies Doing?". Washington, DC: United States House of Representatives, Committee on Science.

Miles, I. (2010). The Development of Technology Foresight: A Review. *Technological Forecasting and Social Change, 77*(9), 1448–1456.

Miles, I., and Saritas, O. (2012). The Depth of the Horizon: Searching, Scanning and Widening Horizons. *Foresight, 14*(6), 530–545.

Miller, C. A., and Bennett, I. (2008, October). Thinking Longer Term about Technology: Is There Value in Science Fiction-Inspired Approaches to Constructing Futures? *Science and Public Policy, 35*(8), 597–606.

National Institute of Advanced Industrial Science and Technology. (2007). *A Nanotechnology-claimed Consumer Products Inventory in Japan.* Retrieved April 30, 2013, from National Institute of Advanced Industrial Science and Technology: http://staff.aist.go.jp/kishimoto-atsuo/nano/

National Intelligence Council. (2012). *Global Trends 2030: Alternative Worlds.* Washington, DC: National Intelligence Council.

National Research Council. (1997). *Maintaining U.S. Leadership in Aeronautics: Scenario-Based Strategic Planning for NASA's Aeronautics Enterprise.* Washington, DC: National Academies Press.

National Research Council. (2009b). *Review of the Federal Strategy for Nanotechnology-Related Environmental Health and Safety Research.* Washington, DC: National Academies Press.

O'Leary, R., and Van Slyke, D. M. (Eds.). (2010, December). Special Issue on the Future of Public Administration in 2020. *Public Administration Review, 70*(S1), S5–S320.

Oppenheimer, M. F. (2016). *Pivotal Countries, Alternate Futures: Using Scenarios to Manage American Strategy.* Oxford, UK: Oxford University Press.

Pang, A. S.-K. (2010). Social Scanning: Improving Futures through Web 2.0; Or, Finally a Use for Twitter. *Futures, 42*(10), 1222–1230.

Pereira, A. G., von Schomberg, R., and Funtowicz, S. (2007). Foresight Knowledge Assessment. *International Journal of Foresight and Innovation Policy, 3*(1), 53–75.

Project on Emerging Nanotechnologies. (2006a, March 10). *First Nanotechnology Consumer Products Inventory Available to Public.* Retrieved November 16, 2015, from Project on Emerging Nanotechnologies: www.nanotechproject.org/events/archive/first_nanotechnology_consumer_products/

Project on Emerging Nanotechnologies. (2006b, March 10). *First-Ever New Nanotechnology Consumer Products Inventory Accessible to Public.* Retrieved November 16, 2015, from Project on Emerging Nanotechnologies: www.nanotechproject.org/process/assets/files/6021/031006nano_product_inven_march09.pdf

Project on Emerging Nanotechnologies. (2008f). *Silver Nanotechnology: A Database of Silver Nanotechnology in Commercial Products.* Retrieved October 8, 2015, from Project on Emerging Nanotechnologies: www.nanotechproject.org/process/assets/files/7039/silver_database_fauss_sept2_final.pdf

Project on Emerging Nanotechnologies. (2015). *Consumer Product Inventory.* Retrieved October 22, 2015, from Project on Emerging Nanotechnologies: www.nanotechproject.org/cpi/about/background/

Quadros, M. E., and Marr, L. C. (2011). Silver Nanoparticles and Total Aerosols Emitted by Nanotechnology-Related Consumer Spray Products. *Environmental Science and Technology*, *45*(24), 10713–10719.

Quadros, M. E., Pierson IV, R., Tulve, N. S., Willis, R., Rogers, K., Thomas, T. A., and Marr, L. C. (2013). Release of Silver from Nanotechnology-Based Consumer Products for Children. *Environmental Science and Technology*, *47*(15), 8894–8901.

Raford, N. (2011). *Large Scale Participatory Futures Systems: A Comparative Study of Online Scenario Planning Approaches.* Department of Urban Studies and Planning. Cambridge, MA: Massachusetts Institute of Technology.

Read, S. A., Kass, G. S., Sutcliffe, H. R., and Hankin, S. M. (2015, September 2). Foresight Study on the Risk Governance of New Technologies: The Case of Nanotechnology. *Risk Analysis*, in press.

Rejeski, D. (2004a, October 11). Memo: Nanotech Initiative—General Policy Environment. Washington, DC.

Rejeski, D. (2004b, November 8). Memo: Nanotech Initiative—Regulation and Oversight. Washington, DC.

Rejeski, D. (2011). Public Policy on the Technological Frontier. In G. E. Marchant, B. R. Allenby, and J. R. Herkert (Eds.), *The Growing Gap Between Emerging Technology and Legal-Ethical Oversight* (pp. 47–60). Dordrecht, The Netherlands: Springer.

Riedy, C. (2009). The Influence of Futures Work on Public Policy and Sustainability. *Foresight*, *11*(5), 40–56.

Ringland, G. (2002). *Scenarios in Public Policy.* Chichester, UK: John Wiley & Sons.

Ringland, G. (2010). The Role of Scenarios in Strategic Foresight. *Technological Forecasting and Social Change*, *77*(9), 1493–1498.

Rip, A., Misa, T. J., and Schot, J. (Eds.). (1995). *Managing Technology in Society: The Approach of Constructive Technology Assessment.* London, UK: Pinter.

Robinson, D. K. (2009). Co-Evolutionary Scenarios: An Application to Prospecting Futures of the Responsible Development of Nanotechnology. *Technological Forecasting and Social Change*, *76*(9), 1222–1239.

Rodemeyer, M. (2009). *New Life, Old Bottles: Regulating First-Generation Products of Synthetic Biology.* Washington, DC: Synthetic Biology Project.

Ronis, S. R. (2010). *Project on National Security Reform: Vision Working Group Report and Scenarios.* Carlisle, PA: Strategic Studies Institute.

Royal Dutch Shell. (2013). *40 Years of Shell Scenarios.* The Hague, The Netherlands: Royal Dutch Shell.

Rushkoff, D., Hammond, R., Thomas, S., and Heitz, M. (2011). *The Tomorrow Project: Bestselling Authors Describe Daily Life in the Future.* Santa Clara, CA: Intel Corporation.

Rycroft, R. W. (2006). Time and Technological Innovation: Implications for Public Policy. *Technology in Society*, *28*(3), 281–301.

Sandler, R. (2009). *Nanotechnology: The Social and Ethical Issues.* Washington, DC: Project on Emerging Nanotechnologies.

Saritas, O., and Miles, I. (2012). Scan-4-Light: A Searchlight Function Horizon Scanning and Trend Monitoring Project. *Foresight*, *14*(6), 489–510.

Saritas, O., and Smith, J. E. (2011). The Big Picture: Trends, Drivers, Wild Cards, Discontinuities and Weak Signals. *Futures*, *43*(3), 292–312.

Schaper-Rinkel, P. (2013). The Role of Future-Oriented Technology Analysis in the Governance of Emerging Technologies: The Example of Nanotechnology. *Technological Forecasting and Social Change*, *80*(3), 444–452.

Schmidt, K. (2007). *NanoFrontiers: Visions for the Future of Nanotechnology*. Washington, DC: Project on Emerging Nanotechnologies.

Schwartz, P. (1996). *Art of the Long View*. New York, NY: Doubleday.

Schwartz, P. (2011). *Learnings from the Long View*. San Francisco, CA: Global Business Network.

Selin, C. (2006). Trust and the Illusive Force of Scenarios. *Futures*, *38*(1), 1–14.

Selin, C. (2008b). *The Future of Medical Diagnostics*. Tempe, AZ: Center for Nanotechnology and Society, Arizona State University.

Selin, C. (2011). Negotiating Plausibility: Intervening in the Future of Nanotechnology. *Science and Engineering Ethics*, *17*(4), 723–737.

Selin, C., and Hudson, R. (2010). Envisioning Nanotechnology: New Media and Future-Oriented Stakeholder Dialogue. *Technology in Society*, *32*(3), 173–182.

Smadja, E. (2006). Four Scenarios Towards More Ethical Futures: A Case Study in Nanoscale Science and Technology. *Foresight*, *8*(6), 37–47.

Society for International Development. (2010). *East African Scenarios to 2040: What Do We Want? What Might We Become?* Rome, Italy: Society for International Development.

Star, S. L., and Griesemer, J. R. (1989). Institutional Ecology, "Translations" and Boundary Objects: Amateurs and Professionals in Berkeley's Museum of Vertebrate Zoology, 1907–39. *Social Studies of Science*, *19*(3), 387–420.

Synthetic Biology Project. (2012b, July 27). *Inventory of Synthetic Biology Products— Existing and Possible*. Retrieved September 30, 2015, from Synthetic Biology Project: www.synbioproject.org/cpi/site/assets/files/1002/synbio_applications_wwics.pdf

Synthetic Biology Project. (2015a). *Synthetic Biology Products and Applications Inventory*. Retrieved September 17, 2015, from Synthetic Biology Project: www.synbioproject.org/cpi/

Taylor, M. R. (2008). *Assuring the Safety of Nanomaterials in Food Packaging: The Regulatory Process and Key Issues*. Washington, DC: Project on Emerging Nanotechnologies.

The European Consumer's Organisation. (2010, October 21). How Much Nano Do We Buy? Retrieved October 8, 2015, from The European Consumer Organisation: www.beuc.eu/publications/2010–00645–01–e.pdf

Turney, J. (2013). *Imagining Technology*. London, UK: NESTA.

Tutton, R. (2011, June). Promising Pessimism: Reading the Futures to be Avoided in Biotech. *Social Studies of Science*, *41*(3), 411–429.

United States Coast Guard. (2009). *U.S. Coast Guard Evergreen II Project Report*. Washington, DC: United States Coast Guard.

United States House of Representatives, Committee on Science and Technology. (2006b, September 21). Opening Statement by Hon. Bart Gordon. Washington, DC.

United States House of Representatives, Committee on Science and Technology. (2007, October 31). Opening Statement by Chairman Brian Baird. Washington, DC.

United States House of Representatives, Committee on Science and Technology. (2008, April 16). Opening Statement by Chairman Bart Gordon. Washington, DC.

van der Heijden, K. (1996). *Scenarios: The Art of Strategic Conversation*. Chichester, UK: John Wiley & Sons.

Vance, M. E., Kuiken, T., Vejerano, E. P., McGinnis, S. P., Hochella Jr., M. F., Rejeski, D., and Hull, M. S. (2015). Nanotechnology in the Real World:

Redeveloping the Nanomaterial Consumer Products Inventory. *Beilstein Journal of Nanotechnology, 6*, 1769–1780.

Walker, R. L., and Morrissey, C. (2012, February). Charting ELSI's Future Course: Lessons from the Recent Past. *Genetics in Medicine, 14*(2), 259–267.

Wiek, A., Gasser, L., and Siegrist, M. (2009). Systemic Scenarios of Nanotechnology: Sustainable Governance of Emerging Technologies. *Futures, 41*(5), 284–300.

Wiek, A., Guston, D., Frow, E., and Calvert, J. (2012, April-June). Sustainability and Anticipatory Governance in Synthetic Biology. *International Journal of Social Ecology and Sustainable Development, 3*(2), 25–38.

Wilkinson, A., and Eidinow, E. (2008). Evolving Practices in Environmental Scenarios: A New Scenario Typology. *Environmental Research Letters, 3*(4), 1–11.

Wilkinson, A., and Kupers, R. (2013, May). Living in the Futures. *Harvard Business Review, 91*(5), 119–127.

World Economic Forum. (2010). *The GCC Countries and the World: Scenarios to 2025.* Geneva, Switzerland: World Economic Forum.

World Economic Forum. (2011). *Scenarios for the Mediterranean Region.* Geneva, Switzerland: World Economic Forum.

World Economic Forum. (2013). *Scenarios for the Russian Federation.* Geneva, Switzerland: World Economic Forum.

5 "A lot of boundary testing going on"

Spanning multiple divides

Boundary-spanning: from the conceptual to the physical

"The room often reached the Standing Room Only status," said one technology journalist, describing the public events that PEN frequently organized to engage people from a range of different sectors, disciplinary backgrounds, and points of view. Taking place mostly in the conference room on the fifth floor of the Wilson Center and often held over a lunch, these gatherings of anywhere from 20 to 50 people served as a key component of PEN's effort to connect with a broad representation of nanotechnology policy stakeholders in government, business, NGOs, and academia. Such events were generally organized to launch newly published reports from PEN, to provide a forum for out-of-town speakers or other researchers to present their latest findings, or to simply offer a venue to another organization—or set of organizations—in need of a space to hold a meeting. The Wilson Center even hosted the United States launch of The Royal Society's often-referenced 2004 report on nanotechnology (The Royal Society, 2004; Responsible Nano Forum, 2009).

The journalist quoted above continued by explicitly noting the sectoral diversity of individuals in attendance at these meetings:

> From Friends of the Earth and other environmental advocacy groups to EPA and FDA, foreign embassy S&T attachés, industry and trade groups, NGOs, congressional staffers, and former scientists and researchers—as well as journalists from the specialist and trade press.

This perspective is substantiated when reviewing the recorded webcasts and pictures taken of the public events PEN hosted. These videos and images often start by focusing on closely cropped shots of speakers at the front of the room and then pan across the audience gathered around the table, often two or three rows of people deep. "If a larger auditorium had been available, I'm sure PEN could have expanded its outreach and the room would [have] reached its Standing Room Only capacity," wrote the journalist as part of the interview process.

Organizing meetings is just one of the many different approaches that NGOs can take to engage multiple stakeholders and leverage their convening capacities to influence policy related to emerging technologies in the United States. Such meetings are a reflection of the impetus by these organizations to situate themselves strategically at the intersection of many conceptual and practical boundaries: between science and policy, between experts and the public, between companies and other NGOs, and between the near-term and long-term, as was discussed in the previous chapter. "There was a lot of boundary testing going on," said David Rejeski, emphasizing the deliberate bridge building approach taken by the organization—and one that is frequently acknowledged and explicitly expressed throughout the internal strategic planning documents and external publications produced by groups such as PEN and ICON.

While PEN, ICON, and the Synthetic Biology Project were often in the spotlight because of this boundary-spanning role, not every effort of this type was always on full public display. Regarding PEN—as is the case with almost all organizations in Washington, DC, aiming to influence policy debates—a substantive component of its effort was spent working behind the scenes. PEN helped to advance partnerships between other organizations, provided background information on request to policymakers, and briefed those who were interested in PEN's view on nanotechnology's potential benefits and risks. In terms of this less visible set of activities that provided targeted policy information on-demand, one former Congressional staffer noted, "We found the Wilson Center very helpful, because they were able to do a lot of essential staff work that we didn't have the resources to do in looking more carefully into what's actually out there, what's being done." ICON also functioned by remaining centrally involved in many technical forums to develop and disseminate best practices, guidelines, and standards across industry, academia, NGOs, and government.

Much of these visible and less visible boundary-spanning roles emerged directly from the mission statements of the Wilson Center and ICON. For example, many interviewees contemplated how the Wilson Center maintains a non-political, neutral disposition. This neutral role was recognized as a core element of ICON's overall mission. To dive deeper into how this positioning was actualized, this chapter examines the different ways in which institutions try to position themselves to play critical boundary-spanning roles—in essence, by becoming *boundary organizations*. The following section will describe the key concepts underlying the academic notion of boundary work, boundary objects, and boundary organizations, with the subsequent section identifying some of the strategies that can be effective in making NGOs well-situated to serve in this capacity with respect to emerging technologies. The chapter concludes with a discussion about the challenges organizations face in functioning in a boundary-spanning modality while simultaneously expressing a distinct point of view on a policy issue.

Boundary work, boundary objects, and boundary organizations

Organizations that undertake *boundary work* and operate at the intersection between two communities of practice have become a focal point in the science and technology policy literature for some time (Gieryn, 1999; Hellstrom and Jacob, 2003). Clark et al. (2012: 12302) provide a general definition of the "central idea of boundary work" as the tensions that "arise at the interface between communities with different views of what constitutes reliable or useful knowledge." A significant focus of early writing on this topic has been on examining the demarcations that are maintained between scientific (e.g. astronomy) and pseudo-scientific (e.g. astrology) topics (Merton, 1973; Gieryn, 1983; Kuhn, 1996), as well on how boundaries between epistemic cultures are created, shaped, maintained, and challenged (Knorr-Cetina, 1999). Gieryn (1999) describes the notion of boundary work in this context as "the discursive attribution of selected qualities to scientists, scientific methods, and scientific claims for the purpose of drawing a rhetorical boundary between science and some less authoritative residual non-science." The related idea of trading zones (Galison, 1997; Gorman, 2004, 2010; Gorman, Groves, and Shrager, 2004) has also been developed to explore how disciplinary boundaries are negotiated among parties, can facilitate collaboration, and lead to the "co-production" of knowledge (Jasanoff, 2004).

The interaction between science and broader policy and social systems has also gained substantial attention in the literature (Kelly, 2003; Webster, 2007; Adams and Bal, 2009). One approach that has been explored is how knowledge is embedded in *boundary objects* that facilitate such interactions across boundaries. One of the first studies to examine how boundary objects enable such interaction comes from Star and Greisemer (1989), who define boundary objects as knowledge products "which both inhabit several intersecting social worlds . . . and satisfy the informational requirements of each of them." They go on to describe boundary objects as being "both plastic enough to adapt to local needs and the constraints of the several parties employing them, yet robust enough to maintain a common identity across sites." Star and Greisemer (1989) deconstruct the example of how the taxonomy and specimen repository system implemented by the University of California's Museum of Vertebrate Zoology served as a boundary object that allowed multiple constituencies— the museum's founder, its administrator, amateur collectors, and university administration—to each realize their own independent vision for the institution while productively contributing to the goals of other groups.

Later research has focused on the role played by boundary objects in different disciplinary contexts. For example, Yakura (2002) studies how project management timelines, called Gantt charts, affect the behavior of different employees within a firm. Bechky (2003) investigates how drawings and machines serve to mediate the relationships between engineer designers and technicians. Kimble et al. (2010) show how an electronic content management system and a healthcare diagnosis protocol can productively connect professionals who work in different disciplines but who are collectively focused on addressing the same problem. White et al. (2010) describe "an interactive simulation model of water supply and demand presented in an immersive decision theater" that acted as a boundary object connecting scientists and local environmental policymakers in the American Southwest. This combination of flexible usage while preserving core characteristics displayed by boundary objects is a good description of the many inventories, reports, and other outputs that became the core components of work undertaken by PEN, ICON, and the Synthetic Biology Project.

Guston (2001) expands the idea of boundary objects in developing the notion of boundary organizations: institutions that encompass boundary-spanning functions to bridge gaps between different actors, stakeholders, and communities. White et al. (2010) write that boundary organizations "serve multiple distinct groups not necessarily by blurring boundaries, but rather by bridging boundaries." They argue that boundary organizations help different stakeholders come together when necessary, while simultaneously allowing "divergent interests and unique social norms to persist" (White et al., 2010). Examples of studied boundary organizations in the literature include the Office of Technology Transfer at the National Institutes of Health (Guston, 1999); the Health Effects Institute that provides independent research on the health effects of air pollution (Keating, 2001); the National Bioethics Advisory Commission (Leinhos, 2005); the United States Department of Agriculture's Cooperative State Research, Education, and Extension Service (Cash, 2011); the International Research Institute for Climate Prediction (Agrawala, Broad, and Guston, 2001); the United Nations Framework Convention on Climate Change's Subsidiary Body for Scientific and Technological Advice (Miller, 2001); the marine agency Sea Grant (Jenkins, 2010); and Arizona State University's Decision Center for a Desert City (Parker and Crona, 2012).

Guston (2001) describes boundary organizations as fulfilling three main criteria: the creation of boundary objects, involving actors from both sides of the disciplinary boundary, and operating at the intersection of different communities of practice. Guston (2001) builds on the definition provided by Star and Greisemer (1989) and notes that boundary objects facilitate the function of institutions as boundary organizations. He argues that this occurs through the production of "standardized packages" that facilitate the productive engagement of representatives from different sides of the disciplinary or sectoral boundary.

The second key dimension of boundary organizations is their ability to involve "the participation of actors from both sides of the boundary, as well as professionals who serve a mediating role" (Guston, 2001: 401). Bringing together professionals with explicitly different, yet complementary, areas of knowledge resonates strongly. For instance, one interviewee alluded that "It was the credibility of the players"—the senior staff at PEN—"who we all knew

[and] respected." David Rejeski reaffirmed that one central element of PEN's effort was to employ staff with experience with different elements of the science policy system as a way of explicitly bridging the boundaries between science and policy communities. "We wanted to be heavily embedded in the community," he commented. "The thing that helped in the long-run, it was hard to ignore the staff because most of the higher level people had been embedded in government," including the EPA, NIOSH, NSF, and OSTP in the White House. "It would have been much easier to blow us off as people who didn't understand government if we hadn't been embedded in it. I actually think that is really important," said Rejeski.

The third critical component of boundary organizations is that they "exist at the frontier of the two relatively different social worlds of politics and science," operating to ensure that the intersections between different communities of practice are productively managed (Guston, 2001: 401). Boundary organizations often come in the form of "hybrid organizations" that combine different institutional components from the public, private, and non-profit sectors (Jasanoff, 1990; Koppel, 2003; Battilana and Dorado, 2010). This hybrid quality accurately describes the quasi-governmental status of the Wilson Center, as the institution is both situated within government as the official "living memorial" to President Woodrow Wilson, yet still remains outside government by operating in the non-partisan and non-political role of a public policy research center or think tank. Many of the aforementioned examples of boundary organizations studied in the science and technology policy literature—ranging from university research centers to national level institutions to international advisory boards—exemplify the characteristics of hybridization and contribute to their roles as effective boundary-spanning agents.

In addition to institutions, individuals can also successfully serve to span disciplinary, conceptual, or operational divides, thereby playing a key role in linking science and policy communities (Collins and Evans, 2007; Collins, Evans, and Gorman, 2007). Pielke (2007) contends that appropriately trained individuals are needed to act as an "honest broker of policy alternatives" in the policymaking process. This does raise a puzzle, however, which will be further addressed at the end of this chapter: How can an institution or an individual try to intervene in a system while simultaneously aiming to function in a neutral, convening capacity? While these two approaches appear contradictory, a central argument here is that it remains possible for an individual or an organization to do both: hold an opinion and provide a space for engagement of different points of view. Pielke argues that this is possible as long as the positions held are acknowledge transparently and do not interfere with functioning in such a convener role. Honest brokers do not merely operate as disinterested bystanders. Instead, by stating their positions up-front, they can simultaneously help others explore a range of governance possibilities, some of which may even go against their preferred perspective.

The practice of boundary-spanning

In general, the organizations studied here adopted boundary-spanning approaches early in their history, and the rationale for this approach is described thoroughly in their earliest planning documents. For instance, ICON's governance documents explicitly note:

> The management of ICON involves all stakeholders in the nanotechnology community in a flexible and transparent structure designed to respond to rapidly changing issues in the area. Decisions about ICON's positions and priorities are made with balanced inputs from four stakeholder communities: government, academia, industry and non-governmental organizations.
>
> (International Council on Nanotechnology, 2009b)

In regards to PEN, planning documents prepared in 2004 as a component of their grant proposal process also emphasized the importance of engaging multiple stakeholders. In one such memorandum, the existing "institutional gap" within nanotechnology policy is cited to augment the case to create the organization that eventually became PEN. "There exists a niche that the Trusts could fill in," the memo states, by "convening the key stakeholders engaged in research activities and providing the necessary overview of the research enterprise" (Rejeski, 2004c). The need for such a boundary-spanning entity to play a watchdog role is also articulated strongly in another planning memo, which claims that, "We need to create a *regulatory panopticon*, where there is a sense that oversight mechanisms and regulations are being rigorously analyzed by some entity that is outside of government (looking in), trustworthy, and independent" (emphasis in the original) (Rejeski, 2004b).

PEN's mission statement also reaffirms the themes raised in these early planning documents. The mission statement declares, for instance, that "the Project will provide independent, objective knowledge and analysis that can inform critical decisions affecting the development and commercialization of nanotechnologies" (Rejeski, 2004a). This theme resurfaced in a publicly available mid-term report produced after PEN's first two years in operation. "The Project has earned its reputation as a trusted source of impartial and highly useful information," it says, highlighting PEN's ability to bridge institutional divides and reach out to a wide range of stakeholders, particularly "policymakers, regulators, and their staffs" (Project on Emerging Nanotechnologies, 2008c).

Building on this aspect of PEN's activities, the Synthetic Biology Project adopted this perspective as well, especially in regards to closely interacting with the DIY synthetic biology community. One Synthetic Biology Project staff member claimed:

> One of the main things that we took from the experience of PEN was how important that actually was … [to bring] together the synthetic

biologists who were developing the applications, the ecologists, the NGOs, and the government regulators into one room ... to have that honest discussion [and] ... to really hash out those questions.

In short, the values espoused by PEN, ICON, and the Synthetic Biology Project—such as being "independent," "trustworthy," and "transparent"— explicitly reflect the positioning of these entities as boundary organizations.

Additionally, Rejeski commented in interviews that, as the leader of both PEN and the Synthetic Biology Project, he aimed to implicitly base the underlying operational strategies of these organizations on a series of interrelated, fundamental operational principles that suggest a boundary-spanning role. Rejeski described three such underlying strategies from "biology, social science, and finance." First, Rejeski underscored the notion of "persistent co-evolution" from biology as being one of the basic organizational principles for both institutions. A second principle relates to the financial idea of "portfolio management," where "an awful lot of stuff ends up on the cutting room floor." This requires the production, testing, revising, and discarding multiple forms and types of information in order to ultimately determine which elements are most effective at achieving a desired end goal. The third tenet, from the social sciences, relates to PEN's role as a participant-observer of the system. He said:

> The idea is that once we decided to do nano, we became part of the system. The recognition that you are part of the system and not just this research think tank changes what you do. It is more participant observation.

Rejeski regularly referred to this strategy as PEN undertaking "action research," where there is an "obligation of people doing the research to intervene" while simultaneously observing the system evolve.

Given that this purpose of boundary-spanning was built into the rationale of these institutions from the start, how did they actually go about putting these ideas into practice? Three primary strategies can be abstracted from examining their activities—leveraging expert credibility, brokering partnerships and facilitating dialogue, and creating boundary objects—that are discussed in the remainder of this section.

Leveraging expert credibility

The first strategy that these entities utilized in their role as boundary organizations was *leveraging the credibility of external experts*. For example, a number of interviewees commented on how PEN engaged many well-known subject matter experts to author reports. For instance, PEN engaged former FDA official Mike Taylor to produce two reports related to nanotechnology's impact on food and drug safety. PEN also worked with Terry Davies, who was involved in authoring the TSCA law, to produce four reports on a range of nanotechnology oversight and environmental issues. One former PEN staff member stressed about engaging Davies on this analysis: "We needed to find someone that could talk about nanotechnology, and who better than the person who wrote TSCA?" Similarly, in responding to interview questions in writing, one NGO representative said that one "thing that PEN did well was to bring authoritative (i.e. 'credentialed') voices to the debate, particularly in order to draw attention to policy gaps/inadequacies." PEN used experts such as Taylor and Davies in multiple ways, not just for preparing substantive reports on these topics. Following the release of their initial reports with PEN, both Taylor and Davies would also typically testify at Congressional hearings, submit comments to federal agencies, and become media spokespersons on the topics they covered.

In addition to these two bold-faced names that PEN engaged from the environmental and health communities, PEN worked with a broad set of experts to produce knowledge in a host of other areas, including public perceptions of nanotechnology, state and local regulation, and nanotechnology's EHS implications. Out of the 19 primary reports PEN published as part of its numbered series, only Andrew Maynard's *Nanotechnology: Research Strategy for Assessing Risk* (2006a) was authored by PEN staff. Six of PEN's 19 major reports were authored either by Davies (4) or Taylor (2). Six other reports were written by individuals from academia, and many of these scholars also had previous government, non-governmental, or private sector experience. Rounding out the sectoral affiliation of report authors, three were from law firms, two from a science journalist, and one from an NGO. Additionally, four of the five shorter research briefs that PEN released were authored by external experts with a social science or legal background. PEN also had a leading survey firm, Hart Research Associates, author studies on public perception almost annually between 2006 and 2010.

The quality and credibility of the experts PEN engaged to produce its reports emerged as a strong theme among interviewees from multiple sectors. One journalist underlined, "PEN's work became distinctive early on because of the timely issue of reports and the use of reputable authors with industry or federal backgrounds." A government representative described how, across a wide range of issues related to nanotechnology policy, "PEN had the advantage of resources and experts" and they "came to the table" with substantive and well-thought out opinions. Similarly, a private sector representative stated:

> One thing [that was] done very, very well, was really trying to make sure that PEN had competent and committed people—I use both of those 'c's— and a sense that folks kind of knew what they were doing and had a sense that they felt it was important, which is important for a group like this.

This interviewee continued that, "I always thought PEN approached these issues from the perspective of an honest broker . . . the identification of the issues were always defined intelligently, and in a relatively neutral way." Finally, one former PEN staff member mentioned, "We brought in outside expertise, people with little knowledge of nanotechnology. This helped us be the facilitators of the conversation in such a new area." This effective combination of engaging well-known experts to produce anticipatory knowledge about nanotechnology's future policy implications helped make PEN's analysis impactful. In short, "nobody else had that," said another NGO representative working on these issues.

The Synthetic Biology Project also followed PEN's approach of leveraging external authors with credibility to produce key reports. Much like PEN engaged external experts such as Terry Davies and Michael Taylor as report authors, the Synthetic Biology Project drew on Michael Rodemeyer to write a systemic overview of the synthetic biology regulatory landscape, primarily due to his experience with regulatory issues associated with food and agriculture biotechnology. Similarly, it also engaged reputable lawyers with expertise in emerging technologies to prepare its more recent report that utilized case studies to examine the relevance of federal regulations for synthetic biology products. In fact, over half of the primary reports released by the Synthetic Biology Project were wholly or predominantly authored by external technology or policy experts not formally on the staff at the project.

Beyond relying on this set of well-regarded experts to strengthen its credibility, groups such as PEN, ICON, and the Synthetic Biology Project also deeply benefited from being housed in non-partisan, non-ideological institutions. Being based at a university facilitated ICON's ability to engage stakeholders from multiple sectors. The reputation of PEN and the Synthetic Biology project was built on the well-regarded perception of the Wilson Center. The Wilson Center's quasi-governmental status was a central component of PEN's and the Synthetic Biology Project's institutional structure and was made explicit at the forefront their boundary-spanning activities. PEN, in particular, placed special emphasis on being headquartered at a quasi-governmental institution, as indicated in frequent references in reports, press releases, agency submissions, and Congressional testimonies. A typical statement to this effect, which reverberates with the PEN's mission statement and organizational goals, appears on the first page of Congressional testimony provided by Andrew Maynard on October 31, 2007. Maynard writes, "As part of the Wilson Center, the Project is a non-partisan, non-advocacy policy organization that works with researchers, government, industry, NGOs, and others to find the best possible solutions to developing responsible, beneficial and acceptable nanotechnologies" (Maynard, 2007: 2).

Similarly, one reporter described how PEN drew credibility from the Wilson Center's strong reputation. This journalist mentioned:

> I had used other people at the Wilson Center as sources when I was in Washington on other policy issues, so perhaps just the fact that the Project was part of that gave it a neutral luster in my mind. I found their information to be pretty reliable, and pretty useful.

Another interviewee describes how the Wilson Center's standing and lack of overt political stance—either liberal or conservative—helped to bolster the credibility of PEN:

> No one starts thinking that the Wilson Center has an axe to grind on nano, and that adds a lot to the credibility [of PEN's work]. I think that was an absolute real plus for the Project. Press, as well as the public, will discount—fairly or not—if a source is advocating a point of view instead of objective information.

Another dimension of this strategy is that at especially critical moments during its work—when looking to augment the visibility and credibility of certain outputs—PEN also secured formal statements of support from a diverse array of high profile institutions and elite individuals. Over the course of its history, PEN secured seven of these commentary statements referencing the quality of its work, coming from Members of Congress (Ron Wyden and a joint statement from Sherwood Boehlert and Bart Gordon), former heads of federal agencies (William Reilly and William Ruckelshaus, both former EPA Administrators), well-known private sector organizations (Intel and the industry trade association the NanoBusiness Alliance), and international bodies such as the Department of Environment, Food, and Rural Affairs (DEFRA) in the United Kingdom.

Such statements of support came at three critical moments relatively early in PEN's history, in 2005 and 2006, all of which focused on issues related to EHS risk management. The first moment came in relation to the release of a web-based inventory that PEN compiled tracking EHS risk research spending across the federal government. This inventory became a key focus in PEN reports and testimony and was used as the primary basis of information for PEN's policy recommendations associated with improving EHS risk research. Like the CPI, PEN championed this inventory as a publicly available and transparent source of information about ongoing research projects directed at illuminating potential EHS risks. PEN then analyzed the data in the inventory to assess whether the portfolio of federally funded EHS risk research was sufficiently relevant to addressing existing information gaps.

The endorsement secured from the NanoBusiness Alliance emphasized:

> The new inventory of research into nanotechnology's potential environmental, human health and safety effects (EH&S) . . . is open and accessible to all, facilitating increased awareness of the projects underway and making it easier for organizations to form partnerships to research and address potential EH&S issues.
>
> (NanoBusiness Alliance, 2005)

The statement went on to say that "we applaud the Woodrow Wilson Center's work as an important step" and that "we encourage our network of corporations, universities, regional initiatives and media to participate and contribute to this growing and open resource." This kind of testimonial from the private sector helps to demonstrate the inventory's value to a wide range of constituencies.

Similarly, following the launch of Maynard's report, *Nanotechnology: A Research Strategy for Addressing Risk* (2006a), PEN secured two endorsements: one from a representative of a leading technology corporation and the other from a foreign government agency. Paolo Gargini, the Director of Technology Strategy at Intel, released a supporting statement stating:

> The Wilson Center report is an important contribution to building much needed consensus around the need for focused research into the implications, as well as the applications, of nanotechnology . . . [the] report coalesces and extends the work of several other groups and illuminates a growing consensus around the need for a more focused, federally-guided nanotech EHS research program.
>
> (Gargini, 2006)

Similarly, DEFRA in the United Kingdom stated:

> We found the Woodrow Wilson Centre report *Nanotechnology: A Research Strategy for Addressing Risk* to be a very helpful contribution to international discussions on research needs . . . and we are particularly supportive of the way in which work has been divided into two categories of short and longer term. Many views are shared between the proposals of the Woodrow Wilson report and our own.
>
> (Department for Environment, Food and Rural Affairs, 2006)

While such statements may, at first glance, seem merely well-intentioned blurbs meant to demonstrate good will among organizations working in the same sector, they do serve a deeper purpose. For an organization still in its early stages, such endorsements help to build its reputation, providing a concrete demonstration of an ability to engage collaboratively across sectors. This benefit is underscored by testimonials coming from organizations from different sectors: a single company, a trade association, a foreign government agency. Additionally, and perhaps most notably, securing these endorsements early in an organization's history helps to attract even higher-profile influencers at a later date.

Perhaps PEN's most effective use of such statements of endorsement came near the end of 2006, following the release of a seminal publication in the journal *Nature*. Andrew Maynard was the lead author, along with 13 experts representing leading nanotechnology researchers on EHS implications, of an article titled "Safe Handling of Nanotechnology" that laid out "five grand challenges for developing safe nanoscience through sound science" (Maynard et al., 2006a: 269). Maynard et al. (2006a) offered a vision for nanotechnology

EHS risk research by producing a forward-looking timeline laying out the "grand challenges" to 2022.

High profile endorsements of this article were secured from key Members of Congress involved in nanotechnology policy, with their release slated to coincide with the launch of this publication. A joint statement released by House Science Committee Chairman Sherwood Boehlert and Ranking Democrat Bart Gordon wrote, "This paper should be a landmark in the history of nanotechnology research . . . This paper should eliminate any remaining excuses for inaction in this vitally important area" (United States House of Representatives, Committee on Science and Technology, 2006a). Such "excuses" referred to the federal government's EHS risk research strategy, which both Members viewed as lagging behind. They wrote, "There is absolutely no reason that those same agencies and the White House should not now quickly put together a plan and a budget to implement the recommendations in the *Nature* paper as part of the fiscal 2008 budget" (United States House of Representatives, Committee on Science and Technology, 2006a). Democrat Senator Ron Wyden—who co-sponsored the 21st Century Nanotechnology Research and Development Act in 2003—also provided an endorsement of his own, stating, "What's great about this *Nature* article is that it provides a much-needed environmental, health, and safety research framework. Its suggested approach presents a solid foundation for developing a short-, mid-, and long-term research strategy" (United States Senate, 2006). Former EPA Administrator Reilly also chimed in, calling the article "an authoritative outline of what that vital research agenda should be. It is a sound, comprehensive proposal that needs early attention" (Reilly, 2006). Such statements helped to solidify PEN's profile, leveraging credibility that it could capitalize on for the remainder of its activities.

A review of PEN's quarterly reports shows that these statements were generally produced after PEN briefed the individual or organization writing the statement, which often took place before a report or article was published. However, the determination as to whether to prepare such statements and what positions to take was left to the authors' discretion. In some instances, such as the Reilly, Gargini and DEFRA examples, the statements of support were released in conjunction with PEN. The release of all these statements made by Members of Congress was timed with the public launch of the *Nature* article. In sum, PEN was able to secure these statements of support using a number of communication strategies. First, PEN had developed previous professional relationships with the individuals and institutions that subsequently might lend a statement of support. Second, PEN sought out statements of support from individuals whose views on an issue carried weight. For example, former EPA Administrator William Ruckelshaus produced a statement in support of Davies's report titled *EPA and Nanotechnology* (2007) that references Ruckelshaus's previous experience at the agency (Ruckelshaus, 2007). Boehlert, Gordon, and Wyden all had salient views on nanotechnology policy given their previous engagement on the issue as Members of Congress. Third, these statements of support were typically pegged to the release of a report or article, maximizing their relevance and helping PEN amplify any buzz surrounding the launch of these materials.

There are no indications from this research of PEN seeking to engage an external expert as an author and not being able to do so, nor are there indications of PEN trying to secure a statement of support and failing to do so. Still, no organization achieves a perfect success rate, either in terms of recruiting external authors for its reports or in terms of meeting no resistance in seeking public statements of support for its work. Presumably, if such rebuffs did occur, PEN did not dwell on them and moved quickly to engage others. If PEN encountered any objections when engaging external authors or securing statements of support, these appeared to have not warranted much attention. The rationale as to why PEN did not seek to engage a group such as ICON formally—either as a partner or secondary supporter of its work—is unclear, especially despite close professional ties between individuals at both institutions. Part of the explanation might be that the organizations operated differently: based on their governance structures, PEN was able to move faster and did not need to get formal approval for its activities from multiple stakeholders that might have very different views on a subject.

Just because an organization such as PEN can leverage expert credibility in this way does not guarantee that these ideas are taken up directly by policymakers or the research community. For instance, just because PEN had Members of Congress and former EPA Administrators call attention to its work did not ensure that the recommendations in the *Nature* paper for an improved EHS risk research plan made their way unaltered into the formal NNI planning documents. However, while no straightforward, one-to-one link connects specific outputs and specific policy impacts, there are still indications that a collective body of analysis can slowly shift the direction of policy or research practices. One former Congressional committee staff member, who worked on the effort to reauthorize the Nanotechnology Research and Development Act, did note "I thought [the Wilson Center] actually played an important role in what ended up in that legislation." Additionally, ICON's 2008 report, *Towards Predicting Nano-Biointeractions*, explicitly mentions that the *Nature* article was one of the key foundational resources that was drawn on to inform the workshop discussions that contributed to that ICON output. This is not surprising, given that Maynard himself was an active participant in ICON as an Advisory Board member. Many groups such as PEN and ICON do undertake their own internal assessments to determine how the outputs they produced were used to inform debates on these topics. PEN even developed an internal document tracking the close parallels in language between a 2009 version of a Senate bill introduced to reauthorize the original 2003 nanotechnology law and how that language compared to rhetoric used in PEN testimonies, reports, and other analyses (Project on Emerging Nanotechnologies, 2009a). Even though neither the House nor Senate versions of this legislation ended up becoming law, this is the kind of sway on the discussion surrounding nanotechnology policy that an NGO such as PEN strives to achieve.

Moreover, organizations such as PEN, ICON, and the Synthetic Biology Project are not the only entities capable of leveraging or adopting this kind of strategy. Many other institutions involved in nanotechnology policy also drew on external experts to expand their footprint and leverage resources on a regular basis. For instance, the National Academies conducts all of its research through independent review committees that involve a range of leading academic and private sector representatives (National Research Council, 2009b; National Research Council, 2012). Similarly, the International Life Sciences Institute organized multi-sectoral working groups involving subject matter experts from different public, private, and academic institutions, with their focus being predominantly on the application of nanotechnology in the food sector and the development of standardized nanomaterial characterization (International Life Sciences Institute, 2013). Chapter 4 also describes how the Center for Responsible Nanotechnology developed an expert-based task force to generate scenarios on the future of nanotechnology and to explore the global policy implications of nanotechnology, with the findings endorsed by a host of representatives from different institutions (Center for Responsible Nanotechnology, 2008a).

Brokering partnerships and facilitating dialogue

In addition to leveraging expert credibility, a second strategy organizations can employ as part of their boundary-spanning efforts is through *brokering partnerships and facilitating dialogue*. This can be done formally, as the coordinator of multi-sectoral collaborations that are acknowledged in public, or informally, through behind the scenes activities. PEN and ICON worked to broker a number of partnerships that brought together organizations from different sectors' advance discussions on nanotechnology policy both in the United States and abroad. For instance, PEN made this partnership brokering responsibility a particularly visible element of its role, noting in its mid-term summary report that, "we often help to build collaborations that span sectoral boundaries, tap into needed sources of expertise, or engage different stakeholder groups to think collectively about nanotechnology-related topics of shared interest" (Project on Emerging Nanotechnologies, 2008c). The report continues: "The Project's 'value added' may be in the form of seed funding, technical assistance, or provision of a neutral forum for exchanges of ideas and viewpoints" (Project on Emerging Nanotechnologies, 2008c).

One influential partnership for which PEN and ICON both played a formative role in fostering was helping to bring together the DuPont Corporation and the Environmental Defense Fund (EDF) that produced one of the most visible nanotechnology voluntary risk management frameworks in the field, known as the *Nano Risk Framework* (Environmental Defense–DuPont Nano Partnership, 2007). While many can take credit for helping to initiate this collaboration, both PEN and ICON were involved in this bridge-building early on. For instance, an individual knowledgeable about ICON speculated that ICON had "built up an enormous amount of good will and trust that, for example, could potentially have laid the ground for the Environmental Defense–DuPont Nano Risk Framework, because both of those groups were heavily involved in ICON." PEN also provided seed funding to DuPont and EDF to work together and produce the main framework document. Fostering this partnership was an explicit goal in PEN's planning documents, which anticipated in its planning memo: "Working with Environmental Defense [to] develop guidelines for voluntary standards of care for nanotechnology and implement those standards with at least one company" (Rejeski, 2004b). Letters and progress reports from EDF to PEN affirm PEN's role as a primary driver of the partnership. Later on, PEN hosted the public launch of the *Nano Risk Framework* and heralded the accomplishment of the EDF-DuPont partnership throughout its internal reporting documents and in the public mid-term report that was published (Environmental Defense–DuPont Nano Partnership, 2007). For example, in the mid-term report, PEN notes:

> [T]o jumpstart actions toward addressing risks . . . we helped to support the first voluntary agreement between a company (DuPont) and an NGO (Environmental Defense Fund). The unusual collaboration produced a pioneering voluntary standard for comprehensively documenting and communicating the steps a user should take to evaluate and address potential risks of nanoscale materials.
> (Project on Emerging Nanotechnologies, 2008c)

PEN's success in bringing together DuPont and EDF was characteristic of the behind the scenes work central to its boundary-spanning efforts. PEN explicitly affirmed this role, acknowledging the "policy-related contributions that result from this behind-the-scenes support," that "range from better communication between organizations to timely, important additions to the nanotechnology literature" (Project on Emerging Nanotechnologies, 2008c). In another example, PEN also referred to this behind the scenes role in helping to inform research undertaken by the GAO in response to a congressionally mandated study on EHS funding levels. PEN notes in its final quarterly report:

> We met with the team from the Government Accountability Office (GAO) that undertook the Senate-mandated research to determine how much is being spent on nano-related EHS research across the entire government and provided GAO with the latest version of our database.
> (Project on Emerging Nanotechnologies, 2010)

This quarterly report continues, "The GAO also found that the federal government was over-estimating the amount of funding for targeted risk research, again supporting the conclusions of our analyses over the past three years" (Project on Emerging Nanotechnologies, 2010).

This kind of role extended to formal participation in review panels and committees. Representatives from PEN and ICON served on two National Academies committees focused on reviewing the federal EHS risk research strategy (National Research Council, 2009b, 2012). PEN was also among a handful of organizations asked to join the Local Advisory Committee formed by the Department of Public Health in Cambridge, Massachusetts to provide guidance in developing and implementing a program to address nanotechnology EHS risks. PEN highlighted this role in its final internal quarterly report, noting that, "we have had on-going conversations with the Cambridge Public Health Department on how to provide technical assistance to nanotechnology firms in the community and to help the city with public outreach" as a way to strengthen the EHS risk management program the city began to put in place (Project on Emerging Nanotechnologies, 2010).

PEN, even more than ICON, also pursued public visibility in its own partnerships with other organizations, in some cases bringing together three or more organizations to produce nanotechnology policy analysis and research that was promoted broadly. The most often-referenced partnership that interviewees mentioned was a project that PEN engaged in with the Grocery Manufacturers Association, a food industry association, to develop case studies related to nanotechnology-based applications in the area of food packaging. This is another good example of where an organization's foresight and boundary-spanning efforts can come together in a synergistic way. The forward-looking hypothetical case studies examining the regulatory adequacy of existing FDA laws were a critical component in PEN's partnership with the Grocery Manufacturers Association. Drawing on plausible information about potential emerging food packaging products—instead of focusing on products that were already being commercialized or coming to market—created a safe space for industry, government, and NGO representatives to engage in the year-long set of discussions and workshops. One former government official said of this partnership, "The [working] committees were a real strength . . . genuinely engaging [diverse] viewpoints" and that the conversations undertaken "proved to be very illuminating. That model of a multi-stakeholder public–private partnership should be done" more frequently, said this interviewee.

Similarly, PEN became involved in a four-way international partnership during the later stages of its work funded by a grant from the European Commission. While the activities supported by The Pew Charitable Trusts were intended to focus almost exclusively on the United States, PEN documents indicate that it became increasingly difficult to ignore the global dimension of nanotechnology. PEN submitted comments on nanotechnology policy issues to agencies in the United Kingdom and held events on the international dimensions of nanotechnology, such as the role of nanotechnology in China's innovation economy and the impact of nanotechnology on challenges facing developing countries. Even the research briefs published as part of the *NanoFrontiers* series—itself the product of a partnership with the NSF and National Institutes of Health—predominantly emphasized international issues. The culmination of these interests was an internationally collaborative project involving three other academic and research centers: the London School of Economics and Political Science and Chatham House in the United Kingdom, and the Environmental Law Institute in the United States. The resulting report, *Securing the Promise of Nanotechnologies*, rivals the report from the Grocery Manufacturers Association partnership in terms of the number of individuals from different institutions involved in its authorship and production (Breggin et al., 2009).

Building these types of multi-sectoral partnerships was also a strategy carried forward into the Synthetic Biology Project. For example, the Synthetic Biology Project collaborated with scholars from the Massachusetts Institute of Technology to study the ecological implications of synthetic biology, leading to both a report by the Synthetic Biology Project on this research (Drinkwater et al., 2014) and a commentary published in *Science* about the oversight of gene drive technology (Oye et al., 2014). The Synthetic Biology Project has also formed partnerships with representatives from the DIY synthetic biology community to survey perceptions and practices of participating researchers (Grushkin, Kuiken, and Millet, 2013). Finally, the Synthetic Biology Project was the only United States partner awarded a grant from the European Union to participate in a consortium with the goal "to foster responsible governance of synthetic biology" (Synthetic Biology Project, 2013b).

Not all such partnerships ultimately succeed or manage to get off the ground fruitfully. One example is that PEN tried to work with a small nanotechnology start-up company, called NanoFilm, to help get the company enrolled in EPA's voluntary information provision program that was designed to share details about the use of nanomaterials in commerce. However, this partnership brokering effort between NanoFilm and EPA ended in March 2009, when the EPA terminated the voluntary reporting program. PEN declares in its final internal quarterly report:

> [U]sing EPA funds and support from PEN, NanoFilm developed an environmental management system to track their progress in terms of reducing waste, energy, etc. NanoFilm submitted their proposal to the EPA, and it was slated for approval in the spring of 2009. They would have been the first nanotechnology company to enter the program.
>
> (Project on Emerging Nanotechnologies, 2010)

Similarly, the idea that Davies (2008) developed to create a "Nanotechnology Effects Institute" that would investigate EHS risks by being co-funded by government and industry never materialized. This notion—drawing on inspiration from the Health Effects Institute, which examines the health impacts of air pollution and is co-funded by the automobile industry and government—did not gain traction or come to fruition. This is, in part, likely due to the challenges associated with generating interest in creating such an entity as well as marshaling the funds needed to make it a reality.

Finally, one additional way organizations can fulfill this partnership brokering and dialogue facilitating role is by serving as event and meeting conveners. Both PEN and the Synthetic Biology Project demonstrated this ability by hosting a multitude of events at the Wilson Center, further demonstrating the ability of these organizations to serve as bridge-building institutions. On a logistical level, these projects were able to use the functional conference space at the Wilson Center—physically located in downtown Washington, strategically located between the White House, Congress, and many federal agencies—to host public events and to invite other organizations to use their facilities for workshops and meetings. On a conceptual level, PEN in particular looked to position itself as a convener early in its lifespan by providing an open venue for discussion among representatives from business, government, and the NGO community. Organizing these kinds of meetings became a commonplace occurrence, with PEN hosting or co-sponsoring over 50 events, an average of nearly one a month over its lifespan, and with the Synthetic Biology Project organizing over 20 such events as well. These include a plethora of presentations (Project on Emerging Nanotechnologies, 2005a, 2007b; Synthetic Biology Project, 2011); report launches (Project on Emerging Nanotechnologies, 2007a, 2008b; Schmidt, 2007; Synthetic Biology Project, 2013c, 2015b); conferences (Project on Emerging Nanotechnologies, 2008a); and socializing and networking events (Project on Emerging Nanotechnologies, 2008e).

Through these types of events, NGOs can gain a reputation and are conferred legitimacy by helping to convene organizations that cut across a spectrum of positions. While judging the impact of these types of public presentations and meetings directly is difficult—one non-governmental representative supposed that "highlighting issues of concern is an infinite task"—representatives from a range of different sectors pointed to the importance of these regular events in helping situate institutions in a boundary-spanning role and promote the view that they are engaged, lively places of thought and action. For instance, one academic researcher stated, "what PEN was able to do, and I think this was a unique role that PEN played . . . [was] in having a convening space . . . a place where people could come and support a convening discussion." Similarly, one private sector representative affirmed the value of organizing such a robust slate of activity:

> All of the reports and all of the webinars and the panel discussions, I have to say when you look at it, you have to see that this group was a very, very active group. They were always releasing a report, or hosting something at the forum there, providing a venue. Overall, in general, the Project was very, extremely influential in the field in that it was very helpful to try to ensure that for the global dialogue there was a comprehensive nature of the dialogue, by providing these different reports or think pieces or panel discussions or letting groups [use the Wilson Center].

Creating boundary objects

The production of *boundary objects* is a third component that can reinforce an institution's boundary-spanning efforts, one that encompasses the multitude of reports, inventories, and events they may undertake over time. The production of boundary objects can raise an organization's public profile and standing considerably by generating new information not yet produced by other stakeholders in the field. One researcher pronounced that PEN's production of fresh information that other stakeholders could use was a key factor in the organization's emergence in the field. This interviewee inferred, "from the outside there was a strong focus on generating information, in the form of reports or databases or events that helped get information out to the hands of policymakers." Similarly, an individual working in the private sector seconded these views, describing PEN as providing:

> information and insight that was helpful to people getting their heads wrapped around these issues and making sure that the people . . . debating these topics had some useful information and insight and analysis to go off of, even though we certainly didn't always agree with it. It was definitely very useful to have.

Of course, PEN was not alone in in the production of boundary objects with respect to nanotechnology policy. Many organizations working in the field also produced reports and informational materials to serve as focal points for policy discussion. ICON published a small number of reports that focused on critical research areas for the field. The International Center for Technology Assessment used legal petitions to bring together other NGOs as signatories to push for greater regulation of nanotechnology in sunscreens (International Center for Technology Assessment, 2006), food and cosmetics (International Center for Technology Assessment, 2008), and nanotechnology-based silver products (International Center for Technology Assessment, 2012b; Center for Food Safety, 2015). Consumers Union and Friends of the Earth Australia used the testing of nano-based sunscreens to engage consumers and scientists in a discussion about the relative merits of the use of nanotechnology (Consumers Union, 2008; Friends of the Earth Australia, 2012). Finally, collaborative standards-setting processes managed by the American National Standards Institute and the International Organization for Standardization positioned debates related to nomenclature to bring together researchers from different countries to aid in the adoption of consistent terminologies and definitions critical to nanotechnology research (International Organization for Standards, n.d.; American National Standards Institute, n.d.).

Interview respondents especially observed how PEN's reports played a valuable role as boundary objects in providing substantive information to multiple constituencies simultaneously. One government interviewee hypothesized about these publications, "The reports are the 'go to' reports." This sentiment was reflected in comments made by a private sector representative, who said that even though many of the reports were published a few years ago—a long time, in a fast-moving field such as nanotechnology—"the work is still good and people refer to it." Another interviewee suggested that stakeholders from a range of sectors found the information provided in PEN reports useful, "providing that sort of next layer of much more detailed policy work. So, it felt to me like it was performing a very valuable service." Finally, a former government representative commented on how the information from PEN's publications synergistically reinforced data emerging from the other types of outputs it produced. This interviewee concluded that "the publications, the forums, and that product list … really had a huge impact on what was happening in the nanotechnology community."

However, both in regards to nanotechnology and synthetic biology, the online databases and inventories perhaps played the leading role as boundary objects. This is likely due to their inherently interactive nature, the ability of users to search for information as needed, and the ease of curating information that could be used for multiple purposes. By touting its EHS risk research inventory as a "unique" informational resource, PEN looked to influence the debate regarding the funding system of governmental EHS risk research, while simultaneously gaining legitimacy by presenting information that others in the field could use for a range of policy purposes (Project on Emerging Nanotechnologies, 2005c).

Speaking at the public launch event for this EHS risk research inventory—which, like many of PEN's activities, was broadcast and recorded for free via online webcast—Rejeski reinforced the idea of developing an information source that could transform discussions about investments in EHS risk research and, in turn, be relevant to the policymaking process. Rejeski began: "We have been batting the number ball across the net for at least a year now," using one of the many metaphors PEN would employ over the years to make the information it produced easier to grasp (Project on Emerging Nanotechnologies, 2005b). He continued by expanding on the metaphor, stating, "What we want to do here is essentially move the game onto a chess board," to determine how the "next research dollar" should be "strategically invested." Rejeski then emphasized the policy relevance of the database, aiming to situate the EHS risk research inventory to stimulate discussions about nanotechnology research funding. "Why are we doing this?" he asks rhetorically:

> Because people have essentially asked us to do this. Over the past three or four months, we have talked to probably hundreds of people about "Should we build a database like this?" We've talked to people in industry and in the NGO community. We've talked to the media. We've talked to a lot of the program managers in the federal government. None of them have said, "Boy that is a really bad idea."
>
> (Project on Emerging Nanotechnologies, 2005b).

Remember that ICON also created an often-used online database to serve as a platform for aggregated information about EHS risk research (International Council on Nanotechnology, 2014). The ICON database was updated monthly to include new scientific publications from a range of sources related to EHS issues, with users having the ability to submit ratings for each paper to indicate its degree of relevance to nanotechnology EHS topics. The development of these informational databases for boundary-spanning purposes also continued with respect to synthetic biology. Similar to PEN's nanotechnology EHS risk research inventory, the Synthetic Biology Project also put together an accounting of federally funded projects focused on synthetic biology risk research (Synthetic Biology Project, 2015c, 2015d). Although this information was simply assembled as a static spreadsheet, instead of displayed as a fully interactive inventory, it served a purpose for the Synthetic Biology Project akin to what the EHS risk research inventory did for PEN: to strengthen the argument that insufficient funds were being spent on synthetic biology risk research.

Moreover, just as PEN produced a map of the most active nanotechnology metropolitan regions—which it called the US NanoMetro Map (Project on Emerging Nanotechnologies, 2009c)—the Synthetic Biology Project also created a map-based inventory of the locations where synthetic biology research and commercialization was taking place (Synthetic Biology Project, 2013a). The Synthetic Biology Project also developed an online "scorecard" (Synthetic Biology Project, 2012a) that tracked the implementation of a series of risk management recommendations published in a 2010 report by the Presidential Commission for the Study of Bioethical Issues, titled *New Directions: The Ethics of Synthetic Biology and Emerging Technologies*. These online information resources from the Synthetic Biology were designed with the same goal in mind as their antecedent inventories from PEN: to provide multifaceted tools that various stakeholders could use to understand and track the progress of developments in synthetic biology.

One indicator of success related to the ability of these organizations to position such inventories as boundary objects is the degree of attention that followed their release. For example, a substantial article on nanotechnology oversight and risk research funding, written by science journalist Rick Weiss, appeared on December 5, 2005 in *The Washington Post* (Weiss, 2005). The article explicitly mentions the funding numbers for nanotechnology risk research represented in PEN's EHS inventory. Rejeski was quoted in this article, along with representatives from environmental organizations such as EDF and the National Resources Defense Council, government officials from EPA, and researchers from national laboratories. This focus of this major newspaper article ultimately revolved around how the findings from the EHS risk research inventory raised broader questions about a range of nano-technology policy issues, such as the application of existing regulations to oversee nanomaterials and the need for better coordination among future risk research projects. Weiss writes:

Amid growing evidence that some of the tiniest materials ever engineered pose potentially big environmental, health and safety risks, momentum is building in Congress, environmental circles and in the industry itself to beef up federal oversight of the new materials, which are already showing up in dozens of consumer products.

(Weiss, 2005: AO8)

Approximately a decade later, on October 8, 2015, another *Washington Post* article with a similar tone was published, reporting on the differing amounts between federal research dollars going to synthetic biology applications versus research attuned to illuminating potentially negative implications. Like the previous article, this one was spurred by the inventory of risk research projects produced by the Synthetic Biology Project, and it quotes representatives from the project throughout the story (Basulto, 2015).

Over time, PEN continually worked to raise the profile of the EHS risk research inventory by referring to information from this database in Congressional testimonies, reports, and press releases, often in conjunction with information from the CPI. For example, in Congressional testimony given in 2006, Andrew Maynard connected information from the CPI with information from the EHS inventory to illustrate what he viewed as key gaps in the federal nanotechnology risk research effort (Maynard, 2006b). In submitted testimony, Maynard writes:

Although this is a very subjective exercise, [the EHS inventory] shows the vast majority of the material-specific risk research is focused—disproportionately it would seem—on carbon-based nanomaterials. At the time of the analysis, carbon-based nanomaterials accounted for just 34% of listed consumer products, while silver accounted for 30% of listed products, and silica and metal oxides such as silica, titanium dioxide, zinc oxide and cerium oxide accounted for 36% of listed products. In other words, risk research does not appear to be in step with current market realities.

Another indicator of how a boundary object such as PEN's EHS risk research inventory operates is how this approach to providing information was adopted by other actors across the nanotechnology policy system. As mentioned previously, one occurrence of this was when Congressional testimony provided by Rejeski helped to spur an analysis of federal nanotechnology risk research by the GAO. The resulting GAO study explicitly adopted an inventorying methodology similar to the one PEN used in producing its EHS risk research database (Government Accountability Office, 2008). GAO presented a detailed, project-by-project accounting of federal funding levels for nanotechnology EHS risk research, mirroring the type of work that PEN had done independently. Confirming PEN's interpretation of the data, the GAO study found that the previously stated funding amounts provided by the NNI overstated the research being undertaken for these purposes (Government Accountability Office, 2008).

PEN also deployed the EHS risk research inventory to try to influence funding practices. One interviewee deduced, "If you look at the budget for the NNI you are starting to see a little bit more money going to EHS and stuff like that, and I think that is partially because of things like [PEN] because they were able to hit that sweet spot," referring to the provision of information in a style that was useful to decision makers. A scientific researcher who focuses on the potential EHS risks of nanotechnology highlighted how informational outputs such as the inventories produced by PEN and ICON generally contributed to changes in perception among policymakers about the importance of EHS issues. "In 2001, this [EHS issues] wasn't a sub-discipline of nano-technology even remotely. This wasn't something that was on the radar screen, really," said the researcher. "I think that they [PEN] were part of a process that—'institutionalized' might be a good word—made it more than just a flash in the pan." Another researcher explained:

> I'm heartened to see that the issues that were so radical in 2002, when CBEN [and ICON] started, are now just very much mainstream academic. [There is] nothing controversial about asking questions about health and toxicity, and about occupational issues. So it's become much more of a mainstream topic.

When PEN began to wind down, its ability to hand over the management of the EHS risk research inventory to another organization further strengthened the inventory's status as a boundary object. Moreover, this transition further positioned this inventory as a platform and opportunity for institutional collaboration. Much like it did in handing over the hosting of CPI to Virginia Tech, in 2009 PEN transferred ownership of the EHS risk research inventory to the Working Party on Manufactured Nanomaterials (WPMN) at the Organization for Economic Co-Operation and Development (OECD), a global forum for leading industrialized countries to harmonize how they address nanotechnology EHS issues.

OECD's WPMN subsequently renamed the database as the OECD Database on Research into Safety of Manufactured Nanomaterials and developed a formal update and information submission process so that representatives from member countries could update inventory entries directly. By handing over the EHS risk research inventory to a global body that served as a liaison among country governments, international NGOs, and businesses, PEN helped to extend the active lifespan of the database and situate the inventory as a central focus of attention in global discussions about nanotechnology. The OECD also upgraded the inventory's functionality to link it more closely with two other informational databases in the field, including the one maintained by ICON. One researcher even remarked on how different institutions attempted to use such digital inventories and databases as boundary objects for their respective purposes. This individual recognized the seeming proliferation of inventories with respect to nanotechnology in the mid-2000s, stating amusingly "there was a time when everybody was developing a database." A summative report produced by the OECD's WPMN alludes to the role that these risk research inventories served in helping countries and other actors work together on this topic. Listed as the first entry under "major outcomes" of the OECD's WPMN, PEN's EHS risk research inventory is described as providing a "global resource for research projects" that will help to "assist researchers in future collaborative efforts" (Organisation for Economic Co-Operation and Development, 2011). PEN's risk research inventory, in its new incarnation, became an integral part of the OECD's broader efforts on addressing nanotechnology EHS issues (Organisation for Economic Co-Operation and Development, 2009b).

While the focus here has been on the EHS risk research inventories produced by PEN and ICON, the role of PEN's CPI as a boundary object in its own right should not be shortchanged either. The CPI was highly effective in engaging stakeholders from different communities, ranging from government representatives to members of the media to the lay public to scientific researchers. For instance, a former Congressional committee staffer described how the CPI was instrumental in helping highlight nanotechnology's commercialization patterns to policymakers. "I remember very well when they came up to the Hill with a whole bunch of products that they had found in the commercial marketplace that had nanomaterials in them," said the former staffer. "The reason that this sort of resonated on the Hill, I think, with Members, is they had the memory of what had happened with genetically modified plants." The interviewee agreed that this type of information was a prominent factor in inspiring additional hearings on nanotechnology's potential societal implications. Similarly, one government official claimed that, especially in terms of providing a line of sight into nanotechnology's commercialization patterns, the CPI "was the only thing out there." A private sector representative underscored that the CPI called attention to "this whole question of what is in the marketplace. [It was] cited and used in so many different places." A city-level government official also said that, "I am simply not aware of any organization that had gone out and done, I call it grunt-work, [tracking] really unregulated products." One NGO representative accentuated this use of the inventory in stressing, "I used the inventory to make a case that nanotech was here and important."

Although tracking how extensively the CPI was used is difficult—since it was referenced in such a wide set of materials and since many of its uses were in items such as reports, workshop summaries, and white papers whose total citation counts are hard to come by—a few proxy indicators illustrate the CPI's reach and utilization by a wide array of stakeholders within the nanotechnology policy community. The extensive engagement by individual and institutional representatives of the US federal government in explicitly referencing CPI statistics has already been discussed (United States House of Representatives, Committee on Science and Technology, 2006b, 2007, 2008). Even critics of the CPI acknowledged the visibility and high levels of attention the CPI garnered. Chapter 4 discussed how this critique focused predominantly on whether the products listed in the CPI were actually an accurate representation of the products on the market using nanomaterials. Even in their article assessing the CPI, Berube et al. (2010: 152) recognize its place as a key reference for the field. Those authors write that the CPI "has been frequently cited in scholarly and popular articles as well as reports from government and industry." Furthermore, in a section titled "The Ubiquitous PEN Inventory," the article notes that "A Google Scholar Search . . . produced over 700 academic publications citing the PEN Consumer Products Inventory" and that "a standard Google Search produced over 13,000 hits" (Berube et al., 2010).

Another indication of the CPI's broader resonance was that other organizations chose to directly imitate the methodology and organizational structure of the CPI in developing other nanotechnology consumer product inventories for their own purposes. One high profile copycat version of the CPI came from the European Consumers' Organisation known as BEUC. In fact, BEUC followed in PEN's footsteps by emulating not one but two of PEN's online inventories. In 2009, BEUC created its own inventory of "products claiming to contain nanoparticles available in the EU market" and explicitly used aspects of PEN's CPI as the basis for structuring this work (The European Consumer's Organisation, 2010). The description of the BEUC inventory expresses, "The different products in our inventory were categorized into products categories and subcategories similar to the ones used in the Woodrow Wilson International Center for Scholars Database" (The European Consumer's Organisation, 2010). Like PEN's, the BEUC inventory grew over time, starting with 151 products in 2009 and rising to 475 products by October 2010, with the inventory's major updates publicized on the organization's website. Additionally, in 2012 BEUC created an online inventory specifically focused on tracking products claiming to contain nanosilver materials that were available on the European market (The European Consumer's Organisation, 2013), emulating a similar inventory on nanosilver products that PEN had previously produced in 2008.

Finally, the best reflection of the CPI's status as a boundary object is perhaps best evident in a tongue-in-cheek reflection on the CPI's ubiquity taken from a short reference made to the CPI in a paper published in the July 2012 edition of *Nature Nanotechnology* (Hansen and Baun, 2012). The authors make a reference about how almost any new report on the topic of nanotechnology "is likely to cite the Consumer Product Inventory maintained by the Project on Emerging Nanotechnologies" (Hansen and Baun, 2012: 409). This line hints at the role played by the many references to the CPI across an array of articles or reports: to serve as a sign of how rapidly nanotechnology was considered to be advancing.

The possibility of positioning "down the middle"?

Although the organizations studied here employed a number of strategies to position themselves as boundary-spanning organizations in regards to emerging technologies, a tension remains between playing a neutral role and being an advocate for a particular viewpoint. Many interviewees, particularly journalists, highlighted this strain. For instance, many interviewees did view PEN and ICON as occupying a relatively impartial position within the spectrum of organizations working on nanotechnology policy. One journalist summed up this idea by noting, "PEN was regarded as an unusual source of neutral but reputable information about nanotechnology." Another journalist said that the information PEN provided was "taken as well-grounded and honest . . . more balanced than some of the environmental groups." A third journalist commented that, "I thought [PEN] was a pretty good bridge between the real advocates who are viewing this very, very skeptically and the industry people who are really pushing this because they see a lot of innovation and a lot of money."

Many interviewees went further in such assessments, placing organizations with different points of view along a spectrum, with groups such as PEN and ICON generally being perceived as being primarily interested in promoting research and evidence-based policymaking. One researcher employed the following image to explain the role that different groups played in the nanotechnology policy landscape: "At one end of the continuum was ICON . . . whose primary interest was trying to figure out what regulatory regimes might be in the future so they could plan things like research protocols." This interviewee continued, "Then at the other end of the spectrum were the folks like ETC Group and Friends of the Earth Australia . . . They were mostly naysayers, opponents." This researcher then suggested, "In the middle, you had folks like Woodrow Wilson and the Environmental Defense . . . who were credentialed and knew what they were doing." Another interviewee stated:

> I think of a lot of the studies that the Wilson Center did as providing more information and analysis and less about advocating for specific policy solutions, which would set them apart from the American Chemistry Council [often viewed as more supportive of nanotechnology] or the ETC Group [often viewed as more negative toward nanotechnology].

One private-sector figure expanded on this idea, noting:

> I think the Wilson Center . . . was probably more sympathetic to the concerns and issues of people who were more worried about the business and commercialization aspects of nanotech. Not to say that the other NGOs were totally unconcerned about that or totally unsympathetic to it, but I think . . . if you are sort of positioning people left, right, and center from the American Chemistry Council or US Chamber of

Commerce on the one extreme or on the one end of things to the ETC Group on the other, the Wilson Center would be a little more down the middle.

However, this perception of neutrality was not universal, and some interviewees did comment that PEN supported some positions more strongly than others. For instance, one private sector representative reflected on the greater attention PEN accorded to discussions of potential nanotechnology risks, as opposed to potential benefits, in the body of its work. "They weren't anti-nano, but paper after paper came out about critical risks," said this interviewee. On the other hand, some NGO representatives commented on what they viewed as PEN having more of a pro-technology or pro-business bias. One NGO representative articulated this view by stating, "Not all of the stakeholders were treated the same way." This comment was in reference to the greater number of government and business stakeholders who this interviewee perceived PEN engaging over those from environmental NGOs. A former government representative nodded toward the strong risk framing that PEN took, especially as its work evolved in its later years. This interviewee stated, "I remain concerned that the balance has shifted very heavily towards the EHS concerns, rather than the benefits of the technology." Another former government representative concurred: "I know that many of the reports issued were scholarly, and had their science behind them, [but], on the other hand, there was a particular bias to it."

Government representatives reflecting this sentiment is not surprising. PEN certainly reserved most of its harshest criticism for federal agencies, particularly in their Congressional testimonies and written comments submitted to agencies. For example, in Andrew Maynard's 2007 Congressional testimony on EHS risk research, he wrote, "When economic interests, people's health and the environment are on the line, to claim 'it's difficult' is a poor excuse for inaction." Maynard continued:

> [O]n the basis of current evidence, the federal government is out of touch with reality and seems to be caught in a bureaucratic process that lacks the responsiveness and vision to address the questions to which nanotechnology stakeholders need answers. There is no sense of urgency to address which new research is needed.
>
> (Maynard, 2007)

Similarly, in Congressional testimony in 2008, Rejeski continued in this critical vein, writing, "At this critical juncture, the federal government has no strategy to engage the public and fill the knowledge gap about nanotechnology, which could have serious implications for nanotechnology's long-term success" (Rejeski, 2008). Furthermore, in earlier public comments written in response to the NNI's revision of its EHS strategy, Rejeski wrote that "the prioritization document lacks the coherence and big-picture view needed to allow the government to strategically address the challenges being faced," noting that "unfortunately, if the suggested 'next steps' are any true indication of future plans . . . the public and interested stakeholders may have to wait a long time before their concerns are addressed. If this document is truly meant to serve as a basis for a risk research strategy, there is a long way to go" (Rejeski, 2007).

This type of critical language is much more prominent in PEN's writings than in ICON's outputs or even in those from the Synthetic Biology Project. PEN evidently did not hesitate to express its opinion, particularly when it came to the role of the federal government in EHS risk research. However, there remains a sense from the interviews conducted that PEN was still less on the extreme than other organizations. One researcher surmised that PEN had:

> A little bit of tight rope to walk here. It didn't want to suggest that the technology was dangerous and become a Cassandra on this, but on the other hand, it did have an immediate result of [wanting to] bring stakeholders together [in a constructive way].

The simultaneous presence of these alternative views raises a puzzle: Can an organization be both neutral and provocative at the same time? Does taking a stance on a policy issue discredit it or render moot efforts to find common ground? There are a number of potential responses to these questions. One possibility is that, for all of its rhetoric, an organization such as PEN actually did not play an effective boundary-spanning role within the nanotechnology policy community. While this is one possible conclusion, the body of evidence does not support this inference to any significant degree. Most of the interviewees did mention PEN's neutral stance in some capacity and recognized its stated approach of trying to help find common ground among stakeholders with different perspectives. A second possibility is that those interviewees who viewed PEN as being more biased somehow are incorrect or had their own skewed view of the organization, colored by frustration or disagreement. While this view likely goes too far as an uncharitable interpretation of the interviewee comments, it remains the case that PEN did take strong stances on different issues and sometimes offered strong critiques of others—particularly entities inside the United States government—for what PEN perceived as the slow federal response to the potential EHS risks posed by nanotechnology.

A third and more likely interpretation is that no inherent contradiction exists between operating in a boundary-spanning role while also taking a point of view on an issue. An organization can take a stand in support of a position while at the same time convene stakeholders with divergent perspectives. An entity such as PEN can serve as a boundary organization, not because it is agnostic on the issues, but exactly *because* a full spectrum of views were given an open forum for debate and dialogue. One academic researcher surmised that before PEN emerged "there wasn't a place in Washington, except for the government" focusing on nanotechnology's EHS issues. This researcher affirmed:

I actually think . . . they brought the issue to the attention of people and kept the issue alive, kept people's interest on it. That is not something [that] could have been done outside of DC . . . Absent that set of folks, it would have been harder to sustain interest in that area, both from a government point of view as well as an academic.

PEN was not the only entity to serve in this role—a small number of other organizations, including ICON, positioned themselves likewise—but its affiliation with the Wilson Center, its strategic positioning in the nation's capital, and its effective communications strategy made PEN one of the most visible institutions operating in such a bridge-building mode.

In conclusion, this boundary-spanning function is a central factor that can give various NGOs outsized influence within their respective policy communities. On a sheer practical level, as organizations also look to maintain their standing and become indispensable in a field, doing so requires exhibiting tangible accomplishments. Engaging experts, brokering partnerships, convening meetings, and creating boundary objects are all tasks that provide these kinds of demonstrable, concrete results. The tangible nature of these deliverables— especially early in an organization's lifecycle—gave entities such as PEN and ICON specific achievements to highlight when reporting to their financial backers, when trying to engage other potential partners, and when communicating externally. One researcher unambiguously stated, "More than any other place that I can think of [PEN] actually kind of occupied the field. I mean it kind of took over this niche." A European policymaker perhaps best summed up how the multiple roles PEN played as a boundary organization accorded it influence:

> Overall, PEN has played a very important role, because it has a very peculiar and unique status. It is governmental and it is non-governmental. It is clearly innovation friendly; at the same time it really pays attention to safety and ethical aspects. It's an activist organization and academic in some ways. It's neutral but engaged at the same time.

These observed dualities, and perhaps even paradoxes, that come with boundary-spanning—being innovation friendly yet paying attention to safety, being activist and academic, being neutral and simultaneously advancing a position—illustrate the complex, critical role that these organizations can play across the landscape of emerging technologies.

Bibliography

Adams, S., and Bal, R. (2009, January). Practicing Reliability: Reconstructing Traditional Boundaries in the Gray Areas of Health Information Review on the Web. *Science, Technology, and Human Values*, *34*(1), 39–54.

Agrawala, S., Broad, K., and Guston, D. (2001). Integrating Climate Forecasts and Societal Decision Making: Challenges to an Emerging Boundary Organization. *Science Technology and Human Values*, *26*(4), 454–477.

American National Standards Institute. (n.d.). *ANSI Nanotechnology Standards Panel.* Retrieved October 8, 2015, from American National Standards Institute: www.ansi. org/standards_activities/standards_boards_panels/nsp/overview.aspx?menuid=3

Basulto, D. (2015, October 8). The Big Trends in Synthetic Biology You Need to Know. *The Washington Post.* Retrieved October 8, 2015, from www.washingtonpost. com/news/innovations/wp/2015/10/08/the-big-trends-in-synthetic-biology-you-need-to-know/

Battilana, J., and Dorado, S. (2010). Building Sustainable Hybrid Organizations: The Case of Commercial Microfinance Organizations. *Academy of Management Journal, 53*(6), 1419–1440.

Bechky, B. A. (2003, November). Object Lessons: Workplace Artifacts as Representations of Occupational Jurisdiction. *American Journal of Sociology, 109*(3), 720–752.

Berube, D. M., Searson, E. M., Morton, T. S., and Cummings, C. L. (2010, Summer). Project on Emerging Nanotechnologies: Consumer Product Inventory Evaluated. *Nanotechnology Law and Business, 7*(2), 152–163.

Breggin, L., Falkner, R., Jaspers, N., Pendergrass, J., and Porter, R. (2009). *Securing the Promise of Nanotechnology: Towards Transatlantic Regulatory Cooperation.* London, UK: Chatham House.

Cash, D. W. (2011). "In Order to Aid in Diffusing Useful and Practical Information": Agricultural Extension and Boundary Organizations. *Science, Technology and Human Values, 26*(4), 431–453.

Center for Food Safety. (2015, July 27). *Groups Sue EPA over Faulty Approval of Nanotechnology Pesticide.* Retrieved October 29, 2015, from Center for Food Safety: www.centerforfoodsafety.org/press-releases/3995/groups-sue-epa-over-faulty-approval-of-nanotechnology-pesticide#

Center for Responsible Nanotechnology. (2008a). *CRN Global Task Force on Implications and Policy.* Retrieved November 10, 2015, from http://crnano.org/CTF.htm

Clark, W. C., Tomich, T. P., van Noordwijk, M., Guston, D., Catacutan, D., Dickson, N. M., and McNie, E. (2012). Boundary Work for Sustainable Development: Natural Resource Management at the Consultative Group on International Agricultural Research (CGIAR). *PNAS, 109*(31), 12302–12308.

Collins, H., and Evans, R. (2007). *Rethinking Expertise.* Chicago, IL: The University of Chicago Press.

Collins, H., Evans, R., and Gorman, M. (2007). Trading Zones and Interactional Expertise. *Studies in the History and Philosophy of Science, 38,* 657–666.

Consumers Union. (2008, December). No-nano Sunscreens? *Consumer Reports, 78*(12), 13.

Davies, J. C. (2007). *EPA and Nanotechnology: Oversight for the 21st Century.* Washington, DC: Project on Emerging Nanotechnologies.

Davies, J. C. (2008). *Nanotechnology Oversight: An Agenda for the Next Administration.* Washington, DC: Project on Emerging Nanotechnologies.

Department for Environment, Food and Rural Affairs. (2006, September 19). *UK Governmental Department Statement on Nanotechnology Report.* Retrieved November 11, 2015, from www.nanotechproject.org/file_download/files/Maynard-UKDEFRA Statement.pdf

Drinkwater, K., Kuiken, T., Lightfoot, S., McNamara, J., and Oye, K. (2014). *Creating a Research Agenda for the Ecological Implications of Synthetic Biology.* Washington, DC: Synthetic Biology Project, Woodrow Wilson International Center for Scholars.

Environmental Defense–DuPont Nano Partnership. (2007). *Nano Risk Framework.* Washington, DC: Environmental Defense–DuPont Nano Partnership.

Friends of the Earth Australia. (2012). *Nano-Ingredients in Sunscreen: The Need for Regulation.* Fitzroy, Australia: Friends of the Earth Australia.

Galison, P. (1997). *Image and Logic: A Material Culture of Microphysics.* Chicago, IL: The University of Chicago Press.

Gargini, P. (2006, July 19). *Intel Congratulates Wilson Center on Publication of New Nano Report.* Retrieved November 13, 2015, from www.nanotechproject.org/news/archive/intel_congratulates_wilson_center_on/

Gieryn, T. F. (1983, December). Boundary-Work and the Demarcation of Science from Non-Science: Strains and Interests in Professional Ideologies of Scientists. *American Sociological Review, 48*(6), 781–795.

Gieryn, T. F. (1999). *Cultural Boundaries of Science: Credibility on the Line.* Chicago, IL: The University of Chicago Press.

Gorman, M. E. (2004). Collaborating on Convergent Technologies: Education and Practice. *Annals of the New York Academy of Sciences, 1013,* 25–37.

Gorman, M. E. (Ed.). (2010). *Trading Zones and Interactional Expertise: Creating New Kinds of Collaboration.* Cambridge, MA: The MIT Press.

Gorman, M. E., Groves, J. F., and Shrager, J. (2004). Societal Dimensions of Nanotechnology as a Trading Zone: Results from a Pilot Project. In D. Baird, A. Nordmann, and J. Schummer (Eds.), *Discovering the Nanoscale* (pp. 63–73). Amsterdam, The Netherlands: IOS Press.

Government Accountability Office. (2008). *Nanotechnology: Better Guidance Is Needed to Ensure Accurate Reporting of Federal Research Focused on Environmental, Health, and Safety Risks.* Washington, DC: Government Printing Office.

Grushkin, D., Kuiken, T., and Millet, P. (2013). *Seven Myths and Realities about Do-It-Yourself Biology.* Washington, DC: Synthetic Biology Project, Woodrow Wilson International Center for Scholars.

Guston, D. H. (1999, February). Stabilizing the Boundary between US Politics and Science: The Role of the Office of Technology Transfer as a Boundary Organization. *Social Studies of Science, 29*(1), 87–111.

Guston, D. H. (2001). Boundary Organizations in Environmental Policy and Science: An Introduction. *Science, Technology and Human Values, 26*(4), 399–408.

Hansen, S. F., and Baun, A. (2012, July). When Enough is Enough. *Nature Nanotechnology, 7*(7), 409–411.

Hellstrom, T., and Jacob, M. (2003, August). Boundary Organisations in Science: From Discourse to Construction. *Science and Public Policy, 30*(4), 235–238.

International Center for Technology Assessment. (2006, May 16). *CTA Petitions on FDA's Failure to Regulate Health Threats from Nanomaterials.* Retrieved November 16, 2015, from International Center for Technology Assessment: www.icta.org/doc/Nano%20FDA%20petition%20final.pdf

International Center for Technology Assessment. (2008, May 1). *Group Demands EPA Stop Sale of 200+ Potentially Dangerous Nano-Silver Products.* Retrieved November 15, 2015, from International Center for Technology Assessment: www.icta.org/files/2011/12/CTA_nano-silver_press_release_5_1_08.pdf

International Center for Technology Asssessment. (2012b, May 2). *Sustained Pressure by Non-Profits Forces Change in FDA Nanotech Policy.* Retrieved November 16, 2015, from www.icta.org/files/2012/05/2012-FDA-Nano-joint-PR_5-2-FINAL_5_2_2012.pdf

International Council on Nanotechnology. (2009b, October 21). *Governance Structure and Operational Plan*. Retrieved September 17, 2015, from International Council on Nanotechnology: http://cohesion.rice.edu/centersandinst/icon/emplibrary/ICON managementv2009_1_Full_Text.pdf

International Council on Nanotechnology. (2014, September 30). *NanoEHS Virtual Journal*. Retrieved November 15, 2015, from The Virtual Journal of Nanotechnology Environment, Health, and Safety: http://icon.rice.edu/virtualjournal.cfm

International Life Sciences Institute. (2013). *NanoCharacter: 2013 Workshop*. Retrieved November 19, 2015, from www.ilsi.org/NanoCharacter/Pages/2013-Workshop.aspx

International Organization for Standards. (n.d.). *ISO/TC 229 Nanotechnologies*. Retrieved November 16, 2015, from International Organization for Standards: www.iso.org/iso_technical_committee?commid=381983

Jasanoff, S. (1990). *The Fifth Branch: Science Advisors and Policymakers*. Cambridge, MA: Harvard University Press.

Jasanoff, S. (Ed.). (2004). *States of Knowledge: The Co-Production of Science and Social Order*. London, UK: Routledge.

Jenkins, L. D. (2010). The Evolution of a Trading Zone: A Case Study of the Turtle Exclude Device. *Studies in the History and Philosophy of Science, 41*(1), 75–85.

Keating, T. J. (2001). Lessons from the Recent History of the Health Effects Institute. *Science, Technology and Human Values, 26*(4), 409–430.

Kelly, S. E. (2003, Summer). Public Bioethics and Publics: Consensus, Boundaries, and Participation in Biomedical Science. *Science, Technology, and Human Values, 28*(3), 339–364.

Kimble, C., Grenier, C., and Goglio-Primard, K. (2010). Innovation and Knowledge Sharing across Professional Boundaries: Political Interplay between Boundary Objects and Brokers. *International Journal of Information Management, 30*(5), 437–444.

Knorr-Cetina, K. (1999). *Epistemic Cultures: How the Sciences Make Knowledge*. Cambridge, MA: Harvard University Press.

Koppel, J. G. (2003). *The Politics of Quasi-Government: Hybrid Organizations and the Dynamic of Bureaucratic Control*. Cambridge, UK: Cambridge University Press.

Kuhn, T. S. (1996). *The Structure of Scientific Revolutions*, (3rd ed.). Chicago, IL: University of Chicago Press.

Leinhos, M. (2005). The US National Bioethics Advisory Commission as a Boundary Organization. *Science and Public Policy, 32*(6), 423–433.

Maynard, A. D. (2006a). *Nanotechnology: A Research Strategy for Assessing Risk*. Washington, DC: Project on Emerging Nanotechnologies.

Maynard, A. D. (2006b, September 21). Testimony on: "Research on Environmental and Safety Impacts of Nanotechnology: What are the Federal Agencies Doing?." Washington, DC: United States House of Representatives, Committee on Science.

Maynard, A. D. (2007, October 31). Testimony on: "Research on Environmental and Safety Impacts of Nanotechnology: Current Status of Planning and Implementation under the National Nanotechnology Initiative." Washington, DC: United States House of Representatives, Committee on Science and Technology.

Maynard, A. D., Aitken, R. J., Butz, T., Colvin, V., Donaldson, K., Oberdorster, G., Philbert, M. A., Ryan, J., Seaton, A., Tinkle, S. A., Tran, L., Walker, N. J., Warheit, D. B. (2006, November). Safe Handling of Nanotechnology. *Nature, 444*, 267–269.

Merton, R. K. (1973). *The Sociology of Science: Theoretical and Empirical Investigations*. Chicago, IL: The University of Chicago Press.

Miller, C. (2001). Hybrid Management: Boundary Organizations, Science Policy, and Environmental Governance in the Climate Regime. *Science, Technology and Human Values*, 26(4), 478–500.

NanoBusiness Alliance. (2005, November 29). NanoBusiness Alliance Announces Endorsement for Inventory of Research on Environment, Human Health, and Safety Effects of Nanotechnology. Retrieved November 15, 2015, from Project on Emerging Nanotechnologies: www.nanotechproject.org/news/archive/nanobusiness _alliance_announces/

National Research Council. (2009b). *Review of the Federal Strategy for Nanotechnology-Related Environmental Health and Safety Research*. Washington, DC: National Academies Press.

National Research Council. (2012). *A Research Strategy for Environmental, Health, and Safety Aspects of Engineered Nanomaterials*. Washington, DC: The National Academies Press.

Organisation for Economic Co-Operation and Development. (2009b). *OECD Database on Research into the Safety of Manufactured Nanomaterials*. Retrieved November 15, 2015, from Organisation for Economic Co-Operation and Development: www.oecd.org/science/nanosafety/42511541.pdf

Organisation for Economic Co-Operation and Development. (2011). *Nanosafety at the OECD: The First Five Years 2006–2010*. Paris, France: OECD.

Oye, K. A., Esvelt, K., Appleton, E., Catteruccia, F., Church, G., Kuiken, T., Lightfoot, S. B-Y., McNamara, J., Smidlre, A., Collins, J. P. (2014, August 8). Regulating Gene Drives. *Science*, 345(6197), 626–628.

Parker, J., and Crona, B. (2012). On Being All Things to All People: Boundary Organizations and the Contemporary Research University. *Social Studies of Science*, 42(2), 262–289.

Pielke, J. R. (2007). *The Honest Broker: Making Sense of Science in Policy and Politics*. Cambridge, UK: Cambridge University Press.

Presidential Commission for the Study of Bioethical Issues. (2010). *New Directions: The Ethics of Synthetic Biology and Emerging Technologies*. Washington, DC: Presidential Commission for the Study of Bioethical Issues.

Project on Emerging Nanotechnologies. (2005a, October 18). *Important First Step to Test Nanomaterials' Toxicity*. Retrieved November 17, 2015, from Project on Emerging Nanotechnologies: www.nanotechproject.org/news/archive/important_ first_step_to_test

Project on Emerging Nanotechnologies. (2005b, November 29). *Live Webcast: First Research Inventory of the Environmental, Health and Safety Impacts of Nanotechnology*. Retrieved November 15, 2015, from Project on Emerging Nanotechnologies: www.nanotechproject.org/events/archive/first_inventory_government_supported/

Project on Emerging Nanotechnologies. (2005c, November 28). *New Inventory of Research into Nanotechnology's Health and Environmental Effects Shows Need for More Resources, Strategy, and Public–Private and International Partnerships*. Retrieved November 16, 2015, from Project on Emerging Nanotechnologies: www.nanotechproject.org/ process/assets/files/6028/112805nanotechnology_inventory.pdf

Project on Emerging Nanotechnologies. (2007a, June 21). *Environmental Defense and DuPont to Jointly Launch Risk Framework*. Retrieved November 15, 2015, from Project on Emerging Nanotechnologies: www.nanotechproject.org/events/archive/ environmental_defense_dupont_to_jointly

Project on Emerging Nanotechnologies. (2007b, March 20). *Life Cycle Assessment Essential to Nanotech Commercial Development.* Retrieved November 15, 2015, from Project on Emerging Nanotechnologies: www.nanotechproject.org/news/archive/life_cycle_assessment_essential_to

Project on Emerging Nanotechnologies. (2008a, January 8). *Food and Drug Law Institute (FDLI), Project on Emerging Nanotechnologies Co-Sponsor Major Conference on Nanotechnology Law, Regulation and Policy.* Retrieved November 15, 2015, from Project on Emerging Nanotechnologies: www.nanotechproject.org/news/archive/food_drug_law_institutefdli_project

Project on Emerging Nanotechnologies. (2008b, May 1). *International Council on Nanotechnology Launched Global Research Needs Assessment.* Retrieved November 15, 2015, from Project on Emerging Nanotechnologies: www.nanotechproject.org/events/archive/6696

Project on Emerging Nanotechnologies. (2008c). *Looking Back on the First Two Years: Biennial Report.* Washington, DC: Project on Emerging Nanotechnologies.

Project on Emerging Nanotechnologies. (2008e, March 11). *New Nanotechnology Television Series Does "Sweat the Small Stuff"; Washington, DC Premiere Event Features U.S. Senator Ron Wyden.* Retrieved November 15, 2015, from Project on Emerging Nanotechnologies: www.nanotechproject.org/process/assets/files/6099/nano_power ofsmall031008.pdf

Project on Emerging Nanotechnologies. (2009a). *Areas of the Senate bill 'S. 1482— National Nanotechnology Amendments Act of 2009' to reauthorize the 21st Century Nanotechnology Research and Development Act that the Project on Emerging Nanotechnologies influenced through testimonies and analyses.* Washington, DC: Project on Emerging Nanotechnologies.

Project on Emerging Nanotechnologies. (2009c, June). *US NanoMetro Map.* Retrieved October 8, 2015, from Project on Emerging Nanotechnologies: www.nanotech project.org/inventories/map/

Project on Emerging Nanotechnologies. (2010, October 15). *Final Internal Quarterly Report, August 1, 2009–October 15, 2010.* Washington, DC: Project on Emerging Nanotechnologies.

Reilly, W. K. (2006, November 15). *Safe and Profitable Nanotechnologies Will Not Become Reality Unless Uncertainties Addressed.* Retrieved November 16, 2015, from Project on Emerging Nanotechnologies: www.nanotechproject.org/file_download/files/REILLYSTATEMENT061116.pdf

Rejeski, D. (2004a, October 11). Memo: Nanotech Initiative—General Policy Environment. Washington, DC.

Rejeski, D. (2004b, November 8). Memo: Nanotech Initiative—Regulation and Oversight. Washington, DC.

Rejeski, D. (2004c, October 19). Memo: Nanotech Initiative—Research. Washington, DC.

Rejeski, D. (2007, September 12). *Prioritization of Environmental, Health, and Safety Research Needs for Engineered Nanoscale Materials: An Interim Document for Public Comment: Comments on Process.* Retrieved November 17, 2015, from Project on Emerging Nanotechnologies: www.nanotechproject.org/process/assets/files/5891/nehi_comments_070912_final.pdf

Rejeski, D. (2008, April 24). Testimony on: "National Nanotechnology Initiative: Charting the Course for Reauthorization." Washington, DC: United States Senate,

Committee on Commerce, Science, and Transportation, Subcommittee on Science, Technology, and Innovation.

Responsible Nano Forum. (2009). *A Beacon or Just a Landmark? Reflections on the 2004 Royal Society/Royal Academy of Engineering Report: Nanoscience and Nanotechnologies: Opportunities and Uncertainties*. London, UK: Responsible Nano Forum.

Ruckelshaus, W. D. (2007, May 23). *Nanotechnology May Pose EPA's Greatest Challenge and Opportunity*. Retrieved November 18, 2015, from Project on Emerging Nanotechnologies: www.nanotechproject.org/process/assets/files/5985/052307 nanotechnology_ruckelshaus.pdf

Schmidt, K. (2007). *NanoFrontiers: Visions for the Future of Nanotechnology*. Washington, DC: Project on Emerging Nanotechnologies.

Star, S. L., and Griesemer, J. R. (1989). Institutional Ecology, "Translations" and Boundary Objects: Amateurs and Professionals in Berkeley's Museum of Vertebrate Zoology, 1907–39. *Social Studies of Science, 19*(3), 387–420.

Synthetic Biology Project. (2011, September 28). *Environmental and Social Issues Arising from Synthetic Biology: Redesigning Life*. Retrieved October 8, 2015, from Synthetic Biology Project: www.synbioproject.org/events/ngo/

Synthetic Biology Project. (2012a, July 16). *Synthetic Biology Scorecard*. Retrieved September 17, 2015, from Synthetic Biology Project: www.synbioproject. org/scorecard/

Synthetic Biology Project. (2013a). *Maps Inventory: Updated Map Tracks Global Growth of Synthetic Biology*. Retrieved September 17, 2015, from Synthetic Biology Project: www.synbioproject.org/inventories/maps-inventory/

Synthetic Biology Project. (2013b, November 18). *Wilson Center Awarded European Union Grant for Synthetic Biology Work*. Retrieved October 8, 2015, from Synthetic Biology Project: www.synbioproject.org/news/project/6674/

Synthetic Biology Project. (2013c, February 26). *Communicating Synthetic Biology: How the Media Covers Emerging Technology*. Retrieved October 8, 2015, from Synthetic Biology Project: www.synbioproject.org/events/6646/

Synthetic Biology Project. (2015b, October 15). *Leveraging Synthetic Biology's Promise and Managing Potential Risk*. Retrieved October 15, 2015, from Synthetic Biology Project: www.synbioproject.org/events/leveraging-synthetic-biologys-promise/

Synthetic Biology Project. (2015c, September 16). *Appendix—Synthetic Biology Research Projects/Programs by Agency*. Retrieved October 8, 2015, from Synthetic Biology Project: www.synbioproject.org/site/assets/files/1386/appendix_projects-1.pdf

Synthetic Biology Project. (2015d). *U.S. Trends in Synthetic Biology Research Funding*. Washington, DC: Synthetic Biology Project, Woodrow Wilson International Center for Scholars.

The European Consumer's Organisation. (2010, October 21). *How Much Nano Do We Buy?* Retrieved October 8, 2015, from The European Consumer Organisation: www.beuc.eu/publications/2010–00645–01-e.pdf

The European Consumer's Organisation. (2013, February 28). *ANEC/BEUC Inventory of Products Claiming to Contain Nano-Silver Particles Available on the EU Market*. Retrieved October 8, 2015, from Safety and Sustainability: www.beuc.eu/ publications/2013–00141–01-e.xls

The Royal Society. (2004). *Nanoscience and Nanotechnologies: Opportunities and Uncertainties*. London, UK: The Royal Society.

United States House of Representatives, Committee on Science and Technology. (2006a, November 15). *Boehlert, Gordon Call for Implementation of New Nanotechnology*

Report. Retrieved November 15, 2015, from Project on Emerging Nanotechnologies: www.nanotechproject.org/file_download/files/BoehlertGordononNanoReport.pdf

United States House of Representatives, Committee on Science and Technology. (2006b, September 21). Opening Statement by Hon. Bart Gordon. Washington, DC.

United States House of Representatives, Committee on Science and Technology. (2007, October 31). Opening Statement by Chairman Brian Baird. Washington, DC.

United States House of Representatives, Committee on Science and Technology. (2008, April 16). Opening Statement by Chairman Bart Gordon. Washington, DC.

United States Senate. (2006, November 15). *Wyden Praises Nature Nanotechnology Article*. Retrieved November 13, 2015, from Project on Emerging Nanotechnologies: www.nanotechproject.org/file_download/files/WydenStatement.pdf

Webster, A. (2007, July). Crossing Boundaries: Social Science in the Policy Room. *Science, Technology, and Human Values, 32*(4), 458–478.

Weiss, R. (2005, December 5). Nanotechnology Regulation Needed, Critics Say. *The Washington Post*, p. A08.

White, D. D., Wutich, A., Larson, K. L., Gober, P., Lant, T., and Senneville, C. (2010, April). Credibility, Salience, and Legitimacy of Boundary Objects: Water Managers' Assessment of a Simulation Model in an Immersive Decision Theater. *Science and Public Policy, 37*(3), 219–232.

Yakura, E. K. (2002). Charting Time: Timelines as Temporal Boundary Objects. *Academy of Management Journal, 45*(5), 956–970.

6 "Near perfect storm of interest"

Engaging the public

Engagement, by all means available

> The interest in trying to develop policy initially came from [what] the Project on Emerging Nanotechnologies had triggered. There was a discussion . . . through the media . . . through an interview on NPR that had gotten the interest of one of our city councilmen, and that had triggered a council order.

This story, told by a public administrator from Cambridge, Massachusetts, provides but a small glimpse into how PEN harnessed media coverage to influence discussions about nanotechnology in the United States. This vignette indicates that the external outreach components of PEN's activities were considerable and took on more than just second-order consequence. More than any of its peer organizations involved in nanotechnology policy, PEN's communications endeavors were ahead of the pack and reflect the organization's strongest area of success, notwithstanding criticism it received due to its ubiquitous presence across the nanotechnology media landscape.

However, PEN faced a quandary that many organizations confront when attempting to engage the media and lay audiences on topics relevant to emerging technologies: how to overcome the inescapable barrier of the public's lack of understanding about the technology and the perception that it is too difficult to grasp. PEN had data from studies it sponsored (Hart Research Associates 2006, 2007, 2008)—findings that have remained generally consistent in the years since PEN closed down (PR Newswire, 2012)—that a majority of the public acknowledges knowing little to nothing about an emerging technology such as nanotechnology, while at the same time still holding strong and divergent opinions about risks, benefits, and how the technology should be managed. Subsequent findings from Hart Research Associates polling found similar results related to synthetic biology, and showed that over the past decade, "there has been only a minor shift in public awareness of nanotechnology" (Hart Research Associates, 2013). Survey respondents indicating that they had heard "a lot" or "some" about nanotechnology only registered between 24 and 31 percent on public understanding studies conducted from 2006–2010, and then again in 2013 (Hart Research Associates, 2013).

PEN's response to this challenge was twofold: adopting an expansive vision of how to interact with the public, including a range of activities that scholars would classify as spanning both public *understanding of* science (PUS) and public *engagement with* science (PES). In the PUS mode, PEN focused on disseminating information about nanotechnology through multiple media channels, both in traditional print formats as well as through online venues. These efforts were more about communicating the results of PEN's research and distributing information about various nanotechnology policy issues. In the PES mode, PEN undertook direct public engagement and deliberation activities, similar to the efforts that many academic researchers have championed, including soliciting public opinion through surveys, holding focus groups, and organizing extended opportunities for in-depth conversations about the technology's societal implications.

On balance, PEN's communication and information dissemination activities outweighed its direct public engagement efforts, and this focus on communications contributed to PEN receiving the degree of attention and notoriety it garnered in the field. On a conceptual level, PEN's distinct emphasis on communications is an element that reflects a slight deviation from the original theoretical description of anticipatory governance as presented in Barben et al. (2008). While the dual thrust of PEN's public outreach approaches—communications and engagement—dovetailed closely with one another, PEN's experience highlights the challenge that exists between the underlying impetus facing NGOs to disseminate their message distinctly and the aspiration to find effective ways of engaging the public in a two-way conversation.

The following section of this chapter provides a brief introduction to the key theoretical concepts underlying the idea of public understanding of science and the shift over time toward the adoption of an engagement-oriented approach. The subsequent section then explores a set of strategies that NGOs can use in developing and implementing a robust public engagement plan, predominantly focusing on PEN, given how extensive its activities were in this area. This chapter then turns toward a reflection on the critiques of PEN's communications approach and considers the view as to whether all the attention it received may have encouraged the organization to skew how it presented information to the media and the public. Throughout this chapter, findings from various comparative media analyses will be presented, including an exploration of the tone of the messages PEN presented in its press releases, a comparison of newspaper coverage of PEN with that received by other NGOs involved in nanotechnology policy debates, and an examination of PEN's online presence. The chapter will conclude with an assessment of the impacts arising from the adoption of such communications and direct deliberation strategies.

From public understanding to public engagement

A transition has occurred over recent decades in prevailing views about how the public relates to and interacts with emerging science and technology issues.

A traditional view on the relationship between science and society—conceptualized in the middle part of the twentieth century, shortly after World War II—was that the expert scientific establishment should retain full decision making authority and autonomy over research processes, following a curiosity-driven path to understand the workings of nature, wherever such lines of inquiry might lead. In exchange for this independence over what research got done, society was expected to benefit from scientific investigation in a myriad of unintended, unexpected, and unpredictable ways. The overall effect would be the advancement of prosperity and economic growth through the development of new products and technologies. Often known as the social contract between science and society, these ideas were most famously articulated in Vannevar Bush's report *Science: The Endless Frontier* (1945). This view that science would be most beneficial to society if left to function on its own also emerged in a number of other prominent publications on the topic, including John Steelman's *Science and Public Policy* (1947), and it strongly underlies Robert Merton's (1973) notion of the "normative structure of science" and Michael Polanyi's (1962) idea of the "republic of science."

Scholars have reassessed this traditional view of the social contract over subsequent decades (Sarewitz, 1996; Stokes, 1997; Guston, 2000a, 2000b, 2012), with scholars questioning the assumption underlying the artificial division of science and society into separate spheres. However, this approach has still greatly impacted perspectives about how the public interacts with science and technology, especially in the United States. Lewenstein (1992) characterizes the 1950s and 1960s as a period where "the term 'public understanding of science' became equated with 'public appreciation of the benefits that science provides to society.'" Bauer, Allum, and Miller (2007) deem this mid-century period the "Science Literacy" era, where improved education was seen as the main response to counteract the presumed lack of information about scientific issues among the general populace.

Bauer, Allum, and Miller (2007) then describe the evolution toward a second phase that took hold from the mid 1980s onward, which they term "Public Understanding." This period focused on tracking changes in public attitudes and knowledge about science and technology topics through methodologies such as surveys. Both the "Science Literacy" and "Public Understanding" periods reflect a rather one-way mentality about how the public relates to science and technology, based primarily on the "deficit model" view of the public's understanding of science (Wynne, 1991; Ziman, 1991; Gregory and Miller, 2000). The deficit model posits that any misunderstandings or controversies surrounding science and technology are merely due to unfamiliarity, illiteracy, or a general lack of awareness about the issues on the part of the greater public. Wilsdon and Willis (2004) write wryly that the default solution to science and technology controversies arising from the deficit model is merely finding ways "to tackle the blight of public ignorance" through the provision of brute facts and irrefutable information from experts.

However, this notion of public understanding of science, grounded in the deficit model, has continued to change and become scrutinized more closely, leading to a more nuanced picture about how science and society interrelate (Sturgis and Allum, 2004). Bauer, Allum, and Miller (2007) call this third period that has emerged the "Science and Society phase," one where the relationship between science and the broader lay public is more interactive and viewed as a two-way street, characterized by questions of how to build trust, understand values, encourage participation, and promote deliberation. Nisbet and Scheufele (2009) contend that this new perspective on engaging the public has begun to take hold firmly. They argue, "One can detect a growing recognition that effective communication requires initiatives that sponsor dialogue, trust, relationships, and public participation across a diversity of social settings and media platforms" (Nisbet and Scheufele, 2009: 1767).

In short, these reflections signify a transition from a PUS mode to one premised on PES. A lexicographical analysis conducted by the journal *Public Understanding of Science* of the vocabulary used in published article abstracts in that journal offers further evidence for this shift. Suerdem et al. (2013) show that articles published during the period of 1992–2001 predominantly use language consistent with the PUS perspective (words such as "public," "model," and "lay"), while articles published during the period of 2002–2010 predominantly use language consistent with the PES perspective (words such as "engage," "citizen," and "participate"). The authors conclude that, "This is consistent with the well-known shift in discourse from a 'deficit model' to a 'dialogical' model of public engagement in science and society relations" (Suerdem et al., 2013: 4).

A number of reasons underlie this change toward a view of public engagement based on dialogue and deliberation. First, the emergence and persistence of high profile science and technology controversies that have few, if any, simple or clear cut solutions. These include debates surrounding genetically modified foods, nuclear power, cloning, and climate change (Funtowicz and Ravetz, 1993; Jasanoff, 2005). The ongoing intractability of such challenges has raised questions about the competing values that motivate advancement in science and technology and better ways to effectively engage the public in decision making about the potential impacts and consequences of related technological development (Winner, 1989; Stone, 2002; Wilsdon, Wynne, and Stilgoe, 2005; Bozeman and Sarewitz, 2005, 2011). Additionally, any related problems become more complex, dynamic, and harder to assess as the speed of scientific and technological change has accelerated (Kayal, 1999; Rycroft, 2007). This accelerating pace has also led to a dwindling of available response time for the design, testing, and implementation of potential solutions (Guston and Sarewitz, 2002; Wilkinson, Kupers, and Mangalagiu, 2013).

Finally, this move toward increased deliberation with respect to science and technology has led to the view that increased public participation has far-reaching benefits in its own right, including the strengthening of democracy and improving socially responsible decision making (National Research

Council, 1996; Kleinmann, 2000; Jasanoff, 2003; Wynne, 2006). For example, Hamlett and Cobb (2006: 630) argue that "effective public deliberations are thought to create civic learning opportunities for participants and observers that presumably add to the health of a democratic polity." Similarly, Brown (2009: 19) argues for a renewed "view of representative democracy that includes a key role for public engagement in science."

Wilsdon and Willis (2004) term this shift the rise of "upstream public engagement," emphasizing the need for substantive public involvement in critical decisions that will guide future trajectories of novel scientific research and technological developments. The authors argue that those involved in scientific and technological endeavors "need to find ways of listening to and valuing more diverse forms of public knowledge," indicating that "only by opening up innovation processes at an early stage can we ensure that science contributes to the common good" (Wilsdon and Willis, 2004: back cover). Leach, Scoones, and Wynne (2005: 3) contend that "proliferating encounters force us to break down established analytical categories to recognize new synergies between expert and lay knowledges—new relationships between state and non-governmental action—and a variety of hybrid forms of public and private control and ownership." Stirling (2012: 5) argues that the main benefit of the expansion of upstream public engagement is that "despite the many different forms, roles, and perspectives around public engagement . . . the real value of more inclusive participation lies in opening up—rather than closing down—a healthy, mature, accountable democratic politics of technology choice."

These conceptual advancements to "open-up" science and technology through public engagement and deliberation are beginning to take hold (Fisher, 2011). Such efforts generally involve employing a variety of engagement methodologies to expand the discourse around science and technology to non-technical audiences. Delli Carpini, Cook, and Jacobs (2004), Dryzek and Tucker (2008), and PytlikZillig and Tomkins (2011) have all begun to track the different approaches to public engagement and explore their implications for public administration broadly. For instance, PytlikZillig and Tomkins (2011: 197) note, "input from the public has been provided via such methods as surveys, legislative hearings, public meetings, and notice and comment opportunities." They describe how in-depth engagement approaches, such as "citizen juries, consensus conferences, and citizen deliberations," have also started to provide a wide range of input into policy processes over recent years.

Many of these different kinds of public engagement efforts have been tested in connection to nanotechnology. Nanotechnology has provided an opportunity to experiment with a wide range of deliberation and engagement techniques, in part because nanotechnology has emerged roughly during the same period as the rise of the PES perspective (Macnaghten, Kearnes, and Wynne, 2005; Kearnes, Macnaghten, and Wilsdon, 2006; Pidgeon, Harthorn, and Satterfield, 2011). Specifically, efforts on nanotechnology public engage-ment include holding nanotechnology-oriented citizen panels, consensus conferences, and technology forums (Gavelin and Wilson, 2007; Powell and

Kleinman, 2008; Hamlett, Cobb, and Guston, 2008; Priest et al., 2011; Guston, 2014a); running web-based and in-person scenario exercises with lay participants (Nanologue, 2007; Selin and Hudson, 2010); arranging focus groups and interviews with members of the public (Rogers-Hayden and Pidgeon, 2007; Throne-Holst and Strandbakken, 2009; Davies and Macnaghten, 2010; Xenos et al., 2011; Grobe et al., 2012; Brown and Kuzma, 2013); and conducting the aforementioned public perception surveys by phone and online about values, risks, and benefits (Siegrist et al., 2007; Siegrist and Keller, 2011; Conti, Satterfield, and Harthorn, 2011; McComas and Besley, 2011; Binder et al., 2012).

These various public engagement efforts have also employed different approaches toward preparing lay-person participants in advance of the engagement process (te Kulve and Rip, 2011) and have considered how to address potential tensions and disagreements that may arise throughout these processes (Joly and Kaufmann, 2008; Delgado, Kjolberg, and Wickson, 2011). Additionally, there have also been concentrated efforts at encouraging scientists and engineers themselves to reflect on the societal implications of nanotechnology (Berne, 2006; Scheufele et al., 2007; Fisher, 2007). For instance, surveys have been used to gauge how scientists view different approaches to regulation and potential EHS risks. Responses from scientists are then contrasted with those of the general public to determine any meaningful differences (Scheufele et al., 2007; Kim, Corley, and Scheufele, 2012; Corley, Kim, and Scheufele, 2013).

One area of intersection among both the PUS and PES is how scientific and technological issues are framed in media and policy contexts. Entman (1993) describes the framing of policy issues as involving an analysis of the various narrative descriptions used to characterize a particular topic. Chong and Druckman (2007: 104) further note, "The major premise of framing theory is that an issue can be viewed from a variety of perspectives and be construed as having implications for multiple values or considerations." Different framings arise in multiple ways and at successive instances throughout the policymaking process, such as when new data or evidence emerges, as new players gain prominence and attention, and as new alliances or coalitions form (Sabatier and Jenkins-Smith, 1999).

Nisbett (2010: 41) claims that framing science and technology issues "is not simply a translation of facts—it is a negotiation of meaning." The suggestion here is that public disputes about science and technology are often not solely disputes about facts, but about how language is used and how such facts are framed. This leads to the recognition that discussions about the societal implications of emerging technologies must addresses an intended audience's values, interests, and worldviews (Nisbet, 2010; von Schomberg and Davies, 2010). Research from communications studies and related disciplines has begun to examine the ways in which the framing of a host of science and technology policy issues pertaining to topics such as climate change (Nisbet and Scheufele,

2009), biotechnology (Nisbet, Brossard, and Kroepsch, 2003), and environmental degradation (Rinfret, 2011) can come to alter public perceptions.

Furthermore, Schon and Rein (1994) argue that disputes over policy options are often really a proxy for disputes about policy framing. They maintain that these disagreements are highly sensitive to key rhetorical factors, such as how particular analogies or metaphors are used to explain a position. This point is directly relevant to topics such as nanotechnology, as discussions about nanotechnology policy regularly use historical analogies drawing on parallels between nanotechnology and biotechnology or other previous technologies. Inevitably, the use of such analogies greatly influences the lens through which any new technology is viewed. For instance, Maynard and the other leading toxicologists who authored the landmark *Nature* article "Safe Handling of Nanotechnology" framed their argument by comparing nanotechnology with biotechnology and asbestos, warning, "We have cautionary examples from genetically modified organisms and asbestos industries that motivate a real interest, from all stakeholders, to prevent, manage and reduce risk proactively" (Maynard et al., 2006: 269). Hodge, Maynard, and Bowman (2014: 2) contend, "Debates concerning nanotechnology are typically constructed through the framework of three distinct languages," which they enumerate as "the language of 'nanotechnology' as a public policy phenomenon; the language of 'nanotechnologies' as a set of multiple scientific frontiers; and the language of regulation." In this view, understanding nanotechnology's societal implications requires gaining a better understanding of all three framings and rhetorical positioning of the technology in different strands of discourse.

The process by which science and technology policy issues are discussed and framed is relevant to activities undertaken within both PUS and PES perspectives. Both points of view are concerned with the factors that affect an individual's response to new information, whether passively (through communications) or actively (through dialogue and deliberation). Schon and Rein (1994: 23) state that regardless of whether the public is engaged in a one-way or two-way process, policy disputes in need of resolution "are resistant to resolution by appeal to facts or reasoned argumentation because the parties' conflicting frames determine what counts as a fact and what arguments are taken to be relevant and compelling." As such controversies evolve over time, new policy framings can emerge that complement, revise, or supplant existing or dominant frames (Pump, 2011).

Additionally, the framing of science and technology policy issues is not just provided by individuals functioning as independent policy entrepreneurs. Instead, scholarship has examined the way that organizations and institutions play important roles in framing complex science and technology issues. This can be seen in the specific practices that organizations adopt, such as how they craft messages or determine their target audiences (Scheufele, 1999). Hoffman and Ventresca (1999) suggest that a greater focus on such institutional dimensions is necessary to understand how issues gain prominence and traction over time. In particular, how individuals and institutions attempt to frame issues related to emerging technologies has received close attention (Cobb, 2005; Castellini et al., 2007; Simons et al., 2009; Anderson et al., 2013). This idea builds on the more general notion of the policy feedback loop, which acknowledges that past policy choices provide the contours for future policy options (Pierson, 1993; Wichowsky and Moynihan, 2008). The very framing and portrayal of an issue—positively or negatively, utopian or dystopian, hyped or downplayed—has a carryover effect. Existing public views about previous technologies will shape how nanotechnology and synthetic biology are perceived: how these technologies are viewed today will serve as precedents that shape how other emerging technologies are regarded going forward.

In sum, this framing feedback loop sets the stage for what follows. Whether nanotechnology and synthetic biology are embraced or rejected, or framed as predominantly risky or beneficial, the resulting view of subsequent technologies will unavoidably be affected. In an era characterized by growing inter-connectivity and the rapid adoption of nearly instantaneous social media communication, this factor could become even stronger, as cultural memes spread faster and messages remain digitally indelible (Shifman, 2013). This makes understanding the strategies that NGOs use to frame emerging technologies ever more important, a topic that will be addressed in the following section.

The centrality of communications and engagement

Evidence shows that PEN, in particular, took a rather inclusive and ecumenical approach toward its interactions with the public, conducting activities that fall across the spectrum of PUS and PES activities, from one-way communication to two-way deliberation. The relative balance among these activities was skewed more towards PUS, with generally favorable results for the organization. Evidence from multiple media analyses, responses from the semi-structured interviewees, and findings that emerged from the document analysis all indicate strongly in the direction that one of PEN's most successful accomplishments—and perhaps more so than other organizations in this space—was in its communications activities.

For instance, multiple interviewees mentioned variations of statements such as "they got all of this attention," "they were everywhere," and, due to the regular dissemination of materials produced by the organization, "they kept me busy." One interviewee with professional experience in government, academia, and civil society espoused, "the communications and press part of it is important . . . laying the foundation for public understanding and accept-ance is awareness." This interviewee continued:

> Elevating the awareness of something like this [nanotechnology] is, I think, a critical part of the process. I think it would not be nearly as useful if it was just reports quietly done and lodged away. I think the more communication the better.

This perspective also comes through strongly in much of PEN's written material. In Congressional testimony, Terry Davies summarizes a view that emerges repeatedly in much of PEN's work. Davies notes:

> The greatest threat to the future of nanotechnology and to nanotechnology-based businesses is not regulation but a collapse in public confidence. Based on polling and focus groups, I believe that the public will hold both government and industry to a higher standard of safety for nanotechnology than it has for any previous technology.
>
> (Davies, 2006)

In large part due to insights such as this one, PEN made strategic communications a core component of its operational and strategic toolkit. Moreover, these efforts were widely recognized as being centrally important to PEN's ability to have policy influence in the field.

ICON did place less of an emphasis on communications, securing media attention, and public engagement than PEN did. This was, in part, due to the need to manage an organization that had formal representation by a diverse array of stakeholders as part of its decision-making structure. Another factor was the extent that PEN made communications such a central element of its activities, to the point that it may have crowded out space for others working in the field to get a similar amount of attention. A third contributing factor is that ICON's role as a primarily research-oriented organization focused predominantly on advancing the scientific examination of potential EHS implications lessened the inclination to conduct broader media outreach. One interviewee with knowledge of ICON's operations perceived:

> That [securing media attention] was a source of constant disagreement within the Council. With the Wilson Center being so out there, so public, so good at getting media attention for its work products, there were some in the Council that thought that we should be right up there with them.

This interviewee continued:

> Because of our niche in this very narrow area of environmental, health and safety research, our target audience was different than the Wilson Center's. And so, instead of trying to get coverage in major media outlets, our primary audience was government regulators, and funding agencies, and companies.

In fact, securing more media attention than it did could actually have been detrimental to ICON's goal of building connections across sectors. This interviewee continued to affirm that members participating in ICON "just wanted to work quietly behind the scenes, to be able to talk to people that

they normally could not talk to, outside of the harsh spotlight of the media."
This interviewee argued:

> That was part of the draw for ICON: "I can talk to people that my
> company won't let me talk to, publically, in this space, because it's a safe
> space." And the more media attention we got, the more that was
> threatened.

Another interviewee familiar with ICON also observed, "I think the Wilson
Center was more savvy. They dealt with media before . . . [with ICON] it
was so hard to get anything done that you would have to get input from all
of these different people."

The Synthetic Biology Project followed very much in PEN's footsteps,
making communications a central component of its activities. Like PEN, the
Synthetic Biology Project held multiple public events tied to the launch of its
reports and maintained an active public presence through the information shared
on its website. One researcher interviewee acknowledged, for instance:

> [O]ne of the things that was noteworthy . . . that people always remark
> on in their synthetic biology work, was that they had a very dynamic
> website that people went to for information. It was really a great resource
> for the whole community, so it performed this unifying function.
> Everybody got their information from there.

The Synthetic Biology Project also paid attention to gauging public opinion
regarding synthetic biology by conducting public perception studies and by
holding smaller-scale focus groups to dive deeper into public views on synthetic
biology (Hart Research Associates 2010, 2013, 2014, 2015). Much like PEN,
the Synthetic Biology Project was also explicitly cognizant of the important
role that framing would play in the eventual societal acceptance or rejection
of synthetic biology. Rodemeyer (2009: 8) presses on this impression strongly
in his report, noting:

> The initial framing of a new technology can have a strong impact on
> regulatory decisions. A new technology that is framed as being similar to
> an existing, familiar product reassures the public about its safety and allows
> policymakers to apply existing regulatory approaches and provides industry
> with a clear and predictable path to market. On the other hand, framing
> a new technology as being truly novel can raise public fears about its safety,
> pose a challenge for regulators, and present an uncertain commercialization
> path for industry.

A more recent report from the Synthetic Biology Project addresses the
issue of framing and communications head-on by providing a "guide for
communicating synthetic biology" (Mazerik and Rejeski, 2014). The report

calls out many of the factors that contribute to effective "message development and delivery," including keeping each distinct audience in mind, appreciating how they might react to different message framings, and realizing that who the actual "messenger" is plays a key role in building and maintaining trust over time (Mazerik and Rejeski, 2014).

However, in an age where any NGO or think tank can use multiple forms of communication and engagement to get their message across, the question becomes: How can organizations utilize effective practices in their work, especially as garnering attention becomes more difficult in a crowded issue and media landscape? The strategies outlined below will document how to implement a sophisticated communications and engagement scheme, capable of framing findings in a way that can be understandable to a broader audience. One interviewee proclaimed:

> The work the Project chose to do initially was very effective in creating a sense of a critical mass that there was something out there to actually talk about and some urgency to do it. [It] was able to do that by using the media to amplify the kinds of reports and messages that PEN was putting out.

This interviewee continued by providing an illuminating and powerful metaphor:

> If a tree falls in the forest and *The Washington Post* doesn't cover it, does it happen? . . . PEN was able to give the sense that [nanotechnology] was easy to report, it's tangible, it's here today. It is sort of saying, "It's here. It's here today. It's not something about tomorrow. It's already in the marketplace." And then to combine that with the science that was beginning to come out expressing concerns about health exposures and environmental exposures. It is a way of sort of saying, "It's here, and you know what? We need to talk. We need to be thinking about what this is doing. We can't put this off."

Framing a clear message

One of the initial tasks any organization involved with emerging technologies likely needs to undertake is *framing a clear message*. A review of PEN's internal records indicates that PEN undertook a message-crafting strategy session shortly after the organization was formed. This resulted in the production of a one page summary sheet that encapsulated the organization's predominant public message: "Get Nano Right, Right from the Start." Supporting this tag line are key bullet points that highlight the kinds of views that PEN would try to advance over the course of its work, such as a "new model" of "smart and sound" regulation that involved "early public engagement," "interdisciplinarity," "disclosure, transparency," and operating in a "proactive, not reactive" manner. Similarly, the Synthetic Biology Project developed an analogous messaging tag-line to what PEN produced, this time featured prominently on the front page of its website: "ensuring benefits are realized through responsible development" (Synthetic Biology Project, n.d.). One individual from the philanthropic sector knowledgeable about PEN's origins noticed the importance of such concise messages. Developing this articulated point of view can help institutions stay "on that very thin line . . . between amplifying a point and calling attention to something," said this interviewee.

The results of this messaging strategy—being cautious about nanotechnology's risks without losing sight of potential benefits—comes through in an examination of the press releases that the organization distributed. A content analysis was conducted on all of the press releases PEN produced and disseminated from 2005 through 2009. This served as a way of exploring the tone of PEN's messaging and helps shed light on the focus between risks and benefits that arose in one aspect of its media outreach. All of PEN's press releases were analyzed along two dimensions: first, as to whether the overall message of the press release was positive, negative, or neutral in tone; second, as to whether the press release predominantly focused on the benefits of nanotechnology, the risks of nanotechnology, or both the benefits and risks of nanotechnology. The findings of this press release content analysis indicates that in terms of tone, 31 percent of PEN's press releases were either positive (using supportive or encouraging language) or neutral (45 percent) in tone (using balanced language that was not overtly critical or challenging), accounting for 76 percent of the press releases. The remainder (24 percent) had a negative or more critical tone. However, most of PEN's press releases had some focus on risk, either as the main emphasis of the press release (25 percent) or in combination with points raised about benefits as well (46 percent). Only 29 percent of the press releases predominantly or wholly focused on the potential benefits of nanotechnology.

It may appear counterintuitive that the largest category of press releases could be either neutral or positive in tone *and* have some focus on risk. However, this lends weight to the view that PEN's messaging aimed for articulating tradeoffs and suggests some degree of balance in addressing benefits and risks. For example, a press release could focus on supporting a federal policy effort (the positive element) in managing EHS risks (the risk element), or promoting work that PEN produced (the positive element) while simultaneously discussing nanotechnology risk-related issues (the risk element). A good example of the first is a January 2008 press release in support of an EPA effort to fill nanotechnology information gaps by encouraging companies to voluntarily provide information on nanotechnology risks. A good example of the second is a July 2008 press release announcing the publication of an editorial co-authored by Andrew Maynard in *Nature Nanotechnology* that focused on learning lessons from previous technologies (Hansen et al., 2008). Furthermore, the previous chapter addressed that while PEN aimed to operate as a boundary-spanning organization, much of the work PEN undertook was still rooted in exploring and addressing EHS issues. This is likely the underlying reason why many of the organization's press releases had a focus on topics related to nanotechnology risks.

Saturating the media landscape

A second strategy used was to *saturate the media landscape* and secure ample press coverage. This helped PEN maintain high visibility in the nanotechnology policy arena. PEN deliberately strived to be referenced or quoted in as many different kinds of sources and publications as possible, ranging from magazines such as *Allure, Consumer Reports,* and *Discover* to newspapers such as *The Boston Globe* and the *International Herald Tribune* to scientific journals such as *Issues in Science and Technology* and *Nature*. PEN heralded its ability to secure high levels of media coverage in the mid-term report it produced after its second year in existence by noting:

> Stories on Project reports and events and interviews with Project staff and consultants have been featured in more than 25 TV and radio programs, 290 print stories, and 750 web stories . . . Over its first two years, news from the Project has resulted in a monthly average of nearly 50 print, broadcast, or web-distributed stories (not including multiple pick-ups, or repeats, of items issued by the Associated Press, Reuters, or other wire services).
>
> (Project on Emerging Nanotechnologies, 2008c)

The wide attention PEN received was also noticed in the nanotechnology community. For instance, nanotechnology law expert John C. Monica wrote in a blog post addressing nanotechnology regulatory matters:

> [W]hile many disagree with some of the approaches and policy positions advocated by PEN, few can argue that PEN has been a key driver in the nano-EHS debate over the past couple of years. One need only "google" the center to see its tremendous influence in the nanotechnology policy arena.
>
> (Monica, 2007)

An editorial in the journal *Nature Nanotechnology* (2007: 257) reinforced these sentiments, stating:

> [L]ow profile is certainly not a problem for the Project on Emerging Nanotechnologies at the Wilson Center in the U.S. . . . Having already taken a lead in efforts to raise the profile of EHS research in the U.S. and beyond.

Similarly, in an analysis of longitudinal newspaper and wire service coverage of nanotechnology risks, Friedman and Egolf (2011) find that PEN was among a small group of organizations outside of a university setting that functioned as source of primary information on nanotechnology EHS issues. Specifically, the authors note that in terms of generating coverage about the regulation of nanotechnology, "PEN played a key role in pushing a legislative program in the United States, with its many reports, news conferences, and testimonies at congressional hearings and in getting media coverage of its activities" (Friedman and Egolf, 2011: 1714). They found that four of the top ten events that took place between 2000 and 2009 driving newspaper coverage of potential nanotechnology risks involved PEN: one was directly related to PEN's work—the launch of the first report written by Terry Davies—and at least three other events included PEN commenting on them in the media.

I also undertook an in-depth review of newspaper articles focused on nanotechnology as one way of exploring PEN's media coverage, an approach that was informed by previous studies of this type (Cukier et al., 2009). The evidence indicates that PEN garnered and received sizable newspaper coverage, particularly when compared to other NGOs involved in nanotechnology policy issues. The primary component of this media analysis involved mining one of the leading research databases assembled containing over 2,000 nanotechnology-related newspaper articles (Dudo, Dunwoody, and Scheufele, 2011). An electronic search of the database text files was conducted for articles in this database covering the 2003–2011 time period—a total of over 1,300 articles—for references to PEN and nine other leading NGOs working on nanotechnology policy and societal issues. These comparison NGOs cover a broad spectrum of perspectives, coming from the environmental community (EDF, Natural Resources Defense Council, and the ETC Group), the business community (NanoBusiness Alliance and the American Chemistry Council), the research community (the National Research Council and ICON/CBEN at Rice University), and nanotechnology issues in general (the Foresight Institute and the Center for Responsible Nanotechnology). The search terms used for this investigation included variations on the name of each organization to ensure the return of comprehensive results. For instance, regarding PEN, this included searching for variations on the names such as "Project on Emerging Nanotechnologies," "Woodrow Wilson International Center for Scholars," and "The Pew Charitable Trusts."

Figure 6.1 indicates that for the timeframe of 2005–2011, the total number of newspaper articles covering all ten organizations is comparatively low in absolute terms, with PEN being mentioned 43 times and the other organizations being mentioned a combined total of 69 times. However, newspaper coverage for PEN during this period far exceeded newspaper coverage of any individual NGO working on nanotechnology policy issues. While more than one organization is often mentioned in an article, for the years examined PEN either had the most newspaper coverage (often by a considerable margin) or was tied for the most coverage for all but one year. In some years—such as in 2006, 2008, and 2009—newspaper coverage for PEN more than doubled, and sometimes tripled, the amount of coverage of the next highest organization.

In fact, the total coverage PEN received in newspapers for the 2005–2011 interval is greater than the next three highest ranked organizations combined.

An interesting trend to also note is that when looking back on the years before PEN was formed, from 2003–2005, the data shows that newspaper coverage for some organizations was higher, especially for the NanoBusiness Alliance, the Foresight Institute, and CBEN at Rice University. But once PEN began in 2005, newspaper coverage for these and other NGOs declined considerably as coverage of PEN rose rapidly. While this finding is correlative and is not necessarily causal—the emergence of PEN did not necessarily lead to the reduction in newspaper coverage of other organizations—the prominence and attention PEN received in the media did have some effect on crowding-out coverage of other organizations.

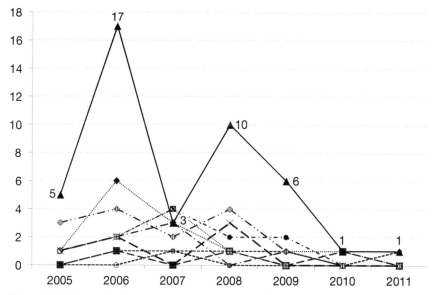

···◆··· NanoBusiness Alliance

--◇-- Center for Responsible Nanotechnology

—▲— Foresight Institute

--◇-- American Chemistry Council

—●— International Council on Nanotechnology/Center for Biological and Environmental Nanotechnology

—✳· National Research Council

—✕· ETC Group

···⬓··· Natural Resources Defense Council

—◆· Environmental Defense Fund

—▲— Project on Emerging Nanotechnologies

Figure 6.1 Nanotechnology newspaper coverage analysis, 2005–2011

Source: Author analysis of data provided by Dietram Scheufele

Finally, the framing of messages in the newspaper articles where PEN is mentioned echoes the findings of the press release review. At least 38 of the 43 newspaper articles in this database referencing PEN are predominantly focused on discussing nanotechnology risks, whether in terms of their potential EHS issues, the emergence of consumer products in the marketplace, or the challenges of developing effective oversight, policy, and regulatory schemes. Although not always mutually exclusive, 19 newspaper articles focused primarily on PEN's work related to consumer products—especially the CPI—followed by 13 articles that focused predominantly on EHS issues. Eight articles focused principally on broader policy and governance issues, two mainly emphasized the science and technological components of nanotechnology, and one article focused largely on nanotechnology public perceptions.

Focusing attention just on coverage in newspapers does not tell the full picture of PEN's approach to saturating the communications landscape with respect to nanotechnology. This is especially true given that the media landscape in the United States changed significantly over the period of PEN's activities, and continued to go through a transformation just as PEN was shifting toward the formation of the Synthetic Biology Project. Over the years when PEN was most active, major newspapers began to have fewer staff dedicated exclusively to covering science and technology issues, and news became increasingly shared through wholly digital means, fracturing the media landscape and making information dissemination harder to track or even quantify. One former PEN staff member reflected:

> When [the work on] nanotechnology started, we were sort of in the beginning of the end of science reporters at major papers and networks. And so, when synbio [synthetic biology] started coming onboard, there [were] not many science desks, or science and technology desks, left at major news outlets. So, that is probably playing some sort of role, in terms of what's getting covered and what's not.

Over time, PEN's robust online presence had the effect of driving most of its media coverage, either through dissemination of its material through other news aggregator websites or just from visits to, and downloads from, its own website. One interviewee commented on the value of PEN's digital media efforts noting, "What impressed me ... was the way they [PEN] got the information out [through] the various modes of communication." This is all the more striking given that PEN's work took place predominantly before many social media sites such as Facebook and Twitter became highly popular, and that PEN was already nearing its halfway mark before web-enabled smartphones, such as the iPhone, entered widespread use.

To provide insight on this web-based component of PEN's communications strategy, all of the press coverage sections from the internal quarterly reports that PEN produced—a total of 15—were collected, reviewed, and analyzed. Data about the page views and unique users of the PEN website were extracted and compiled to produce Figure 6.2, which shows usage and access of PEN's website by quarter or year, depending on data availability, both during and after PEN's lifetime. PEN's initial website was launched on November 28, 2005 and redesigned late in 2007 with an updated layout and improved graphics. The information compiled indicates that PEN's website had over 9 million page views and close to 1.5 million unique users since launching.

A spike in usage at the end of 2006 occurred, which corresponds to a number of high-profile activities that were indicated on the timeline provided in Chapter 1, including an update of the CPI, the publication of the *Nature* article "Safe Handling of Nanotechnology" (Maynard et al., 2006), and Congressional testimony during that period by Maynard (Maynard, 2006b). This timeframe also corresponds to the release of three prominent reports: Maynard's PEN report on nanotechnology risk research (Maynard, 2006a), the release of PEN's research tracking public perceptions of nanotechnology (Hart Research Associates, 2006), and Michael Taylor's report on nanotechnology and the FDA regulatory system (Taylor, 2008). Additionally, for the period of 2005 through March 2008, PEN documented in its quarterly reports that its website was the eighth most visited site for nanotechnology as rated by Google Page Rank.

Beyond the visibility that PEN's website received, press coverage of PEN elsewhere online further demonstrates the strengths of its web-based media strategy. Again, while comprehensive data for this dimension of PEN's work is hard to come by, analysis of the organization's quarterly reports indicate that, for certain periods, web coverage of PEN's research led to hundreds of mentions or links across the Internet. For example, the quarterly reports indicate that PEN had close to 1,000 press hits from the period between March 15 and June 15 in 2007. Such coverage mostly resulted from a handful of press releases being reposted across multiple websites. For example, for the first quarter of 2008 (January 15–March 15), online reposting of just five press releases collectively accounted for 101 web-based articles, which were usually replications or slight variations on the original press releases. One press release ("Nanotechnology's Future Depends on Who the Public Trusts") alone accounted for 30 instances of online coverage. Online coverage of PEN during the second quarter of 2008 (March 15–June 15) tells a similar story, with five different press releases also accounting for at least 100 mentions across the web, with one press release ("New Nanotech Products Hitting the Market at a Rate of 3–4 Per Week") achieving 30-plus web re-postings alone.

Building a brand, institutionally and for key individuals

The third strategy employed was to *build a brand* for the institution and for key, affiliated individuals. Of the 43 newspaper articles covering PEN, 30 of them (nearly 70 percent) make reference to the Wilson Center in some way, either jointly with reference to PEN (17 articles with dual mentions) or just with a mention of the Wilson Center on its own, without referring to PEN.

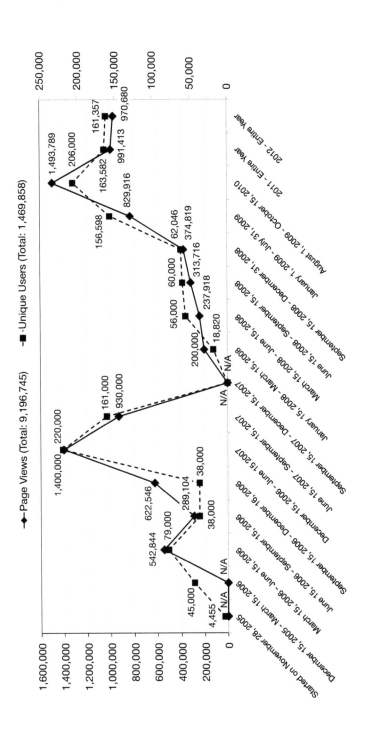

Figure 6.2 PEN website page views and unique users, by quarter or year, 2005–2012

Source: Author analysis

No apparent pattern is evident for when PEN is mentioned separately from, or together with, the Wilson Center. However, one likely explanation for the Wilson Center's frequent appearance is that the Wilson Center, as the larger host institution for PEN, was likely a more broadly well-known organization. Of interest is that PEN's main funder, The Pew Charitable Trusts, was referenced in only seven of the 43 articles, and never by itself. Mentions of The Pew Charitable Trusts either occur in conjunction with PEN and the Wilson Center (five times) or with just the Wilson Center (two times) alone.

Not having "Pew" formally at the beginning of PEN's name—unlike some of the other science-related projects that The Pew Charitable Trusts supported on agricultural biotechnology and climate change—likely provided PEN with greater freedom to operate more independently than would have otherwise been possible. Findings from the interviews bear this out, with one respondent suggesting there is a "blessing and curse of having Pew in your name." Using the "Pew" name formally might have had the advantage of bringing even greater media coverage to PEN's work, given that the funder is known well within policy circles. However, Pew's stances in other areas of environmental and health policy might have created difficulty for PEN to operate in a neutral, boundary-spanning role. One interviewee with deep knowledge on this issue responded that not using "Pew" in PEN's name "was wise in a whole variety of perspectives," because it provided additional "leeway" in how PEN could message and position its work to the public.

For those articles where individuals from PEN are quoted, instead of just references to PEN at the organizational level, Andrew Maynard is cited the most times by far, in 22 articles, followed by David Rejeski (eight articles), PEN advisors Terry Davies (six) and Michael Taylor (three), and staff member Julia Moore (one). The previous chapter described how PEN derived legitimacy and leveraged credibility from deploying a wide range of experts (such as Davies and Taylor) as spokespersons for the organization beyond its senior staff members (Rejeski, Maynard, and Moore). This strategy had a distinct benefit in terms of how some of PEN's outputs were received in the media. When desired, PEN could align itself with the finding of an external author's report and associate itself with a particular view. But, in the event that PEN wanted to distance itself from a particular idea, it could then lean on the fact that, more likely than not, an external author (not a staff member) wrote the report. One interviewee commented directly on the effectiveness of this strategy: "Most of them were PEN reports and they weren't PEN reports. They had deniability if they needed it . . . but they got the credit because it had PEN's logo on the front that said it was a PEN publication." This interviewee continued by describing how PEN managed this delicate situation effectively by commenting:

> This is not at all a unique situation, but it's still a very hard one to play because the press tends to say, "Well yeah, sure you have an individual author," but it wouldn't have been issued by PEN if PEN didn't agree with it.

Combining scientific credibility with metaphorical language

A fourth strategy that was utilized was the ability to *combine scientific credibility with metaphorical language* as a way of presenting a more understandable description of the policy and societal issues surrounding nanotechnology to lay audiences. This strategy also served PEN's role as a boundary organization, reflecting the organization's ability to function with authority in the scientific community while also being able to communicate effectively with the lay public. Specifically, PEN's Chief Science Advisor Andrew Maynard embodied this boundary-spanning role between these two worlds of science and the public, a characterization that emerged multiple times from interviewees and that was often raised with a high degree of appreciation for the difficulty of filling this gap. One interviewee stated directly that "Andrew is Mr. Communications," and another interviewee with a background in government bestowed him the title of "Nano King." A journalist who was interviewed said, "To the extent that consumers that are looking for a source that is as neutral as humanly possible . . . Andrew Maynard puts those pieces together really, really well." An example of this combination of scientific credibility and communications ability is apparent in Maynard being listed as one of the top nanotechnology EHS risk experts in a *Nanotechnology Law and Business* (2009) article. Maynard's 2006 PEN report on risk research was also listed in a 2012 National Research Council report as one of the earliest "key reports that assess or provide information on research needs and strategies for addressing the environmental, health, and safety implications of engineered nanomaterials" (National Research Council, 2012).

Another important indicator of Maynard's scientific credibility emerged from a citation analysis conducted of scientific papers contained in the Scopus database (Elsevier, 2013). As of December 2012, the *Nature* article "Safe Handling of Nanotechnology" (Maynard et al., 2006), on which Maynard was the lead author with 13 other well-known nanotechnology toxicologists, ranked as the 274th most cited article out of 75,496 articles in the Scopus database with the term "nanotechnology" in the title, abstract, or keyword. This paper jumped to the 64th most cited nanotechnology article out of 55,378 articles since its date of publication in 2006. Similarly, a well-known empirical research article that Maynard co-authored in *Nature Nanotechnology* (Poland et al., 2008), which found that some carbon nanotubes behave like asbestos when introduced into the abdominal cavity of mice, ranked as the 174th most cited article out of over 89,057 articles in the Scopus database among articles using the term "nanotubes" in the title, and reached the tenth most cited article out of 53,045 articles using the term "nanotubes" since its publication in 2008. As of September 2013, the *Nature* article was ranked in the top 0.1 percent of articles published since 2006 with the keyword "nanotechnology" in the title and the *Nature Nanotechnology* article was ranked in the top 0.01 percent of articles published since 2008 with the keyword "nanotubes" in the title.

In tandem with this scientific credibility, Maynard also regularly deployed metaphors, analogies, and other rhetorical devices intended to help make the complexities of nanotechnology understandable to lay audiences. The utilization of these effective public communications skills evolved during Maynard's time at PEN, helping to add another dimension to his scientific output and spurring him to become more prominent over time as his profile began to rise. While the adoption of these tactics was not unique to Maynard or PEN—and were also carried over to a degree in the work of the Synthetic Biology Project— they were particularly valuable in helping to explain the difficult characteristics of a technology that cannot be seen with the naked eye or manipulated without advanced machinery. In Congressional testimony provided in 2008, Maynard likened the difficulty in developing a comprehensive federal EHS risk research for nanotechnology to navigating the twists and turns of a car driven by a blindfolded driver. "Moving towards the nanotechnology future without a clear understanding of the possible risks, and how to manage them, is like driving blindfolded," wrote Maynard (Maynard, 2008).

> The more we are able to see where the bends in the road occur, the better we will be able to navigate around them to realize safe, sustainable and successful nanotechnology applications. But to see and navigate the bends requires the foresight provided by strategic science.
>
> (Maynard, 2008)

In the same testimony, Maynard used an analogy to kitchen utensils in order to describe how nanomaterials can both behave similarly and differently to everyday objects. "Imagine picking up two common kitchen implements—a skillet and a knife. Each can be used for very different purposes . . . Likewise, each implement can cause harm in different ways." Maynard continues:

> Yet the chemical makeup of each implement is very similar—it is predominantly iron . . . Nanomaterials are the same, in that how they behave—for good or bad—depends on their shape as well as their chemistry. But this is where nanotechnology becomes counterintuitive. Because we cannot see these intricate nano-shapes unaided, we forget that they are important.
>
> (Maynard, 2008)

Another example shows Maynard's use of a bit of whimsy and irreverence, in combination with metaphors, as an effective communications tool to explain the distinct properties of nanomaterials. In 2007, Maynard recorded a downloadable video of a talk, posted on the PEN website and heralded in a press release, titled "The Twinkie Guide to Nanotechnology." Maynard used the metaphor of a Twinkie to describe how nanomaterials can be similar to or different from the iconic American snack food. The accompanying press release also adopts a humorous tone and announces that this presentation "serves up the complexities of nanoscience in enticing, digestible, bite-size morsels." In his presentation, Maynard adopts this amusing set-up as a way to make nanotechnology understandable to a lay audience. "Putting a nanoparticle on a Twinkie," he explains, "is comparable in scale to putting a Twinkie on the moon" (Project on Emerging Nanotechnologies, 2007c).

Creating a "coherent design philosophy"

Finally, a subtle and easy-to-overlook strategy that PEN employed as part of its communications tactics was, as one interviewee coined the term, *creating a "coherent design philosophy,"* one that came to encapsulate the appearance of all of its outputs, from its website down to written research reports. At first glance, there may be an inclination to dismiss this component of PEN's work as being merely unimportant packaging for the substantive commentary that such materials contain. However, the need to make information about complex areas of science and technology accessible and compelling to the public affirms the importance of paying attention to visual and stylistic appeal. Reports from PEN had a consistent design theme that made them easy to recognize quickly and potentially pick out from a crowded table or bookshelf. A former PEN staff member indicated how the organization used design to "bundle together" elements across different media platforms to ensure consistency, from the look of a banner placed across the top of a newsletter to the artwork accompanying a podcast download to an image on the cover of a report. "The bundling of various media was useful," continued this former staff member, "because people would enter the system from different perspectives. They would listen to the podcasts, and then read something." Summarizing the value derived from effective layout, presentation, and design, David Rejeski synopsized as follows:

> The basic rule was we don't want to go much over 30 or 40 pages. I remember one time I went up to the Hill one day, it may have been Terry [Davies] and I went, to follow up on his report. And the guy came in, and there his report was there with 15 sticky notes in it. The guy said, "I just read this at Starbucks." And at that point, I knew we succeeded. I mean, we actually produced something that he could read over a cup of coffee. And he paid enough attention to mark a lot of the stuff. You know, we did enough Congressional testimonies, and a lot of that stuff was integrated into legislation. But, actually seeing that on the desk next to the coffee, full of sticky notes, was a sign that we kind of hit the sweet spot.

Most PEN reports used either a two-toned design cover or employed stylized artwork that called to mind the specific topic of the report, with easily identifiable visual cues related to science and technology, such as microscopes or magnifying glasses. These branding schemes were repeated in the design of PEN's website, filled with pictures of consumer products to publicize the CPI and using commissioned drawings across many media platforms, visually tying and linking print and online activities. In particular, variations of the organization's logo, based upon a three-circle motif with the organization's full name or its acronym standing out boldly, adorned all of PEN's report covers and became a commonplace visual cue reproduced on many PEN materials, signaling that the particular output was a product of the organization. The distinctiveness of PEN's visual style in helping to advance its communications strategy did not go unnoticed, with the importance of these design components resonating across a spectrum of interviewees. Respondents indicated that this close attention to imaging and branding helped create an underlying cohesiveness to PEN's work, especially as the organization branched out to analyze different sub-topics within nanotechnology policy. More than one interviewee effectively made the exact same exclamation about the PEN reports, saying: "I still have them . . . on my shelf." Many interviewees remarked that the aesthetically pleasing nature of PEN's outputs legitimately helped contribute to the institution's staying power in the field. One veteran journalist contemplated this design element rather expansively, indicating how crucial these seemingly second-order, "trivial," or "silly" visual considerations can be to advancing an organization's impact. This interviewee expanded:

> Having that level of branding gave it a much more professional appearance. It was of course professional, but it had that formalness to it. And if you're trying to get the attention of policy makers, and even journalists, perception is 99 percent of the issue here. So if it's looking formal and looking authoritative, then it's going to instantly be given that benefit of the doubt that this [report] is carrying weight. So yeah, you may have to spend a lot of time on branding, and logos, and making sure your reports had nice glossy covers. I'd argue that it's probably worth it. You know, it seems trivial and it seems kind of silly in a lot of ways, but I think it does make a difference.

Similarly, the design and branding of outputs from the Synthetic Biology Project borrow many traits from PEN. The organization's logo, use of images, document layout and style, and even color palette are consistent across the Synthetic Biology Project's digital platforms and printed reports. The Synthetic Biology Project also created a distinctive logo that was emblazoned on all of its major outputs, again serving as an easy short-hand indicator that the output was produced by the project. On the other hand, while ICON's use of branding and visual design was less extensive and integrative than PEN's, instances exist when ICON did use this tactic to good effect. For example, ICON's 2008 report exploring information gaps related to the interactions between nanotechnology and biological systems (International Council on Nanotechnology, 2008) contains a detailed chart that helps to visualize the near-term, mid-term, and long-term research needs in this area. This style of this chart has elements that are similar to a "heat map" image included in Maynard's PEN report of 2006 (Maynard, 2006a), which used this chart style to help underscore research priorities across potential nanotechnology EHS risk areas. This may not be surprising, given that Maynard participated in the workshop that led to that ICON report. However, the key takeaway is that different institutions often adopted common approaches to visualizing these kinds of findings and, in doing so, utilized comparable design motifs to express similar ideas.

Outside of PEN, other organizations involved in nanotechnology policy also made a concerted effort to deploy images and visualizations powerfully. Perhaps the other organization that best put this practice to use at the forefront of its activities was the ETC Group, a NGO that advocated for a moratorium on all nanotechnology product commercialization. The ETC Group made use of incisive drawn cartoons to accompany its policy positions. One often-seen image was a drawing of a scientist looking down into a microscope, with his shadow reflected on the wall as an ostrich with its head buried in the ground under the caption "Nano Particle Safety Test" (ETC Group, 2009). Additionally, the ETC Group commissioned a public graphic design contest in 2007 to develop a symbol that would stand as a warning sign for hazards arising from nanotechnology. About 480 images were submitted from 24 countries during this contest, with the three winning entries showing various depictions of small dots to represent nanomaterials and the iconic yellow hazard triangle often used as a warning for dangerous materials in other technological realms (ETC Group, 2007).

These cartoons and symbols were a somewhat arch way for the ETC Group to reflect their strong stance against the advancement of nanotechnology. This imagery was also indicative of how NGOs can use visual cues and colorful pictures to make their outputs distinctive. Although PEN did not utilize a similar cartoon strategy, its particular design and branding elements did help to make their outputs easily identifiable. This also had the effect of differentiating PEN materials from the multitude of other reports on nanotechnology that were being published during this period. One government respondent said of PEN's branding, "it was very useful . . . otherwise you become more of a cacophony of general noise." Another respondent from the private sector summarized PEN's look as:

> The best that can be done, in terms of image and branding . . . just the look of and the feel of and the heft of the material itself was formidable. So, I think the message—whether people agreed with it or not—the message was put forth in a format that made it very striking.

Experimenting with direct deliberation

In addition to its extensive communications pursuits, PEN also undertook a handful of activities that involved *experimenting with direct deliberation* to round out its toolset of public engagement efforts. These kinds of direct deliberation activities were generally outside the scope of ICON's mission, leading to little or no focus on such activities over the course of its history. While the majority of PEN's resources devoted to interacting with the public did focus on communications-style activities, PEN's experiments in direct public engagement and deliberation offer insights into the opportunities and challenges that similar organizations will face in adopting such practices in the future. In essence, the main motivation behind PEN's deliberation efforts was to learn about people's expectations and concerns about nanotechnology. PEN often then interwove the voices and views unearthed from these direct deliberation activities into its policy analysis activities, presenting this information as an important source of evidence about how nanotechnology policy might be most effectively advanced.

One form of public engagement that PEN utilized regularly was working with the survey firm Hart Research Associates to conduct yearly polls that tracked public values and views on nanotechnology policy. PEN surveyed over 5,000 people in total from 2006 to 2010—and then another 800 people in 2013 as part of a follow-up survey undertaken by the Synthetic Biology Project—to measure public perceptions, both before and after information about the technology was provided to these participants. The Synthetic Biology Project continued this tradition of conducting national surveys, doing so at least three times to track public perception of synthetic biology along with specific issues such as genome editing technologies. However, surveys are only one, minimal form of public engagement, taking place at a low, light-touch level. They do not get too deep into two-way conversation, even when they address more complicated issues, such as exploring differing levels of trust across federal agencies or calibrating public opinions on particular commercial applications of nanotechnology, such as nanotechnology-engineered food packaging products.

Reflecting a slightly more in-depth level of direct deliberation, PEN and the Synthetic Biology Project both organized a number of focus groups with members of the general public to discuss a variety of nanotechnology and synthetic biology policy issues. In fact, PEN's first published report highlighted findings from 12 focus groups involving just over 175 people in three sites across the country, with discussions centered on topics such as nanotechnology commercialization and trust in government and industry (Macoubrie, 2005). On an annual basis from 2006–2008, PEN arranged in-person focus groups in Baltimore, Maryland in collaboration with Hart Research Associates as a way of learning more about public views on specific nanotechnology issues, such as the use of nanotechnology in cosmetics. The Synthetic Biology Project followed suit, with a set of focus groups conducted to get a nuanced sense of how people perceive neural engineering issues (Hart Research Associates, 2014). These focus groups were all conducted on a relatively small scale, with each discussion involving approximately ten people, totaling no more 50 individuals over the full course of these engagements. In a number of instances, PEN integrated videos from these focus groups into the public launch events of the findings (Project on Emerging Nanotechnologies, 2006c, 2008d). They also excerpted quotes and insights garnered from these activities into their Congressional testimonies, agency submissions, and organizational reports. An interviewee from another NGO mentioned, "The public voice piece was [particularly] useful" in providing a snapshot about how non-experts perceive nanotechnology and its potential risks and benefits. A private sector representative similarly mentioned:

> It was an important and valuable source of information for us in terms of some of the studies that they sponsored . . . in particular, the studies that they did on public perceptions of nanotechnology, some of the research that they did on supporting some kind of consumer surveys and focus groups.

Beyond these surveys and focus groups, PEN's largest-scale efforts designed to engage the public directly did not take place on a face-to-face basis but instead occurred through a variety of web-based mechanisms. For instance, PEN held a two-day, web-based discussion titled Consumers Talk Nano that engaged over 250 people with the stated goal of providing "an easily accessible venue for the public to discuss information and share their thoughts about the usage and potential benefits and risks of consumer products made with nanomaterials" (Web Dialogues, 2007). Beyond this web chat, PEN supported and worked with researchers at the Cultural Cognition Project at Yale Law School to investigate "the cultural cognition of nanotechnology risks," which "refers to the tendency of people to form beliefs about the risks and benefits of an activity that fit their cultural evaluations of it" (Kahan and Rejeski, 2009: 2). Three web-based engagements were conducted that involved over 5,000 people with the goal of understanding:

> Whether and how cultural cognition might be expected to affect public opinion toward nanotechnology and, just as important, to generate insights that might be used to form strategies for communicating scientifically sound information about nanotechnology in forms that make it accessible to citizens of diverse cultural outlooks.
>
> (Kahan and Rejeski, 2009: 2)

In turn, these efforts looked to illuminate how different cultural values held by participants, different message framings, and different views about the expert providing the message might shape, change, or steer the receptivity of nanotechnology information by the public.

These direct deliberation activities had a dual role of being research studies in their own right and engaging the public about nanotechnology. For instance, one of the Cultural Cognition Project efforts on which PEN collaborated presented a set of four different hypothetical newspaper articles to gauge public response to different message framings about nanotechnology's potential benefits and risks. One such hypothetical article was framed around the need for additional research to understand nanotechnology's role in improving the environment, while another hypothetical article was framed around the use of nanotechnology for national security purposes. A separate Cultural Cognition Project study that involved PEN as a partner presented individuals with hypothetical profiles and pictures of "culturally identifiable policy advocates" to determine how these different types of message-bearers might shape people's views on nanotechnology (Kahan and Rejeski, 2009). Specifically, this research showed images and provided descriptions of different experts sharing messages about nanotechnology. This included an image of a fictitious elderly male dressed in a suit whose favorite books were listed as "Selfishness is Not a Vice" and "Why Big Government Doesn't Work." Another image was of an (again, fictitious) smiling, bearded, glasses-wearing male whose favorite books were listed as "Society as Family" and "People Before Profit." The goal here was twofold, involving elements of both PUS and PES: the use of different hypotheticals provided an opportunity to explore how people might respond to varying message framings while these studies also engaged the public in open-ended discussions about dilemmas regarding nanotechnology's potential societal implications.

Of course, PEN was not unique in terms of undertaking direct deliberation activities with the public. In fact, many other organizations involved with nanotechnology placed an even stronger emphasis on undertaking direct deliberation activities. For instance, CNS-ASU, discussed in Chapter 3, organized the National Citizens' Technology Forum in 2008, concentrating on the topic of nanotechnology and human enhancement (Hamlett, Cobb, and Guston, 2008). This activity involved engaging 74 individuals in six locations around the country through multiple, in-depth, face-to-face discussions and regular virtual communications. Similarly, a local citizens consensus conference on nanotechnology that took place in Madison, Wisconsin, led to the formation of a small NGO, called the Nanotechnology Citizen Engagement Organization, that eventually came to submit comments and testimony on nanotechnology policy issues to the Wisconsin State Legislature, the NNI, and the EPA. In fact, representatives from this organization were sometimes the only members of the general, lay public to submit comments and participate at such open hearings (Colin, 2007).

At a larger scale, the Nanoscale Informal Science Education Network (NISE Net) was launched in 2005 to improve direct public engagement around nanotechnology by promoting discussions at science museums, research institutions, and other informal science organizations. NISE Net organizes an annual weeklong program of events, called NanoDays, and distributes nanotechnology information kits to help raise public awareness about the technology (Nanoscale Informal Science Education Network, n.d.). Outside of the United States, the British think tank Demos has conducted similar public engagement exercises. For example, Demos organized a "people's inquiry" on nanotechnology and the environment, including conducting focus groups that linked members of the public with research funding bodies, organizing stakeholder workshops in developing countries, and structuring dialogue between nanotechnology companies and consumers (Stilgoe, 2007).

Guston (2014a) notes one challenge that these efforts face in terms of direct public engagement around emerging technologies: determining how to best scale such activities and expand their reach to larger numbers of people. Many of these well-intentioned direct deliberation efforts are only able to involve a small number of individuals at any one time. For instance, 13 people participated in the meeting in Madison, Wisconsin that led to the formation of the Nanotechnology Citizen Engagement Organization (Kleinmann and Powell, 2005). The various public engagement projects that Demos undertook on nanotechnology ranged from a low of six people in discussion workshops organized in Zimbabwe to a high of 28 in dialogues held between consumers and corporations (Stilgoe, 2007). The participation numbers of the focus groups that PEN and the Synthetic Biology Project organized—talking to a dozen or so individuals at any one time—are similar in size and scale to many of these other direct public engagement efforts. This should not be surprising: participating in a constructive deliberation around nanotechnology, synthetic biology, or any other emerging technology is not straightforward. It requires a fair amount of preparation and time from individuals who do not have a technical background and who are often balancing multiple demands on their personal time. The organizing institutions also need to secure substantive financial resources in order to implement these efforts (Kleinman, Delborne, and Anderson, 2011). It may just be that an immutable, inverse relationship endures between the time spent in deliberation and the number of people that can be effectively engaged. Organizations can hold extended discussions with a few members of the public, but the logistics and costs of engaging larger numbers of people—in the thousands and beyond—may inevitably require a switch to mostly online means, such as through "keyboard-to-keyboard" interactions (Guston, 2014a).

However, innovations aiming to overcome these limitations of direct public engagement at-scale are being tested. One effort that signals a potential way forward regarding how to combine the intimacy of small-scale deliberative efforts with sufficiently large numbers of people is the World Wide Views project led by The Danish Board of Technology. World Wide Views is a global effort founded on the Danish citizen consensus conference model that has coordinated simultaneous, country-level dialogues across the world on a single day related to different science and technology topics, including climate change (The Danish Board of Technology, 2009), biodiversity (The Danish Board of Technology Foundation, 2012), and energy (The Danish Board of Technology Foundation, 2015). Doing so allows for the intimacy of smaller-scale engagements, on the order of 100 people per dialogue, to be aggregated across multiple sites in different countries, leading to participation numbers in the thousands to tens of thousands of people. These dialogues are also structured to provide structured input at key moments in global policymaking processes. For instance, the World Wide Views dialogue focused on biodiversity was designed to integrate citizen views into global climate discussions held in India in October 2012 focused on the Convention on Biological Diversity. The dialogue focused on energy and climate held in 2015 was designed to provide input into global climate talks held in Paris later in the year. This deliberation process includes the development of substantive background materials to inform local face-to-face discussions at each site, which are then linked together via a web tool that aggregates citizen voting on previously determined questions in real-time.

Efforts such as these offer an early glimpse into how direct engagement with the public around emerging technologies could be more effectively structured. Still, such large-scale deliberation efforts will likely remain few and far between, in part because the human and financial resources required to organize these projects are substantial. For instance, the World Wide Views project on biodiversity entailed two years of planning and the coordination of 42 national and regional partners for one day of networked, face-to-face deliberation.

Even without orchestrating such a large-scale direct deliberation endeavor—which is likely beyond the scope of most individual NGOs working on emerging technologies—these examples indicate there remained potential for an institution such as PEN to do more in terms of direct public engagement and deliberation. For instance, PEN could have expanded the number of focus groups it conducted and linked them together more thoroughly. Additionally, while PEN's emphasis on communications helped to disseminate the information it produced and build the organization's reputation, this likely created a situation in which more extensive, two-way engagement with the public was less robust than optimal. Despite this untapped potential, among the NGOs involved in nanotechnology policy, PEN still maintained a considerable public profile, leveraging its website, media coverage, and in-person public events to become a hub of activity within this community.

Temptation to "skew the information a little bit"?

One natural question that arises here is how the adoption of such communications and direct deliberation techniques might influence the substantive content and findings that an organization produces. For instance, critiques of PEN's communications and engagement strategy emerged from both the interviews and document analysis. These critiques indicate some degree of concern about the effect that PEN's communications efforts had on the information it disseminated and the ways in which PEN went about securing media coverage. One former government official wondered about the presence of "tension between their [PEN's] need to get coverage . . . to show they were doing something with the money they received and the more straightforward communications about the field." This criticism possibly arises from PEN's tendency to reserve its harshest criticisms for what it viewed as the slow progress that federal agencies were making on developing effective nanotechnology EHS risk research plans. This interviewee continued:

There is always a temptation to get coverage to skew the information a little bit, to spin it so it is attractive to the media, putting the concerns ahead of the scientific stage. I tend to think that colored the good work that was done . . . I really thought that where the pressure needed to go was on business.

Similarly, a journalist commenting on the volume of PEN's output recalled "becoming almost desensitized" to the amount of material PEN produced. This interviewee stated that it seemed as if a PEN report or press release was issued almost "every week," surmising that the constant flow of press-oriented activities could have led to a "dilution of the message."

Along the lines of the critique of the CPI discussed in Chapter 4, PEN also received criticism surrounding the degree of publicity it received related to the various updates to the number of products listed in the CPI. A 2007 blog post by Dexter Johnson professed: "Now, of course, everybody quotes this number as solemn gospel truth. But, now some folks are beginning to look at the validity of this list" (Johnson, 2007). The blog author then presents another quote from a different outlet:

It is important to remember that its Project on Emerging Nanotechnologies exists as a self-appointed watchdog for environmental and health risks. The more nanotech products it can claim, the higher the public alarm. The higher the alarm, the more the media and citizens are going to come to the Wilson Center for "answers."

(Johnson, 2007)

In 2009, Johnson continued:

Last month I ignored the announcement of The Project on Emerging Nanotechnologies' (PEN) nanotech-enabled consumer product list. To be honest, I've pretty routinely ignored their yearly announcement of the ever increasing number of products that supposedly contain nano, except, of course, to make fun of the whole idea.

(Johnson, 2009)

This blog post continues by stating:

One nanotech blog that is no longer with us had the temerity to suggest that the cause of the spiraling number of products on the PEN list might have less to do with being able to buy nanotech-enabled product at your local retail store and more to do with PEN trying to secure a place in the government feeding trough of nanotech.

(Johnson, 2009)

While this criticism takes umbrage at PEN's media saturation strategy, a number of interviewees emphasized the value to the field as a whole in having

PEN receive generous media attention. One private sector representative articulated:

> I thought that [PEN] did a really good job of sending things out and framing the issues and the results in a way that was really compelling to journalists and to readers in general. I would imagine, and I would say my qualitative impression from what I saw, is that really did have a role in driving a lot of nanotechnology coverage in the press.

Similarly, many interviews also indicated that having individuals from PEN speak at major nanotechnology conferences conferred a degree of credibility and attention on these forums. One former PEN staff member further exclaimed, "All of us were all over the world, [we were] invited every place to give this perspective." Another interviewee described that because representatives of PEN were present at many events, discussions, and gatherings outside of the Wilson Center, "everybody knew about it" and, in turn, "paid attention when something came out." Finally, another respondent who works frequently with the private sector summarized this idea, saying that PEN was "one of the top voices" in the world of nanotechnology policy and you "can't ask for a higher profile and notoriety," concluding that the presence of PEN representatives at many major discussion forums helped to position the organization as "a leader on the policy level."

Which side of the line did PEN fall: Being sufficiently ubiquitous so that they could be heard in a small but crowded landscape of actors, or stretched too thin as they chased the spotlight of media attention? The ability to tout high levels of coverage across many media platforms, from newspapers to magazines to websites, is important for preserving any organization's leadership in a field. The value of repetition here is not to be underestimated. Nanotechnology is a rather niche issue in the policy landscape. PEN's ability to create and regularly reinforce a few key themes and data points—such as the number of consumer products on the market or the need for additional EHS research—provided a well-defined message that could be reported on, whether from radio spots at the cosmetics counter of local department stores to the pages of *Consumer Reports* magazine.

By regularly producing easily digestible information on a complex technology policy issue, PEN was able to position itself as a big fish in a rather small pond, and in turn generate substantial attention. The quotations above indicate that PEN may have developed a reputation as attention seekers within the confines of the nanotechnology policy community. The rapid pace of releasing materials may also have led journalists who cover nanotechnology policy to become mildly "desensitized" to successive PEN reports. However, especially for reporters based at large, national newspapers who are either on deadline or need an illustrative statistic to flesh out a feature story on a topic that most of their readers had likely never heard about, it appears that PEN's approach more often than not provided just what was needed to secure high volumes of media coverage.

PUS, PES, or both?

What, then, do these experiences imply for the implementation of anticipatory governance practices in the policymaking process? First, the kind of public efforts undertaken by groups such as PEN demonstrate that the language and practice of engagement is becoming increasingly embedded into organizational activities. Second, these examples foreshadow that many organizations working on emerging technologies may take an expansive view of the concept, incorporating both PUS and PES efforts into their work plans. It may be challenging to restrict the public engagement concept inherent in anticipatory governance to PES alone, especially as the framework begins to inform the practices of organizations operating in different sectors, including civil society and government. Elements of PUS—such as raising awareness, communicating information, and gaining attention—will continue on as central components of how organizations approach the public going forward. However, unlike the prevailing views from decades ago, this is not due to outdated views about public irrationality or illiteracy that characterized the old deficit model. Instead, technologies are changing so rapidly, becoming so much more complex, and becoming even more interconnected that these PUS-like activities are important foundational complements—some might say level-setting necessities —that can complement and facilitate direct, two-way public engagement efforts.

Third, the current period is characterized as an exploratory phase about how to deeply engage larger numbers of people effectively through substantive direct deliberation modalities. Doing so is not easy. The advent of effective web-based collaboration technologies almost makes certain that these components will become an increasingly central part of public engagement efforts going forward. Scaling direct deliberation processes without employing sophisticated web-based collaboration tools in one way or another is hard to imagine. In short, the anticipatory governance framework has laid out the conceptual rationale as to why such a public engagement stance and commitment to direct deliberation activities are necessary. Working through the intricacies of realizing this vision, in practice, consists of the task moving ahead.

The centrality of PEN's public persona to its overall effectiveness was widely noticed by the broader nanotechnology policy community and often emerged when interviewees gave an assessment of PEN's work overall. One interviewee with experience in both government and academia reflected on how PEN was the "only game in town" that cut across these various dimensions. Another interviewee argued, "One of the hallmarks of a project like this, there is a substance side, but the strategic side has to be about leveraging your targets out of their comfort zone and making them moveable objects." Finally, a former government official perhaps best summed up the impact of PEN's communications efforts by remarking, "I mean the kind of visibility per dollar of the Wilson Center was amazing to me."

Just as the replication of PEN's CPI was one indicator demonstrating the broader influence of PEN's foresight and boundary-spanning activities, another example involving a parody of PEN's communication activities provides another powerful indication of PEN's influence within the nanotechnology policy community. On April 1, 2008, as part of an annual April Fool's Day satire of nanotechnology policy debates, Michael Berger—writing on a nanotechnology policy news aggregator website called Nanowerk—lampooned how a hypothetical entity with the mocking acronym "PEN" might respond to the implementation of a fictitious regulation addressing the imaginary discovery of "nanoassemblers" (Berger, 2008). Berger's parody states, in mock serious journalistic tone:

> The Project for Exposing Nanotechnologies (PEN) issued a statement in which it said that this new regulation has been overdue. Coincidentally, PEN already has scheduled a press conference and webinar to introduce the release of its new report "Do nanobots dream?—The philosophical and ethical issues surrounding molecular assemblers."
>
> (Berger, 2008)

That Berger poked fun at the meaning of the (real) PEN's name and acronym, its supportive response to the (fake) regulation, and the (presumed) reliance on attention-grabbing strategies that included a quickly arranged press conference, webinar, and report release speaks volumes about how others in the nanotechnology policy community perceived PEN's role and mode of operating in the public sphere. Of course, neither communications nor engagement alone is enough to have lasting influence on policy. PEN's actions indicated that the development of substantive information and effective outreach needed to work hand-in-hand in order to ensure its effectiveness. Taken together, these factors were complementary components that contributed to PEN's largely successful efforts to influence debate and raise the profile of nanotechnology policy issues in the United States.

In summary, the main argument in this chapter is that PEN viewed its interactions with the public along a continuum, including PUS elements of disseminating information and PES elements of direct deliberation and public participation. Especially on the PUS end of the spectrum, PEN's adoption of multiple strategies—framing a clear message, saturating the media, building a brand institutionally and for key individuals, effectively combining scientific credibility with metaphors and analogies, and creating a "coherent design philosophy"—demonstrates how an organization situated at the boundary between different communities of practice can effectively interact with the public on issues surrounding emerging technologies.

Bibliography

Anderson, A. A., Brossard, D., Scheufele, D. A., Xenos, M. A., and Ladwig, P. (2014). The "Nasty Effect": Online Incivility and Risk Perceptions of Emerging Technologies. *Journal of Computer-Mediated Communication, 19*(3), 373–387.

Barben, D., Fisher, E., Selin, C., and Guston, D. H. (2008). Anticipatory Governance of Nanotechnology: Foresight, Engagement, Integration. In E. J. Hackett, O. Amsterdamska, M. Lynch, and J. Wajcman (Eds.), *The Handbook of Science and Technology Studies*, 3rd ed. (pp. 979–1000). Cambridge, MA: The MIT Press.

Bauer, M. W., Allum, N., and Miller, S. (2007, January). What Can We Learn from 25 Years of PUS Survey Research? Liberating and Expanding the Agenda. *Public Understanding of Science, 16*(1), 79–95.

Berger, M. (2008, April 1). *Newly Formed Nanotechnology Protection Agency (NPA) to Regulate Molecular Assemblers.* Retrieved November 18, 2015, from Nanowerk: www.nanowerk.com/spotlight/spotid=5145.php

Berne, R. W. (2006). *Nanotalk: Conversations with Scientists and Engineers about Ethics, Meaning, and Belief in the Development of Nanotechnology.* Mahwah, NJ: Lawrence Erlbaum Associates.

Binder, A. R., Cacciatore, M. A., Scheufele, D. A., Shaw, B. R., and Corley, E. A. (2012). Measuring Risk/Benefit Perceptions of Emerging Technologies and Their Potential Impact on Communication of Public Opinion Toward Science. *Public Understanding of Science, 21*(7), 830–847.

Bozeman, B., and Sarewitz, D. (2005, April). Public Values and Public Failure in US Science Policy. *Science and Public Policy, 32*(2), 119–136.

Bozeman, B., and Sarewitz, D. (2011). Public Value Mapping and Science Policy Evaluation. *Minerva, 49*(1), 1–23.

Brown, J., and Kuzma, J. (2013). Hungry for Information: Public Attitudes Toward Food Nanotechnology and Labeling. *Review of Policy Research, 30*(5), 512–548.

Brown, M. (2009). *Science in Democracy: Expertise, Institutions, and Representations.* Cambridge, MA: MIT Press.

Bush, V. (1945). *Science: The Endless Frontier.* Washington, DC: United States Government Printing Office.

Castellini, O., Walejko, G., Holladay, C., Theim, T., Zenner, G., and Crone, W. (2007). Nanotechnology and the Public: Effectively Communicating Nanoscale Science and Engineering Concepts. *Journal of Nanoparticle Research, 9*(2), 183–189.

Chong, D., and Druckman, J. N. (2007). Framing Theory. *Annual Review of Political Science, 10*, 103–126.

Cobb, M. D. (2005). Framing Effects on Public Opinion about Nanotechnology. *Science Communication, 27*(2), 221–239.

Colin, M. (2007, January 8). *PRESS RELEASE: "Madison's resident's lone citizen voice in the Halls of Washington."* Retrieved November 10, 2015, from Nanopublic: http://nanopublic.blogspot.com/2007/01/press-release-madison-residents-lone.html

Conti, J., Satterfield, T., and Harthorn, B. H. (2011). Vulnerability and Social Justice as Factors in Emergent U.S. Nanotechnology Risk Perceptions. *Risk Analysis, 31*(11), 1734–1748.

Corley, E. A., Kim, Y., and Scheufele, D. A. (2013). The Current Status and Future Direction of Nanotechnology Regulations: A View from Nano-Scientists. *Review of Policy Research, 30*(5), 488–511.

Cukier, W., Ngwenyama, O., Bauer, R., and Middleton, C. (2009). A Critical Analysis of Media Discourse on Information Technology: Preliminary Results of a Proposed Method for Critical Discourse Analysis. *Information Systems Journal, 19*(2), 175–196.

Davies, J. C. (2006, February 2015). Testimony on: "Developments in Nanotechnology." Washington, DC: United States Senate, Committee on Commerce, Science and Transportation.

Davies, S. R., and Macnaghten, P. (2010). Narratives of Mastery and Resistance: Lay Ethics of Nanotechnology. *Nanoethics*, *4*(2), 141–151.

Delgado, A., Kjolberg, K. L., and Wickson, F. (2011). Public Engagement Coming of Age: From Theory to Practice in STS Encounters with Nanotechnology. *Public Understanding of Science*, *20*(6), 826–845.

Delli Carpini, M. X., Cook, F. L., and Jacobs, L. R. (2004). Public Deliberation, Discursive Participation, and Citizen Engagement: A Review of the Empirical Literature. *Annual Review of Political Science*, *7*, 315–344.

Dryzek, J. S., and Tucker, A. (2008, September–October). Deliberative Innovation to Different Effect: Consensus Conferences in Denmark, France, and the United States. *Public Administration Review*, *68*(5), 864–876.

Dudo, A., Dunwoody, S., and Scheufele, D. A. (2011). The Emergence of Nano News: Tracking Thematic Trends and Changes in U.S. Newspaper Coverage of Nanotechnology. *Journalism and Mass Communication Quarterly*, *88*(1), 55–75.

Elsevier. (2013). *Scopus*. Retrieved November 14, 2015, from www.elsevier.com/online-tools/scopus

Entman, R. M. (1993). Framing: Toward Clarification of a Fractured Paradigm. *Journal of Communication*, *43*(4), 51–58.

ETC Group. (2007, January 24). *Winners of Nano-Hazard Symbol Contest Announced at World Social Forum*. Retrieved November 13, 2015, from ETC Group: www.etcgroup.org/content/winners-nano-hazard-symbol-contest-announced-world-social-forum

ETC Group. (2009, October 15). *Nanoparticle Safety*. Retrieved November 16, 2015, from ETC Group: www.etcgroup.org/content/nanoparticle-safety

Fisher, E. (2007). Ethnographic Invention: Probing the Capacity of Laboratory Decisions. *NanoEthics*, *1*(2), 155–165.

Fisher, E. (2011). Public Science and Technology Scholars: Engaging Whom? *Science and Engineering Ethics*, *17*(4), 607–620.

Friedman, S. M., and Egolf, B. P. (2011). A Longitudinal Study of Newspaper and Wire Service Coverage of Nanotechnology Risks. *Risk Analysis*, *31*(11), 1701–1717.

Funtowicz, S. O., and Ravetz, J. R. (1993, September). Science for the Post-Normal Age. *Futures*, *25*(7), 739–755.

Gavelin, K., and Wilson, R. (2007). *Democratic Technologies? The Final Report of the Nanotechnology Engagement Group (NEG)*. London, UK: Involve.

Gregory, J., and Miller, S. (2000). *Science in Public: Communication, Culture, and Credibility*. New York, NY: Perseus Publishing.

Grobe, A., Rissanen, M., Funda, P., De Beer, J., and Jonas, U. (2012). *Nanotechnologies from the Consumers' Point of View*. Bern and St. Gallen, Switzerland: Federal Office of Public Health and Risk Dialogue Foundation.

Guston, D. H. (2000a). *Between Politics and Science: Assuring the Integrity and Productivity of Research*. Cambridge, UK: Cambridge University Press.

Guston, D. H. (2000b, Summer). Retiring the Social Contract for Science. *Issues in Science and Technology*, *16*(4), 32–36.

Guston, D. H. (2012, September). The Pumpkin or the Tiger? Michael Polanyi, Frederick Soddy, and Anticipating Emerging Technologies. *Minerva*, *50*(3), 363–379.

Guston, D. H. (2014a, January). Building the Capacity for Public Engagement with Science in the United States. *Public Understanding of Science*, *23*(1), 53–59.

Guston, D. H., and Sarewitz, D. (2002). Real-time Technology Assessment. *Technology in Society*, *24*(1–2), 93–109.

Hamlett, P. W., and Cobb, M. D. (2006, November). Potential Solutions to Public Deliberation Problems: Structured Deliberations and Polarization Cascades. *Policy Studies Journal, 34*(4), 629–648.

Hamlett, P., Cobb, M. D., and Guston, D. H. (2008). *National Citizens' Technology Forum: Nanotechnologies and Human Enhancement.* Tempe, AZ: The Center for Nanotechnology in Society, Arizona State University.

Hansen, S. F., Maynard, A., Baun, A., and Tickner, J. A. (2008). Late Lessons from Early Warnings for Nanotechnology. *Nature Nanotechnology, 3*(8), 444–447.

Hart Research Associates. (2006). *Attitudes Toward Nanotechnology and Federal Regulatory Agencies.* Washington, DC: Project on Emerging Nanotechnologies.

Hart Research Associates. (2007). *Awareness of and Attitudes Toward Nanotechnology and Federal Regulatory Agencies.* Washington, DC: Project on Emerging Nanotechnologies.

Hart Research Associates. (2008). *Awareness of and Attitudes Toward Nanotechnology and Synthetic Biology.* Washington, DC: Project on Emerging Nanotechnologies.

Hart Research Associates. (2010). *Awareness and Impressions of Synthetic Biology.* Washington, DC: Synthetic Biology Project.

Hart Research Associates. (2013). *Awareness and Impressions of Synthetic Biology.* Washington, DC: Synthetic Biology Project.

Hart Research Associates. (2014). *Perceptions of Synthetic Biology and Neural Engineering.* Washington, DC: Synthetic Biology Project, Woodrow Wilson International Center for Scholars.

Hart Research Associates. (2015). *Public Attitudes Regarding New Technology from Editing DNA.* Washington, DC: Synthetic Biology Project, Woodrow Wilson International Center for Scholars.

Hodge, G. A., Maynard, A. D., and Bowman, D. M. (2014). Nanotechnology: Rhetoric, Risk, and Regulation. *Science and Public Policy, 41*(1), 1–14.

Hoffman, A. J., and Ventrescra, M. J. (1999). The Institutional Framing of Policy Debates. *American Behavioral Scientist, 42*(8), 1368–1392.

International Council on Nanotechnology. (2008). *Towards Predicting Nano-Biointeractions: An International Assessment of Nanotechnology Environment, Health and Safety Research Needs.* Houston TX: International Council on Nanotechnology.

Jasanoff, S. (2003). Technologies of Humility: Citizen Participation in Governing Science. *Minerva, 41*(3), 223–244.

Jasanoff, S. (2005). *Designs on Nature: Science and Democracy in Europe and the United States.* Princeton, NJ: Princeton University Press.

Johnson, D. (2007, September 4). *Five Hundred Consumer Applications for Nanotech?!!* Retrieved November 15, 2015, from IEEE Spectrum: http://spectrum.ieee.org/tech-talk/semiconductors/devices/five_hundred_consumer_applicat

Johnson, D. (2009, September 10). *Reconsidering The One Thousand Nanotech Consumer Product Inventory.* Retrieved November 17, 2015, from IEEE Spectrum: http://spectrum.ieee.org/nanoclast/semiconductors/nanotechnology/reconsidering-the-one-thousand-nanotech-consumer-product-inventory-

Joly, P.-B., and Kaufmann, A. (2008). Lost in Translation? The Need for "Upstream Engagement" with Nanotechnology on Trial. *Science and Culture, 17*(3), 225–247.

Kahan, D. M., and Rejeski, D. (2009). *Toward a Comprehensive Strategy for Nanotechnology Risk Communication.* Washington, DC: Project on Emerging Nanotechnologies.

Kayal, A. (1999, March). Measuring the Pace of Technological Progress: Implications for Technological Forecasting. *Technological Forecasting and Social Change, 60*(3), 237–245.

Kearnes, M., Macnaghten, P., and Wilsdon, J. (2006). *Governing at the Nanoscale: People, Policies, and Emerging Technologies*. London, UK: Demos.

Kim, Y., Corley, E. A., and Scheufele, D. A. (2012). Classifying US Nano-Scientists: Of Cautious Innovators, Regulators, and Technology Optimists. *Science and Public Policy, 39*, 30–38.

Kleinmann, D. L. (Ed.). (2000). *Science, Technology and Democracy*. Albany, NY: State University of New York Press.

Kleinman, D. L., Delborne, J. A., and Anderson, A. A. (2011, March). Engaging Citizens: The High Cost of Citizen Participation in High Technology. *Public Understanding of Science, 20*(2), 221–240.

Kleinmann, D., and Powell, M. (2005). *Report of the Madison Area Citizen Consensus Conference on Nanotechnology*. Madison, WI: Madison Area Citizen Consensus Conference.

Leach, M., Scoones, I., and Wynne, B. (Eds.). (2005). *Science and Citizens: Globalization and the Challenge of Engagement*. London, UK: Zed Books.

Lewenstein, B. V. (1992). The Meaning of "Public Understanding of Science" in the United States After World War II. *Public Understanding of Science, 1*(1), 45–68.

McComas, K., and Besley, J. C. (2011). Fairness and Nanotechnology Concern. *Risk Analysis, 31*(11), 1749–1761.

Macnaghten, P., Kearnes, M. B., and Wynne, B. (2005, December). Nanotechnology, Governance, and Public Deliberation: What Role for the Social Sciences? *Science Communication, 27*(2), 268–291.

Macoubrie, J. (2005). *Informed Public Perceptions of Nanotechnology and Trust in Government*. Washington, DC: Project on Emerging Nanotechnologies.

Maynard, A. D. (2006a). *Nanotechnology: A Research Strategy for Assessing Risk*. Washington, DC: Project on Emerging Nanotechnologies.

Maynard, A. D. (2006b, September 21). Testimony on: "Research on Environmental and Safety Impacts of Nanotechnology: What are the Federal Agencies Doing?." Washington, DC: United States House of Representatives, Committee on Science.

Maynard, A. D. (2008, April 16). Testimony on: "The National Nanotechnology Initiative Amendment Act of 2008." Washington, DC: United States House of Representatives, Science and Technology Committee.

Maynard, A. D., Aitken, R. J., Butz, T., Colvin, V., Donaldson, K., Oberdorster, G., Philbert, M. A., Ryan, J., Seaton, A., Tinkle, S. A., Tran, L., Walker, N. J., and Warheit, D. B. (2006, November). Safe Handling of Nanotechnology. *Nature, 444*(7117), 267–269.

Mazerik, J., and Rejeski, D. (2014). *A Guide for Communicating Synthetic Biology*. Washington, DC: Synthetic Biology Project, Woodrow Wilson International Center for Scholars.

Merton, R. K. (1973). *The Sociology of Science: Theoretical and Empirical Investigations*. Chicago, IL: The University of Chicago Press.

Monica, J. J. (2007, October 12). *Andrew Maynard Starts New Nanoblog*. Retrieved November 18, 2015, from Nanotechnology Law Report: www.technologylaw source.com/2007/10/articles/nanotechnology/andrew-maynard-starts-new-nanoblog/

Nanologue. (2007). *The Future of Nanotechnology: Why We Need to Talk*. Wuppertal, Germany: Wuppertal Institute.

Nanoscale Informal Science Education Network. (n.d.). *NanoDays: The Biggest Event for the Smallest Science!* Retrieved November 16, 2015, from Nanoscale Informal Science Education Network: www.nisenet.org/nanodays

Nanotechnology Law and Business. (2009). Top Ten Experts in Environmental, Health, and Safety Issues Related to Engineered Nanomaterials. *Nanotechnology Law and Business*, 6(1), 133–138.

National Research Council. (1996). *Understanding Risk: Informing Decisions in a Democratic Society*. Washington, DC: National Academies Press.

National Research Council. (2012). *A Research Strategy for Environmental, Health, and Safety Aspects of Engineered Nanomaterials*. Washington, DC: The National Academies Press.

Nature Nanotechnology. (2007). Room for Improvement. *Nature Nanotechnology*, 2(5), 257.

Nisbet, M. C. (2010). Framing Science: A New Paradigm in Public Engagement. In L. A. Kahlor, and P. A. Stout (Eds.), *Communicating Science: New Agendas in Communication* (pp. 40–67). New York, NY: Routledge.

Nisbet, M. C., and Scheufele, D. A. (2009). What's Next for Science Communication? Promising Directions and Lingering Distractions. *American Journal of Botany*, 96(10), 1767–1778.

Nisbet, M. C., Brossard, D., and Kroepsch, A. (2003). Framing Science: The Stem Cell Controversy in an Age of Press/Politics. *Harvard International Journal of Press/Politics*, 8(2), 36–70.

Pidgeon, N., Harthorn, B., and Satterfield, T. (2011). Nanotechnology Risk Perceptions and Communication: Emerging Technologies, Emerging Challenges. *Risk Analysis*, 31(11), 1694–1700.

Pierson, P. (1993). When Effects Becomes Cause: Policy Feedback and Political Change. *World Politics*, 45(4), 596–628.

Poland, C. A., Duffin, R., Kinloch, I., Maynard, A., Wallace, W. A., Seaton, A., Stone, V., Brown, S., MacNee, W., and Donaldson, K. (2008). Carbon Nanotubes Introduced into the Abdominal Cavity of Mice Show Asbestos-like Pathogenicity in a Pilot Study. *Nature Nanotechnology*, 3(7), 423–428.

Polanyi, M. (1962). The Republic of Science: Its Political and Economic Theory. *Minerva*, 1(1), 54–74.

Powell, M., and Kleinman, D. L. (2008). Building Citizen Capacities for Participating in Nanotechnology Decision-making: The Democratic Virtues of the Consensus Conference Model. *Public Understanding of Science*, 17(3), 329–348.

PR Newswire. (2012, September 6). *Nanotechnology Awareness May Be Low, But Opinions Are Strong*. Retrieved November 14, 2015, from PR Newswire: www.prnewswire.com/news-releases/nanotechnology-awareness-may-be-low-but-opinions-are-strong-168750156.html

Priest, S., Lane, T., Greenhalgh, T., Hand, L. J., and Kramer, V. (2011). Envisioning Emerging Nanotechnologies: A Three-Panel Study of South Carolina Citizens. *Risk Analysis*, 31(11), 1718–1733.

Project on Emerging Nanotechnologies. (2006c, September 19). *Public Awareness of Nanotechnology: What Do Americans Know? Who Do They Trust?* Retrieved November 15, 2015, from Project on Emerging Nanotechnologies: www.nanotechproject.org/events/archive/public_awareness_nanotechnology_what_do/

Project on Emerging Nanotechnologies. (2007c, October 22). *The Twinkie Guide to Nanotechnology*. Retrieved November 18, 2015, from Project on Emerging Nanotechnologies: www.nanotechproject.org/news/archive/the_twinkie_guide_to_nanotechnology

Project on Emerging Nanotechnologies. (2008c). *Looking Back on the First Two Years: Biennial Report.* Washington, DC: Project on Emerging Nanotechnologies.

Project on Emerging Nanotechnologies. (2008d, September 30). *Nanotechnology? Synthetic Biology? Hey, What's That?* Retrieved November 15, 2015, from Project on Emerging Nanotechnologies: www.nanotechproject.org/events/archive/synbio_poll_event/

Pump, B. (2011). Beyond Metaphors: New Research Agendas in the Policy Process. *Policy Studies Journal, 39*(S1), 1–12.

PytlikZillig, L. M., and Tomkins, A. J. (2011). Public Engagement for Informing Science and Technology Policy: What Do We Know, What Do We Need to Know, and How Will We Get There? *Review of Policy Research, 28*(2), 197–217.

Rinfret, S. R. (2011). Frames of Influence: U.S. Environmental Rulemaking Case Studies. *Review of Policy Research, 28*(3), 231–246.

Rodemeyer, M. (2009). *New Life, Old Bottles: Regulating First-Generation Products of Synthetic Biology.* Washington, DC: Synthetic Biology Project.

Rogers-Hayden, T., and Pidgeon, N. (2007, July). Moving Engagement "Upstream"? Nanotechnologies and the Royal Society and Royal Academy of Engineering's Inquiry. *Public Understanding of Science, 16*(3), 345–364.

Rycroft, R. W. (2007, June). Does Cooperation Absorb Complexity? Innovation Networks and the Speed and Spread of Complex Technological Innovation. *Technological Forecasting and Social Change, 74*(5), 565–578.

Sabatier, P. A., and Jenkins-Smith, H. C. (1999). The Advocacy Coalition Framework: An Assessment. In P. A. Sabatier (Ed.), *Theories of the Policy Process* (pp. 117–168). Boulder, CO: Westview Press.

Sarewitz, D. (1996). *Frontiers of Illusion: Science, Technology and the Politics of Progress.* Philadelphia, PA: Temple University Press.

Scheufele, D. A. (1999, Winter). Framing as a Theory of Media Effects. *Journal of Communication, 49*(1), 103–122.

Scheufele, D. A., Corley, E. A., Dunwoody, S., Shih, T.-J., Hillback, E., and Guston, D. H. (2007). Scientists Worry about Some Risks More than the Public. *Nature Nanotechnology, 2*(12), 732–734.

Schon, D. A., and Rein, M. (1994). *Frame Reflection: Toward the Resolution of Intractable Policy Controversies.* New York, NY: Basic Books.

Selin, C., and Hudson, R. (2010). Envisioning Nanotechnology: New Media and Future-Oriented Stakeholder Dialogue. *Technology in Society, 32*(3), 173–182.

Shifman, L. (2013). Memes in a Digital World: Reconciling with a Conceptual Troublemaker. *Journal of Computer-Mediated Communication, 18*(3), 362–377.

Siegrist, M., and Keller, C. (2011). Labeling of Nanotechnology Consumer Products Can Influence Risk and Benefit Perceptions. *Risk Analysis, 31*(11), 1762–1769.

Siegrist, M., Keller, C., Kastenholz, H., Frey, S., and Wiek, A. (2007). Laypeople's and Experts' Perception of Nanotechnology Hazards. *Risk Analysis, 27*(1), 59–69.

Simons, J., Zimmer, R., Vierboom, C., Harlen, I., Hertel, R., and Bol, G.-F. (2009). The Slings and Arrows of Communication of Nanotechnology. *Journal of Nanoparticle Research, 11*(7), 1555–1571.

Steelman, J. R. (1947). *Science and Public Policy: A Report to the President.* Washington, DC: Government Printing Office.

Stilgoe, J. (2007). *Nanodialogues: Experiments in Public Engagement with Science.* London, UK: Demos.

Stirling, A. (2012, January). Opening Up the Politics of Knowledge and Power in Bioscience. *PLoS Biology, 10*(1), 1–5.

Stokes, D. (1997). *Pasteur's Quadrant: Basic Science and Technological Innovation.* Washington, DC: Brookings Institution Press.

Stone, D. (2002). *Policy Paradox: The Art of Political Decision Making,* (2nd ed.). New York, NY: WW Norton & Company.

Sturgis, P., and Allum, N. (2004, January). Science in Society: Re-Evaluating the Deficit Model of Public Attitudes. *Public Understanding of Science, 13*(1), 55–74.

Suerdem, A., Bauer, M. W., Howard, S., and Ruby, L. (2013). PUS in Turbulent Times II—A Shifting Vocabulary that Brokers Inter-Disciplinary Knowledge. *Public Understanding of Science, 22*(1), 2–15.

Synthetic Biology Project. (n.d.). *About the Synthetic Biology Project.* Retrieved September 17, 2015, from Synthetic Biology Project: www.synbioproject.org/about/

Taylor, M. R. (2008). *Assuring the Safety of Nanomaterials in Food Packaging: The Regulatory Process and Key Issues.* Washington, DC: Project on Emerging Nanotechnologies.

te Kulve, H., and Rip, A. (2011). Constructing Productive Engagement: Pre-engagement Tools for Emerging Technologies. *Science and Engineering Ethics, 17*(4), 699–714.

The Danish Board of Technology. (2009). *World Wide Views on Global Warming: From the World's Citizens to the Climate Policy-Makers.* Copenhagen, Denmark: The Danish Board of Technology.

The Danish Board of Technology Foundation. (2012). *World Wide Views on Biodiversity.* Copenhagen, Denmark: The Danish Board of Technology Foundation.

The Danish Board of Technology Foundation. (2015). *World Wide Views on Climate and Energy: From the World's Citizens to the Climate and Energy Policymakers and Stakeholders.* Copenhagen, Denmark: The Danish Board of Technology Foundation.

Throne-Holst, H., and Strandbakken, P. (2009). "Nobody Told Me I was a Nano-Consumer": How Nanotechnologies' Might Challenge the Notion of Consumer Rights. *Journal of Consumer Policy, 42*(4), 393–402.

von Schomberg, R., and Davies, S. (2010). *Understanding Public Debate on Nanotechnologies: Options for Framing Public Policy.* Luxembourg: European Commission.

Web Dialogues. (2007, October 23). *Consumers Talk Nano.* Retrieved November 15, 2015, from *Nanotechnology and the Public: A Dialogue*: www.webdialogues.net/cs/pen-consumer-home/view/di/95?x-t=home.view

Wichowsky, A., and Moynihan, D. P. (2008, September-October). Measuring How Administration Shapes Citizenship: A Policy Feedback Perspective on Performance Management. *Public Administration Review, 68*(5), 908–920.

Wilkinson, A., Kupers, R., and Mangalagiu, D. (2013, May). How Plausibility-based Scenario Practices are Grappling with Complexity to Appreciate and Address 21st Century Challenges. *Technological Forecasting and Social Change, 80*(4), 699–710.

Wilsdon, J., and Willis, R. (2004). *See-Through Science: Why Public Engagement Needs to Move Upstream.* London, UK: Demos.

Wilsdon, J., Wynne, B., and Stilgoe, J. (2005). *The Public Value of Science, Or How to Ensure that Science Really Matters.* London, UK: Demos.

Winner, L. (1989). *The Whale and the Reactor: A Search for Limits in an Age of High Technology.* Chicago, IL: University of Chicago Press.

Wynne, B. (1991, Winter). Knowledges in Context. *Science, Technology and Human Values, 16*(1), 111–121.

Wynne, B. E. (2006, May). Public Engagement as Means of Restoring Trust in Science? Hitting the Notes, but Missing the Music. *Community Genetics*, *9*(3), 211–220.

Xenos, M. A., Becker, A. B., Anderson, A., Brossard, D., and Scheufele, D. A. (2011, December). Stimulating Upstream Engagement: An Experimental Study of Nanotechnology Information Seeking. *Social Science Quarterly*, *92*(5), 1191–1214.

Ziman, J. (1991, Winter). Public Understanding of Science. *Science, Technology, and Human Values*, *16*(1), 99–105.

7 Foreshadowing the future

Learning lessons for the next wave of emerging technologies

"A model for other emerging areas?"

"Are you thinking of seeing how this could be used as a model for other emerging areas?" One interviewee at a leading independent research organization asked this question of me at the very beginning of a conversation, emphasizing an interest in lesson drawing across a range of emerging technologies. A key finding here is that the various foresight, boundary-spanning, and combined communications and engagement strategies employed by organizations such as PEN, ICON, and the Synthetic Biology Project can be helpful in informing the practices of other NGOs in response to future, forthcoming technological advancements. There is substantive value in building on previous experiences—whether successes or failures—even if the process of transferring such lessons is not a simple or straightforward endeavor. This ability to draw lessons from one policy situation to another becomes particularly urgent when an issue might change rapidly, when resources are limited, and when a close conceptual connection exists between topics—all characteristics of emerging technologies.

While there is often an interest in drawing lessons and transferring policy learning from one geographical or institutional policy context to another (Dolowitz and Marsh, 1996), or from one time period to another (Neustadt and May, 1986), lesson-drawing remains a contested and challenging process. Oliver and Lodge (2003) note that these attempts can easily devolve into rather generic "how to" guides that strip away important contextual information about specific systemic, temporal, or geographic dimensions of policy design and implementation. Rose (1991) also emphasizes that there can be a fair amount of uncertainty when attempting to transfer a set of solutions from one policy problem to another. However, Evans and Davies (1999) argue that such lesson learning is critical to policy innovation across multiple scales, from national and international levels all the way down to cross-organizational sharing.

The importance of the lesson-learning components from these case studies must not be underestimated. One interviewee reaffirmed, "it's incumbent on any of us who've been involved in these things over any sustained period to try and do more to draw out systematic lessons, themes, commonalities—and also, of course, differences and discontinuities, which are equally interesting." What can be said about the overall performance of institutions studied here? What overarching takeaways arise that are applicable and generalizable to other emerging technologies? This final chapter will address these questions. The next section will synthesize the overarching findings from the cases discussed throughout this book, highlighting instances that confirm initial expectations, point to surprising results, and consider what the tensions identified in this book imply for future areas of investigation. The chapter will then turn toward abstracting a series of cross-cutting operational, conceptual, and society-wide lessons that arise from this analysis as a whole. The chapter finishes by posing a set of questions that can guide future research and considers what may lie ahead for institutions that aspire to anticipate the societal implications of emerging technologies.

Looking back, projecting forward: from ag biotech to nano to synbio to . . .

Throughout this book I have shown that NGOs involved in emerging technologies aim to accomplish an array of multifaceted goals, from exploring a technology's future to bringing together organizations with different points of view to expanding dialogue with the public. PEN in particular generally succeeded at influencing nanotechnology policy in the United States, in the sense that it expanded discussion, debate, and deliberation about the technology's societal implications. One interviewee with a background in the NGO sector emphasized that "at the end of the day, the real objective was smart, highly informed, well-resourced policymaking on this issue." This interviewee stressed that due to PEN:

> There is a more organized conversation around [nanotechnology policy] with a larger body of work available to support intelligent policymaking . . . and a community that now has shared understanding of issues, risks, players, how far and wide the technology was able to reach. PEN laid that landscape out and made a more intelligent discourse possible.

Another researcher commented on PEN's outsized influence on the issue overall, indicating:

> There was sort of an advantage of having the size and funding from Pew that gave them the space to really kind of take over that field early on. And I think it was very successful in bringing industry to the table, and certainly engaging the agencies.

This interviewee continued by claiming that PEN's ultimate legacy was in "forcing the agencies to take a hard look . . . at the regulatory authorities, and really kind of pushing them to begin to develop some policies. So, I think that happened a lot more quickly than otherwise would have happened." Yet another researcher echoed this idea, "I think they were a major force at the time," with a former government official commenting that, "certainly the PEN database of nanomaterials, and products that involved nanotechnology, I think without question . . . it impacted the whole policy look at the environmental, health and safety implications of nanotechnology." This government official surmised, "I think it really brought the attention to the impact that the field was having on the actual products that people were coming in contact with." In sum, these notions of making "more intelligent discourse possible," pushing discussions forward "a lot more quickly than otherwise would have happened," and influencing "the whole policy look" are exactly the type of results that speak in favor of PEN accomplishing its overarching goals.

This is not to say that the ideas and policy-oriented contributions by institutions such as PEN, ICON, or the Synthetic Biology Project were necessarily adopted by other actors. Nor is it that such institutions were always able to identify to a specific development and say unequivocally that it was the sole reason for the change. While the body of evidence indicates that PEN, and to some extent ICON, contributed extensively to shaping nanotechnology policy, attributing any single policy or regulatory change to PEN or ICON alone is too strong a claim. In fact, unambiguous attribution is hard to come by for any NGO working on technical problems with multiple stakeholders over an extended period of time. For example, one former senior-level US government official provided a particularly nuanced view on this matter, confirming PEN's influence while simultaneously indicating the difficulty in ascribing direct policy change to any one actor. "I think it's an extraordinary testimony . . . that PEN established itself quickly and as solidly as they did, [becoming] the place to go on nano as quickly and as well as they did," said the interviewee. The official continued, "Having said that, it's much harder to answer the question of 'Did they really have an impact on policy?' I mean I've spent longer than I like to think about dealing with that question."

While other NGOs can learn much from the institutions studied here, a cautionary note is warranted. Despite the inevitable inclination to compare the context of one emerging technology with another, the unavoidable differences of each must still be recognized. Despite the inevitable inclination to look at these technologies together, the unique characteristics of each domain must also be taken into account. For example, while many interviewees acknowledged that the potential societal implications of nanotechnology were difficult to address, many also commented that synthetic biology could potentially raise even more fundamental questions. One staff member of the Synthetic Biology Project commented as much in reflecting:

> Nano was more sort of just a chemical kind of issue, in terms of ecological and environmental safety issues. Synbio sort of broaches all sorts of different types of environmental health and safety issues that it sort of blows my mind that there are not more NGOs trying to jump into that space.

Another academic researcher reiterated:

> Nano is sort of like chemical risk assessment on steroids. You may not know what the right dose is because it is nano-scaled, but at least you have a starting point for crying out loud. For a gene drive system, you don't even really have a starting point . . . then the ethical issues are much bigger, too. It blends environmental ethics with bioethics with agricultural ethics.

Similarly, the beginning of this book covered the differences among the federal funding, research prioritization, regulatory regime, and innovation system in the United States for nanotechnology and synthetic biology. This alternative backdrop implies that NGOs moving on to address one area of emerging technology to another must still consider such differences in determining how to best handle each new field. One interviewee highlighted the importance arising from these potentially subtle yet salient differences, remarking:

> There is no executive agency backstop [for synthetic biology]. There is no surrogate to the National Nanotechnology Initiative, for example. There is no international competitiveness angle. There is no, "If we don't get our arms the synthetic biology and what it means to the global economy, we're going to be left in the dust." I think absent connecting all of those dots, there will continue to be a denigration of this constellation of technologies that will continue to be kind of put in "the land of misfit toys," as opposed to in the heart of innovation going forward.

The situation may slowly be changing, at least with respect to synthetic biology. Due to considerations such as those mentioned above, an announcement from the United States government in July 2015 indicated the beginning of a process to update the Coordinated Framework for the Regulation of Biotechnology so that participating agencies can become better prepared to address the regulatory and oversight challenges brought on by new developments in synthetic biology (Holdren et al., 2015). Through this review process, the regulatory implications of synthetic biology may begin to get the type of scrutiny at the federal level that the regulatory implications of nanotechnologies began to receive nearly a decade ago.

Additionally, differences in the size and structure of the industry looking to commercialize different emerging technologies can also affect the roles that NGOs can play in the system. For instance, in the early days of nano-technology, many companies were less averse—or at least agnostic—toward using the term "nanotechnology" to market or advertise their products. This does not appear to be the case with respect to synthetic biology, with companies seemingly less willing to adopt that moniker when starting to sell or distribute their novel applications. Perhaps this is because of negative connotations or perceptions that the term "synthetic biology" might raise in the marketplace or because of the term's presumed close affiliation with agricultural bio-technology. A case in point: consider the way in which EPA retitled the public dialogue project it launched related to the environmental impacts of syn-thetically engineered algae, an application that is being promoted as potentially providing a source of renewable biofuels and other chemicals (Wang et al., 2012). This public outreach project was initially called the "GM/Synbio Algae Project" (Morris, McClung, and Segal, n.d.), but the title changed and it subsequently became the "Biotechnology Algae Project" (Environmental Protection Agency, 2015b), avoiding all use of the phrase "synthetic biology" anywhere in the description of the project. One interviewee suggested that this change was due, at least in part, to an uneasy reaction by the private sector community looking to commercialize these technologies. One interviewee surmised:

> The Synthetic Biology Algae Project that quickly morphed into the Biotechnology Algae Project, seemingly overnight, I found that very telling, in that the community just really reacted quick, and immediately viscerally to any association between algae and synbio. And I think EPA literally got an earful . . . and the subsequent posting was completely scrubbed of any of the synbio language. It's a little bit of a teachable moment for me, anyway, as to why the industry is objecting to that charac-terization, or why those terms are thought to be so radioactive.

Former senior staff and advisors from the three institutions studied here were cognizant of these differences and were familiar with the societal pushback and the challenges faced by other previous technologies. I mentioned earlier that many of these individuals had worked on such controversial science and technology issues throughout their careers, creating a keen realization that policy processes to address societal concerns often lag behind the development of the technology. The staff members I spoke with expressed a genuine concern that nanotechnology and synthetic biology could quickly reach an inflection point as they transition from the laboratory to the marketplace, with the pace of the technology outstripping the speed of policymaking. These institutions viewed the creation of platforms for early dialogue among different stakeholders as preparatory work that might bear fruit once greater attention was paid to the opportunities and risks arising from these technological developments.

For instance, one individual affiliated with ICON extrapolated:

> ICON, Wilson Center, and others had a model that said, "Let's not wait for the bad things to happen and clean them up afterwards. Let's be proactive, and imagine what could happen, and figure out what needs to be done to make it not happen." And if that becomes the model going forward, then I think that would be a tremendous legacy to have left.

Similarly, a former PEN staff member argued that "nanotechnology has influenced dialogue around to other emerging technologies just as GMOs influenced the early dialogue around nanotechnology." This interviewee continued:

> If you look at how people talk about understanding the benefits and risks around emerging technology, thinking about responsible development and responsible innovation, and thinking about new models of governance, almost everything is grounded at some point in what worked and what didn't with nanotechnology.

One government representative also hypothesized on this lesson-learning dimension, stating that, "I don't think you are going to get a pass, like they did with ag-biotech [agricultural biotechnology], and GMOs in this country early on . . . maybe [these organizations] ought to be like a canary in the coal mine." The efforts put forth by these organizations, therefore, carried high stakes: the intention was to speed the policymaking process along and help to lay the groundwork by providing a precedent for similar types of activities that would inevitably be needed again in the future.

So, if groups such as PEN and ICON were successful in achieving their goals, at least to some extent, it raises the question: why did they close and why did their work end? Interestingly, many interviewees shared the view that while these organizations may have helped to sustain and propel a broader discussion about the societal issues associated with emerging technologies, their very accomplishments could have actually weakened their rationale to remain in existence. One interviewee suggested that groups such as PEN helped nanotechnology "cross the valley of death" and retain a degree of prominence among ever-competing science and technology priorities for attention. One academic interviewee even pondered a hypothetical world in terms of what would have happened if an NGO such as PEN was not formed and gotten started in the first place. This interviewee postulated: "What would have happened had they not been there? I think the answer is it may have been that this community may not have sustained. It would have been a little blip."

It was also suggested that such NGOs can ultimately become "a victim of their own success," as one interviewee stated, with their ability to seed ideas and drive attention to a topic eventually making them seem less critical over time. While changes in funding availability and shifting interests among key staff were commonly cited reasons as to why ICON and PEN closed their doors around 2010, the changing institutional setting brought on by the very work these groups undertook was a critical factor as well. One interviewee involved with ICON stated as much, noting that, "the landscape was so different in 2011 than it was in 2005 . . . that people were doing other things." This interviewee continued, "As those activities gained traction, there was less time and funding available for companies to come in to ICON."

Alternative explanations are possible, however, regarding the key factors that led to the winding-down of these institutions. Simply put, the extensive degree of popular backlash and policy confusion that was expected to arise from advancements in nanotechnology just did not seem to materialize, and any skirmishes that did arise never became elevated into full-scale battles. This view, espoused by a handful of interviewees, posits that the extensive worry associated with these technologies early-on was ultimately unfounded or misplaced. One government representative surmised:

> Where we are right now with synbio is, there is the warning that we are likely to see all sorts of substances that are very different, will challenge our ability to review them for environmental behavior and potential hazard, and there's going to be a lot of them. That may be the case, but it's the same thing we heard with nano; it didn't really work out that way.

Another interviewee suggested that this very lack of a resulting catastrophe essentially forced these NGOs working on nanotechnology to either close down, change their focus, or move on to other matters. This individual reflected:

> A lot of these institutions were created in anticipation of a public reaction that never really seemed to develop . . . I think what really it comes down to is: one, nanoscale materials aren't just one thing, they're everything. It's very hard to pick anything in particular that embodies them in a way that would provoke public fascination or fear. Second, there hasn't been an incident which could tantalize public interest in a way that commands broad attention. If there had been an explosion associated with nanoscale aluminum that was unique, if there had been a toxic release that had caused wide-scale damage in a way that nanoscale materials exacerbated, we might be having a different story here. Lacking that type of flashpoint, nanoscale materials just became more and more routine. Those flashpoints might still occur in the future, but for now people seem to be quietly putting away the emergency response gear and be more business as usual.

Regardless of which of these explanations rings true, since the closing of PEN and ICON very few NGOs currently exist that can play an anticipatory role with respect to nanotechnology. One interviewee astutely cautioned, "Nothing filled that void when PEN left." A private sector representative said bluntly, "I hear this big sucking sound with PEN and ICON gone." Many interviewees were also bothered by how quickly discussions about nano-technology's societal implications began to fall off the radar and take a back seat to discussions related to synthetic biology, geoengineering, and other emerging technologies once institutions such as PEN and ICON wound down. Organizations such as the ETC Group and the International Center for Technology Assessment have begun to turn their attention to these other topics. Groups such as the Foresight Institute and Center for Responsible Nanotechnology have also either curtailed the scope of their work or focused predominantly on promoting nanotechnology's advancement. Some environmental organizations with expansive mandates to cover a wide range of topics have become less engaged with emerging technologies in general, especially as nanotechnology EHS issues have begun to fade somewhat from view. The National Academies serves as a source of neutral, credible information on such issues, but they generally only produce reports sporadically and on-demand, with much of their nanotechnology-oriented studies focused on fulfilling their mandate to review the performance and progress of the NNI periodically. Technical and standards-setting discussions do continue to take place, but these undertakings have a more narrow focus and are unlikely to have a strong public engagement component along the lines of what a group such as PEN might try to emphasize.

The tensions identified throughout this book are helpful in identifying potential areas for further examination going forward. One of these tensions is the challenge organizations face in striking a balance between considering *the future and the present*. For instance, more interviewees than expected characterized the value of PEN's work as focusing on rather proximate policy concerns and emphasized less the forward-looking nature of PEN's activities. Chapter 4 discussed that PEN did not explicitly use many traditional foresight methodologies, such as scenario planning or trend monitoring, as stand-alone activities. Instead, much of its foresight work was often subsumed in a secondary role, placed at the edges to augment policy analysis contained in other work products. One implication of this finding for the anticipatory governance conceptual framework is that as the application of this concept becomes more commonplace in a wider range of sectors and contexts, organizations may adjust the degree to which the foresight component is at the center of their efforts. For NGOs working in this space, less emphasis might be places on what might be called "foresight for foresight's sake" and, instead, this component might become more subtly interwoven with other types of traditional research activities. At the most extreme, the continual pressure to focus on the near-term could even make entities scale back on the "anticipatory" elements that lie at the heart of the theory. This could lead to a slippery slope where the forward-looking component is diminished or outright lost. Organizations that begin with a future-oriented disposition will face a continual challenge that is unlikely to dissipate: ensuring an ability to influence the present while envisioning multiple future alternatives that are needed to undergird a robust and informed debate. Attention is needed so that a focus on the future is not wholly sacrificed for immediate concentration on the present.

How could this tension be explored in the context of other emerging technologies going forward? One area to examine is the explicit possibility of combining visionary forms of non-predictive, non-probabilistic foresight with near-term strategic planning efforts that are intended to develop actionable policy solutions. For instance, developing effective mechanisms to combine long-term foresight with near-term action is particularly relevant for planetary-wide challenges, such as climate change, and therefore may arise more strongly in the context of geoengineering. It remains unclear as to whether geoengineering will be able to combat the effects of climate change, and, even if this is possible, the full impacts of geoengineering will likely only be fully realized in decades or centuries to come (Stilgoe, 2015). However, since present-day steps are to address climate risks, different visions about how a technology such as geoengineering might play out could helpfully be combined with concrete plans that can be actualized in the near term.

One suggestion Fuerth (2012: 54) makes to help bridge this gap between the long-term and near-term is a notion called "component-level implementation process (CLIP)." This idea is similar to the strategic planning steps that are typically taken following a scenario planning exercise, when narratives of the future are used to develop signals and signposts that can suggest adjustments in present-day planning or action. Fuerth (2012: 54) writes that the idea behind CLIP is to translate long-term visions into "a series of short-term goals to be implemented in components." This approach would ensure that "Each component is valuable in its own right and can stand on its own so that benefits are achieved regardless of whether the final goal is achieved" (Fuerth, 2012: 54). Organizations involved with emerging technologies such as nanotechnology, synthetic biology, or geoengineering could find ways of testing whether marrying near-term actions with alternative visions of the future can help realize tangible accomplishments even when, as Fuerth (2012: 54) reminds, "the final results may not be seen for decades."

A second tension that warrants additional consideration is how to balance *neutrality and interestedness*. While I find that all three organizations successfully functioned in a boundary-spanning role to a greater or lesser degree, a tension continues in terms of how institutions can operate as a neutral convener while also adopting a point of view on an issue. In Chapter 5, I argue that these positions are not mutually exclusive: transparently holding a point of view does not preclude an organization from brokering partnerships or creating boundary objects that can engage multiple parties effectively. This consideration becomes complicated, however, when the uncertainties, promises, and fears surrounding new technologies are taken into account. Approaching these intricate science and technology policy questions without some perspective about how they should be addressed is hard, if not impossible. Organizations involved with emerging technologies will continually have to grapple with this tension and will need to regularly reassess whether their stated preferences are interfering with their ability to bridge the gap across sectors and institutions that may hold different points of view.

On this theme, another area to explore going forward is the question of whether newly formed institutions can operate more neutrally than previously existing institutions. The findings show that although PEN was sometimes viewed as taking a strong stance on nanotechnology policy, it was often still viewed as operating in a more neutral role than similar organizations with a longer history of working on environmental or health issues. It remains an open question as to whether new institutions are needed that are uniquely devoted to exploring each emerging technology or whether existing institutional arrangements can evolve into effective venues for addressing different technologies successively. The stances taken by previously existing institutions may also hinder the ability of these entities to successfully span boundaries in other areas. Alternatively, it might also be that the experience that these institutions accrue from working on one area of emerging technology might make them better prepared to investigate another. This is an interesting conundrum that warrants further attention.

A third tension is one related to understanding the relationship between *communications* and *engagement*. While a distinct shift from a PUS model to a PES model has occurred in the academic literature—and in much of the practice related to interacting with the public regarding emerging technologies—many organizations involved with emerging technologies will continue to blur the boundaries between the two. Undertaking PUS activities alongside or in conjunction with PES activities is inevitable. Recent literature also indicates that to effectively engage the public in constructive and productive deliberations, organizations will have to take better account of how science and technology issues are framed and how pre-existing perceptions can lead individuals to process new information in unexpected and perhaps counterintuitive ways.

What could arise next from this nexus of communications and engagement is the emergence of a new era of what some have called "mass customization." Much like the manufacturing sector is being transformed by on-demand production and is moving into a phase where customized design specifications can be quickly combined with large-scale production systems (McCarthy, 2004; Piller, 2004; Kaplan and Haenlein, 2006; Reeves, Tuck, and Hague, 2011; Gannes, 2014), so too is public engagement with emerging technologies likely moving into an era of on-demand interaction, more immediate access to individualized messaging and imagery, and the potential advent of customized deliberation models. New ideas related to deliberation that have emerged in recent years, such as midstream modulation (Fisher, Mahajan, and Mitcham, 2008) and socio-technical integration (Fisher and Guston, 2012; Flipse, van der Sanden, and Osseweijer, 2013), are beginning to steer in this direction as well. Designing large-scale public engagement opportunities that are also capable of being tailored and customizable at the individual level remains a challenge and warrants additional exploration.

NGOs will increasingly be able to bypass all media channels in favor of direct interaction with the public that will involve a mixture of what was traditionally viewed as one-way communication and two-way deliberation. The ongoing fracturing of the media landscape also implies that how the impact of communications activities is assessed must also change. Counting newspaper articles or the number of radio and television spots mentioning an organization will no longer be an accurate or comprehensive indicator of an institution's influence or clout. Instead, measuring the number of followers on Twitter, the number of "likes" on Facebook, or the number of views of a YouTube video may be far better indicators of organizational reach. This merging of communications with direct public deliberation implies that engagement efforts will continue to morph as well, evolving from time-limited, place-based, face-to-face discussions to virtual, ongoing, digitally based conversations. Chapter 6 describes how the combined in-person and online deliberation elements showcased in efforts such as the World Wide Views project are indicative of this way forward. Moving ahead, it will be useful to examine how these shifts change the behavior of NGOs involved in anticipating the societal implications of emerging technologies. It will be critical to study how the capacity for real-time engagement is being impacted as organizations take to social media to provide regular streams of bite-sized information, receive constant feedback on the materials they disseminate, and work to connect with their ever-more self-selected communities of interest.

Cross-cutting lessons for the field: operational, conceptual, and societal

In addition to the specific tactics identified by contemplating the activities of PEN, ICON, and the Synthetic Biology Project in detail, abstracting a set of broader, cross-cutting lessons is also possible. Table 7.1 organizes these lessons into three categories that will each be addressed in turn: operational, conceptual, and societal.

One of the principal operational lessons to arise is how key it is to *build a protected space that promotes individual and institutional experimentation*. PEN and Synthetic Biology Director David Rejeski intimated that "we were outliers at the Wilson Center," commenting on how these two projects differed in many ways from the Wilson Center's other programs. Complex institutional

Table 7.1 Cross-cutting lessons: operational, conceptual, and societal

Operational	Conceptual	Societal
Build a protected space for individual and institutional experimentation • Promotes the ability to fail rapidly as new ideas are tested	*Take a systems approach* • Allows for the exploration of a wide portfolio of governance options	*Immediate salience of specific technologies can be fleeting* • Risk of fast-fading relevance, with the next wave of new technologies always on the horizon
Promote reiteration of critical information • The recurring use and presentation of information promotes continued relevance in a field	*Recognize the difficulty in judging success* • Diffuse goals, multiple expectations, and many degrees of freedom makes assessing influence challenging	*Effective policymaking is dependent on "a moment in time"* • Policy windows open only infrequently—and then never for long

arrangements can therefore arise between a host organization and the project embedded within it. Chapter 5 highlighted how PEN and the Synthetic Biology Project benefitted greatly from being housed at the Wilson Center. They were able to partake in the Center's narrative of providing non-partisan policy analysis. They were able to function independently when necessary, but retained the operational benefits of being based in a larger institution with a ready-made reputation for quality and substance. They were physically and metaphorically situated at the heart of policy debates surrounding emerging technologies, with the Wilson Center located between Congress, the White House, executive agencies, and other NGOs, all factors helping to enhance and amplify their role as a convener of disparate positions.

This is not to say that these derived benefits come without their own peculiarities. For instance, the Wilson Center had little previous history working on science and technology policy issues, let alone on issues related to emerging technologies. This is what made PEN and the Synthetic Biology Project somewhat of an odd fit, subject matter-wise, among the Wilson Center's many geographically oriented programs focused on international affairs. While the type of public events PEN and the Synthetic Biology Project held were typical of the kinds arranged by other programs at the Wilson Center, the rate of output and high volume of media coverage that PEN, in particular, received was unusual. PEN's independently active web presence was also atypical, which contributed to providing PEN with its own brand alongside the Wilson Center. This helps to explain the finding, discussed in Chapter 6, that the most frequent kind of institutional reference in newspaper stories about PEN's work were joint mentions of PEN and the Wilson Center. Finally, some of the activities PEN undertook—such as inventory development, analysis of hypothetical products, web dialogues, focus groups and public perception surveys—were also uncommon when compared with the Wilson Center's other customary policy analysis work. The topics that PEN and the Synthetic Biology Project covered, their prodigious output, and the courting of extensive media attention all made these projects rather different from the many others housed at their host institution.

However, this odd fit was not insurmountable nor did it get in the way of a fruitful and productive relationship between PEN, the Synthetic Biology Project, and the Wilson Center. The combination of Wilson Center affiliation, reputable senior project staff, and the extensive use of credible external experts were central to this strategic and productive arrangement. Many interviewees actually acknowledged that one of PEN's primary achievements derived from a tightly coupled combination of the quality of people involved and its organizational set-up. One researcher argued, for instance, that the "strengths of PEN were the people involved," with the ability to draw on "the right people at the right time" to advance its stated goals. One interviewee with deep experience in the federal government stressed that this high degree of trust is critical to successfully adopting a forward-looking mentality. Creating and maintaining a "safe" atmosphere promotes the ability to fail rapidly as new ideas are tested. This interviewee implied that this kind of environment is lacking in many such organizations today, but persists as a key element of creating an effective policy foresight system. The interviewee warned about the need to maintain "a protected, non-judgmental space in which neither you nor any of your peers self-censor or rule out possibilities because they are professionally risky, or they are unorthodox, or they expose you to even office ridicule or conference table ridicule." This interviewee continued: "Either you must tolerate that, if you're operating alone, or the people around you have to be conditioned to tolerate that, or the penalty is going to be that you will only look at incremental change and incremental responses." Openness to trial and error, therefore, and the ability to fail safely must be implicitly and explicitly supported in organizations that try to creatively anticipate the many ways that emerging technologies can impact society.

A second operational lesson is the need to *promote reiteration of critical information* to maximize opportunities for policy influence. While a stand-alone report may make the proverbial splash in the news or trade press, regularly updating information is a central ingredient in building a reputation and staying relevant in a field. Out of the organizations studied here, their best-known successes are characterized by a process of establishing a toe-hold in a policy ecosystem and then providing recurring updates—with each update helping to build awareness of the organization. This process helps to solidify the place of such information within any particular community of practice and draws attention to other areas of work that may have previously been less visible. When an institution such as PEN found leverage points that gained traction, such as its CPI and EHS risk research inventories, they continued to return to them over time. One interviewee put it that information from these inventories were released "like clockwork." PEN's annual public perception surveys and regularly produced agency-oriented policy analyses became their calling cards and helped to define and solidify the organization's public identity. Even ICON utilized this strategy to its advantage over its history, regularly focusing on similar EHS issues in the reports it released. In adopting this strategy, NGOs with a focus on emerging technologies can help to bolster their relevance and maintain influence for an extended period of time.

One conceptual lesson that unambiguously arises is the value in *taking a systems approach* in analyzing the issue at hand. For example, when beginning to address a new sub-topic of nanotechnology policy, PEN often began by undertaking a broader systems analysis of a particular regulatory system or agency, such as the FDA (Taylor, 2006), before diving into greater depth on specific laws, such as dietary supplements (Schultz and Barclay, 2009) or food packaging (Taylor, 2008). The Synthetic Biology Project followed suit and also took a strong systems-oriented view, demonstrated most distinctly in the analysis presented in one of its 2015 reports that looked across the oversight system to examine how a range of potential products from different sectors— including agriculture, healthcare, chemicals, and energy—might interact with different laws at different stages of their development (Bergeson et al., 2015).

Similarly, ICON adopted this systems-oriented disposition in its two later reports that, respectively, examined nanotechnology's potential interactions with biological systems and the environment, with each report presenting a series of overarching typologies and analytic frameworks designed to help provide a holistic, comprehensive perspective on these issues (International Council on Nanotechnology, 2008, 2010).

Rejeski explained, "We started with the system and then drilled down" into the details of individual regulations. For instance, reflecting on the importance of these foundational systems analyses related to various domains, Rejeski highlighted the importance of one particular image that was included in Taylor's report examining nanotechnology's potential systemic impact on the FDA. "I mean, Taylor's report, you could see the whole report on one page. You know those heat maps? You want a classic example of one graphic that works," said Rejeski. "Here's the entire FDA," he continued, "this is all of the things they regulate. These are all the tools they have, pre-market, post-market. Here's where they fail, here's where they're good." One interviewee based at an independent research institution reaffirmed this idea as follows:

> Having a systems approach is very helpful, since it allowed [PEN] to be set up in a way to take the whole system into account and provides a balanced approach . . . It helps both deepen understanding, but it also helps to create an avenue for the broad range of stakeholders that have an interest in certain policy outcomes to be at least keeping track of the work that you do, if not also get actively involved when there are opportunities to do so.

PEN also demonstrated this systems approach by investigating a range of governance options that could be potentially relevant, depending on how nanotechnology evolved over time. Many NGOs involved in nanotechnology had a tendency to focus on or advance views about specific laws or rule interpretations. Additionally, a number of other organizations took strongly fixed policy positions, such as the ETC Group's suggestion to place a freeze or moratorium on all nanotechnology research activities or the International Center for Technology Assessment's legal petition against federal regulatory agencies to try to limit the commercialization of silver nanotechnology. PEN took a different approach. It examined and explored the potential impacts and consequences of a wide array of oversight and governance options, ranging from creating new regulations to adapting existing regulations to developing new voluntary systems. Maintaining a wide view and retaining flexibility as debates about emerging technologies evolve can provide these institutions with a more robust ability to contribute across a wide-ranging set of discussions as the development of the technology progresses.

A second conceptual lesson is *recognizing the difficulty in judging success* of the types of efforts undertaken by these NGOs. All three institutions studied here had relatively broad and diffuse organizational goals: to facilitate dialogue, build an evidence-base, present a range of policy options, and in some cases, engage the public. While multiple pathways can be pursued to achieve these kinds of overarching goals, challenges arise when trying to judge the success of entities guided by such broad, vague mission statements. Formally engaging experts in the field and tracking demonstrable indicators of influence—such as mentions in the media or report citations—offer some markers of success. However, these indicators likely do not tell the full story and can lead to mischaracterizations about how an organization has operated in a particular field. Perhaps the best way to guard against this risk is by regularly documenting accomplishments and adopting transparent practices so that any activities undertaken can be more formally assessed later on, after the work has wrapped. Moreover, the outputs produced by projects such as PEN, ICON, and the Synthetic Biology Project can have long tails of relevance, so the mark of their legacy could remain even if the institution has faded away. Periodically reassessing impacts of these institutions at different time periods, then, is a sensible idea.

A confounding factor in judging success is that boundary-spanning organizations such as PEN, ICON, and the Synthetic Biology Project continually face the pressure of managing expectations of both internal and external constituents. For instance, PEN faced critiques from external actors as to what the organization should do, what it was not doing well, or what it needed to do better. ICON's governance structure required that it integrate perspectives from multiple sectors through a consensus-building process, leading some in the field to characterize it as being slow to respond to immediate developments. Some interviewees from NGOs and academia charged that PEN and ICON were too closely aligned with the interests of corporations and did not as fully reflect the points of view of smaller, advocacy-oriented organizations. On the other hand, more than one government representative thought that PEN was too focused on advocating for specific positions or emphasizing risks. While it may be tempting to say that this criticism from many different sides is a good indicator that a group such as PEN was effective in being "neutral," a more accurate conclusion is that organizations must constantly be aware of the different stances they take and how these positions will be interpreted by different stakeholders. Walking this fine line can be tricky. Boundary management processes need to be regularly assessed so that interested parties are continuously willing to engage in productive dialogue that involves contested claims about the future.

Finally, society-wide lessons are apparent that can inform how other emerging technologies are addressed going forward. The first of these lessons is that the *immediate salience of specific technologies can be fleeting*. Organizations, and even individuals, winning notice and gaining notoriety on specific science and technology policy issues can be vulnerable to fading fast, especially given that the "next wave" of emerging technologies is always on the horizon. With the pace of technological development speeding up, the race by individuals and organizations to stay ahead of the curve and move on to the next technology coming over the horizon has also accelerated. One interviewee reckoned with the enticing pull of making such transitions quickly in acknowledging:

> It's no accident that it was very much the same community of people who piled into the nanotech debate as had been involved in varying degrees with biotech debates, and indeed other emerging tech debates. In an entrepreneurial and opportunistic sense [we all] have to seize the opportunities as they arise to both ask the same sets of related questions about anticipatory governance and broader societal, political, and ethical dimensions of new technologies.

Choices—financial, logistical, and otherwise—are always pressing, and turning to focus on the "the next big thing" is often a rather appealing option. Another interviewee suggested as much, stating that NGOs and the institutions that fund them are often looking for "an opportunity to intervene and make change happen, to get in and usually to do it in a fairly big way, and then make the change happen and then get out." Another interviewee from government remarked how this transition has taken place between nanotechnology and synthetic biology: "The societal implications folks had tapped into nano, and built up publications and programs in nano, and are basically taking and converting those activities, or modifying them, to get grant money for synbio now as well." This individual continued, "It's not clear, although they're trying really hard, whether they will get the same response out of the government for societal implications funding for synbio." Finally, one academic researcher readily admitted that for both practical and intellectual reasons, these kinds of shifts among scholars and practitioners happen regularly and are likely unavoidable:

> I think there is this tendency with people who work on emerging technologies or environmental problems, that if you see a new issue arise, you say, "Okay, well, there are so many people working in nanotechnology. I think we have something really important to say here in this new area that could raise attention." It's just the tendency for us to want to jump into these new and emergent areas to be first movers, so to speak. The reason for that is because at the surface, the issues are different. [But,] once you get down to kind of the fundamental problem, they remain the same in a way. You always have a problem with: What do you do in the face of uncertainty? What do you do in the face of missing information? What do you do with intellectual property and confidential business information? How do you treat it? What is this business about open access or closed access? How do you fund a research program? Should it be basic research driven, or applied and societally driven? Some of those fundamental technology policy problems remain largely the same.

These shifting interests, coupled with the challenge of securing funding for any such effort, ultimately raise questions about the sustainability and viability of NGOs engaged with emerging technologies over the long term.

In fact, as interests move on to the next technological frontier—from nanotechnology to synthetic biology to geoengineering to whatever may come afterwards—the number of projects or institutional arrangements needed to address each successive area of innovation could proliferate as well. This is especially true given the lack of an existing federal government body, at least in the United States, tasked with addressing the societal implications of multiple emerging technologies simultaneously. This returns to the theme raised in the first chapter of this book: even if one could establish a single government entity for this purpose, such an approach is likely outmoded already. One interviewee remarked that developing a network of NGO-based anticipatory governance institutions is likely a more optimal solution:

> It's almost like you need parallel tracks of projects [for] the big picture thinking and the elements within it. It's almost like you would need three or four PENs . . . sort of orchestrating how all the changes in all those areas are going to come together to affect society.

A second, related societal lesson is that *effective policymaking is dependent on "a moment in time."* Factors including funding availability, staffing, and receptivity of ideas within a policy environment are all critical to the successful initiation and staying power of projects such as PEN, ICON, and the Synthetic Biology Project. One respondent even commented on the generally short duration of existence for entities such as these, which in this individual's words, tend to come and go "in a blink of an eye." Another interviewee similarly argued: "The competition in this arena isn't for money, really, it is for time [and] people's engagement." An additional interviewee reaffirmed:

> Even before implementation, you may have a sense of the rate at which circumstances may be creating an alignment, or an opening where implementation becomes possible. Solutions that work today or tomorrow might have been totally impossible earlier. There is a sense of rightness and readiness. When the situation is right, you better be ready.

It will not always be possible to seize the moment when the confluence of forces and prescient timing allows for an entity such as those studied here to form for other emerging technologies. Kingdon (1995) famously notes that policy windows of opportunity only open infrequently—and then never last for long. Future opportunities to establish an entity such as PEN, ICON, or the Synthetic Biology Project with respect to other emerging technologies vitally depends on preparations made sufficiently in advance and the ability of individuals and institutions to actualize available resources quickly. Because of this context dependency, once policy influence or impact is achieved—

however vaguely defined—this very success may make it appear that such an entity is no longer needed on a particular issue. Individuals and institutions can change their focus—as PEN did in transitioning into the Synthetic Biology Project—but given the short half-life of policy and technology "windows," quick wins will inevitably become a top priority. The provision of in-depth analysis will become rarer still, and whether sustained inquiry, exploration, and examination over a period of years, if not decades, will be possible as this new pattern takes hold remains unclear.

Setting a precedent for the future

In conclusion, this book charts a course about how to put into practice strategies that are capable of addressing the societal implications of emerging technologies. PEN, ICON, and the Synthetic Biology Project offer real-world examples about how the anticipatory governance conceptual framework can be applied to better understand organizational behavior, offering a kind of roadmap that other institutions can follow, at least to some degree, as a way of influencing other areas of science and technology in the future. Chapter 3 commented on how the concept of anticipatory governance can be compared to a regular exercise routine, one of preparation. Building on this metaphor, these case studies offer insight into how some real-world "exercise" regimens have played out and show the results arising from different ways of actualizing foresight analysis, boundary-spanning, and a combination of communications and public engagement activities.

In their own concluding thoughts, many interviewees judged that even though these anticipatory governance practices may slowly be gaining traction, there persists a concern that society is still collectively unprepared for the unforeseen impacts of various technological developments. Many respondents were apprehensive about the fading possibility of creating the next PEN- and ICON-like organization. The closing of PEN and ICON foreshadows the likely fate of efforts such as the Synthetic Biology Project, especially as technological advancement churns forward. The shift of technology assessment functions away from their historical roots in government not only portends the loss of public support, both symbolically and literally, but also runs the risk that NGOs—for all of their best intentions—may not be up to the task at hand. Questions linger about whether such entities can be sustained at a sufficiently large enough scale, arise at the right moment in time, and bring to bear the appropriate constellation of skills and capacities needed to address the intricate, interconnected science and technology challenges that are starting to face society today and will likely continue to do so in the years and decades to come.

While turning back the clock and re-creating another centralized OTA-like entity is unlikely, many respondents almost nostalgically yearned for and held on to the promise of such an institution, imperfections and all. One journalist who regularly covers this issue lamented: "Without the benefit of an OTA, the

United States has few resources that can offer the type of useful analysis, review and compilation of material on emerging technologies that PEN achieved on a continuing and timely basis." A representative from the private sector reiterated this longing, asserting that "in a perfect world, there would be a free-standing, dedicated entity to help navigate, both domestically and internationally, how to deal with these issues in a public and transparent" manner.

The main challenge to overcome is disaggregated, siloed analysis of individual technologies and transition toward a more integrated, all-inclusive perspective. Research institutions, NGOs, philanthropies, businesses, governments, and everyday citizens can no longer afford the luxury of exploring the societal effects of each new technology separately. One academic researcher conjectured:

> The problem we face in terms of funding models is that people will tend to fund the particular technology one-by-one and aren't so interested in funding the connective tissue . . . that in many ways is the more important area of learning . . . but [there is] very little investment in systematic learning from bio, nano, and other debates.

The institutions studied here lay the foundation for progress in the direction of developing this "connective tissue." The notion of anticipatory governance has reached a stage where many subtle variations on the original formulation are appearing, particularly as the conceptual framework is beginning to get applied toward understanding activity that is taking place across academia, government, and non-governmental sectors. In Chapter 3 I argued, and I have co-authored elsewhere, that anticipatory governance has the potential to update "canonical theories of the policymaking process" by augmenting the "standard, stepwise models that conceptualize how policy is made," thereby underscoring that "publicly developed, interdisciplinary visions of plausible futures greatly influence the framing of policy problems" (Guston and Michelson, 2015: 93). This research suggests that understanding organizational practices is a necessary component to better respond to the myriad, interwoven societal and policy issues that will be brought on by emerging technologies. One interviewee shared in writing:

> The challenge that we face as a society is to figure out a way to move beyond "crisis management" tech assessment, where the products of a technology have come to market and then *ex post facto* we try to assess and/or deal with their impacts.

This interviewee continued, "The point is we have to figure out a way to assess technologies before they've been dumped on society instead of always being in the position of trying to play catch-up." The institutions studied here tried to do just that.

To conclude, additional follow-up paths of inquiry abound and flow directly from this research. On the narrower side, more can be done to mine these case studies and the wealth of collected qualitative data even further. Other potentially valuable avenues for additional probing include an exploration of PEN's use of new media outlets during its history, an examination of the ways ICON managed diverse multi-sectoral representation as part of its governance structure, or an assessment of the ultimate impact of the Synthetic Biology Project once that effort ends. Broader questions are pressing as well. For example, how are democratically elected leaders responding to the increased role that these kinds of NGOs are playing in the policymaking process? How can organizations best adapt the approaches traced here to better function in different operating environments? What will be the extended influence of these institutions, especially as many of them recede farther into the past? What other variations on the anticipatory governance framework can be gleaned from empirical qualitative or quantitative studies? What are the conceptual links between ideas such as anticipatory governance and responsible innovation with other relevant strands of the science and technology policy literature, such as complexity theory or resilience theory? Going forward, what factors might hinder or enhance the effectiveness and ability of a networked, non-governmental approach to anticipating the societal implications of emerging technologies? The hope is that the insights gained throughout this book can serve as a jumping off position for such analysis and help seed answers to these and other pressing questions as future emerging technologies continue to unfold.

Bibliography

Bergeson, L. L., Campbell, L. M., Dolan, S. L., Engler, R. E., Baron, K. F., Auerbach, B., Backstrom, T. D., Vergnes, J. S., Bultena, J. P., Auer, C. M. (2015). *The DNA of the U.S. Regulatory System: Are We Getting It Right for Synthetic Biology?* Washington, DC: Synthetic Biology Project, Woodrow Wilson International Center for Scholars.

Dolowitz, D., and Marsh, D. (1996). Who Learns What from Whom? A Review of the Policy Transfer Literature. *Political Studies*, 44(2), 343–357.

Environmental Protection Agency. (2015b, August 5). *US Environmental Protection Agency Biotechnology Algae Project*. Retrieved October 21, 2015, from Environmental Protection Agency: www2.epa.gov/sites/production/files/2015–09/documents/biotechnology_algae_project.pdf

Evans, M., and Davies, J. (1999). Understanding Policy Transfer: A Multi-Level, Multi-Disciplinary Perspective. *Public Administration*, 77(2), 361–385.

Fisher, E., and Guston, D. H. (2012). *STIR: Socio-Technical Integration Research*. Tempe, AZ: Arizona State University.

Fisher, E., Mahajan, R. L., and Mitcham, C. (2008, December). Midstream Modulation of Technology: Governance from Within. *Bulletin of Science Technology Society*, 26(6), 485–496.

Flipse, S. M., van der Sanden, M. C., and Osseweijer, P. (2013, Spring). Midstream Modulation in Biotechnology Industry: Redefining What is "Part of the Job" of Researchers in Industry. *Science and Engineering Ethics*, 19(3), 1141–1164.

Fuerth, L. (2012). *Anticipatory Governance: Practical Upgrades*. Washington, DC: Project on Forward Engagement.

Gannes, L. (2014, February 4). *3-D Printing's Next Frontier: Mass Customization*. Retrieved October 22, 2015, from Re/code: http://recode.net/2014/02/04/3-d-printings-next-frontier-mass-customization/

Guston, D. H., and Michelson, E. S. (2015). Anticipatory Governance. In J. Holbrook, and C. Mitcham, *Ethics, Science, Technology, and Engineering: A Global Resource*, 2nd ed. Farmington Hills, MI: Macmillan Reference.

Holdren, J. P., Shelanski, H., Vetter, D., and Goldfuss, C. (2015, July 2). *Modernizing the Regulatory System for Biotechnology Products*. Retrieved October 20, 2015, from Office of Science and Technology Policy: www.whitehouse.gov/sites/default/files/microsites/ostp/modernizing_the_reg_system_for_biotech_products_memo_final.pdf

International Council on Nanotechnology. (2008). *Towards Predicting Nano-Biointeractions: An International Assessment of Nanotechnology Environment, Health and Safety Research Needs*. Houston TX: International Council on Nanotechnology.

International Council on Nanotechnology. (2010). *Advancing the Eco-Responsible Design and Disposal of Nanomaterials*. Houston, TX: International Council on Nanotechnology.

Kaplan, A. M., and Haenlein, M. (2006, March). Toward a Parsimonious Definition of Traditional and Electronic Mass Customization. *Journal of Product Innovation Management, 23*(2), 168–182.

Kingdon, J. (1995). *Agendas, Alternatives, and Public Policies*. New York, NY: Addison-Weseley.

McCarthy, I. P. (2004). Special Issue Editorial: The What, Why and How of Mass Customization. *Production Planning and Control: The Management of Operations, 15*(4), 347–351.

Morris, J., McClung, G., and Segal, M. (n.d.). U.S. EPA GM/Synbio Algae Guidance Project. Retrieved October 20, 2015, from Arizona State University College of Law: http://conferences.asucollegeoflaw.com/get2015/files/2011/12/Morris.Jeff_.pdf

Neustadt, R. E., and May, E. R. (1986). *Thinking in Time: The Uses of History for Decision-Makers*. New York, NY: The Free Press.

Oliver, J., and Lodge, M. (2003). The Limitations of "Policy Transfer" and "Lesson Drawing" for Public Policy Research. *Political Studies Review, 1*(2), 179–193.

Piller, F. T. (2004). Mass Customization: Reflections on the State of the Concept. *The International Journal of Flexible Manufacturing Systems, 16*(4), 313–334.

Reeves, P., Tuck, C., and Hague, R. (2011). Additive Manufacturing for Mass Customization. In F. S. Fogliatto, and G. J. da Silveira (Eds.), *Mass Customization: Engineering and Managing Global Operations* (pp. 275–289). London, UK: Springer.

Rose, R. (1991). What Is Lesson-Drawing? *Journal of Public Policy, 11*(1), 3–30.

Schultz, W. B., and Barclay, L. (2009). *A Hard Pill to Swallow: Barriers to Effective FDA Regulation of Nanotechnology-Based Dietary Supplements*. Washington, DC: Project on Emerging Nanotechnologies.

Stilgoe, J. (2015). *Experiment Earth: Responsible Innovation in Geoengineering*. Oxon, UK: Routledge.

Taylor, M. R. (2006). *Regulating the Products of Nanotechnology: Does FDA Have the Tools it Needs*. Washington, DC: Project on Emerging Nanotechnologies.

Taylor, M. R. (2008). *Assuring the Safety of Nanomaterials in Food Packaging: The Regulatory Process and Key Issues*. Washington, DC: Project on Emerging Nanotechnologies.

Wang, B., Wang, J., Zhang, W., and Meldrum, D. R. (2012, September). Application of Synthetic Biology in Cyanobacteria and Algae. *Frontiers in Microbiology, 3*(344), 1–15.

8 Methodological appendix

The research approach primarily taken in this book involved interpretative qualitative case study analysis (Lincoln and Guba, 1985; Stake, 1995; Yanow, 1996, 2000; Yin, 2003). Qualitative methods enable researchers to understand a wide range of complex phenomena, including illuminating the context of particular policy situations, understanding key organizational strategies and processes, and enhancing and building on theory. Multiple modes of data collection were used to inform the exposition presented here, including document analysis, semi-structured interviews, and a set of media analyses.

The application of in-depth organizational case studies employing diverse qualitative data collection methods demonstrates the significant contribution that qualitative research can make in advancing knowledge related to emerging technologies. The details of the three primary data collection methodologies used in this project are described further in this appendix. Since this research project was initially undertaken when the author was affiliated with New York University, the research protocol was reviewed and deemed exempt by the university's institutional review board, known as the University Committee on Activities Involving Human Subjects, in November 2011.

Document analysis

Document analysis is often used to collect data for qualitative research projects (Scott, 1990; Prior, 2003; Mogalakwe, 2006), generally in tandem with interviews or observations. By examining documents as a main evidence base, the body of materials produced by the organizations studied here were effectively treated as an archive of information from which conclusions could be drawn. Ventresca and Mohr (2001: 806) argue that these types of written materials are particularly "consequential and strategically useful" sources of data and information, enabling "researchers to view the ebb and flow of organizational life, the interpretations, the assumptions, the actions taken and deferred from a range of differing points of view as events unfold." Bowen (2009: 30) highlights the value of qualitative document analysis as a primary data collection approach, noting that document analysis can "provide background and context, additional questions to be asked, supplementary data, a means of tracking change and development, and verification of findings." While these strengths do recommend qualitative document analysis as a primary data collection methodology, acknowledged limitations do exist. For instance, some important yet intangible aspects related to an institution's evolution over time are never captured in written materials. Moreover, elements of policy influence can occur informally or through back channels that leave little or no formal trace or written record. However, by complementing the document analysis component of this research with two other modes of data collection, the design of this research ensures that the findings are sufficiently triangulated and that no major themes are missed.

A comprehensive approach was taken to construct the archive of documents for analysis. I used the computer-aided qualitative data analysis software Atlas.ti, version 6.2.28, to help organize the collection of documents and the analytic coding scheme that was subsequently developed (Friese, 2012). I analyzed a total of 117 documents in Atlas.ti—along with additional materials analyzed outside of Atlas.ti, as described below—in the primary research phase of the project, which took place from 2011–2013. Another 18 documents in total were reviewed outside of Atlas.ti in the secondary, follow-up phase of the research project that took place in late 2015, including ten documents related to ICON and eight documents related to the Synthetic Biology Project.

Most of the documents analyzed were related to PEN, in large part because PEN serves the primary focal point of analysis and because PEN published such a wide-ranging set of materials over its lifespan. All of PEN's primary public materials were contained in the dataset that I analyzed, broken down into the following categories: commissioned external reports (19), research briefs (8), Congressional testimonies (8), submissions to domestic and international government agencies (17), statements of support for PEN reports from influential leaders in the field (8), and background materials on the eight web-based inventories that PEN hosted. I also included in this database a number of additional journal articles, speeches, images, and reports produced by and about PEN. I also analyzed a number of early documents produced by the Synthetic Biology Project and the Science and Technology Innovation Program in the main Atlas.ti document set as well. In total, I reviewed, analyzed, and coded over 2,200 pages of material in Atlas.ti in the primary research phase. Almost all of the materials that PEN produced for public consumption were downloaded from its website, which has effectively become a static record of the project's outputs since it closed in 2010.

Many of PEN's public reports follow a similar structure that is typical of such documents. They usually begin with a foreword by PEN Director David Rejeski, then a biography indicating the author's expertise in the field, followed by an executive summary. The main body of each report usually starts with an introduction to nanotechnology, an overview of the specific policy problem or topic under investigation, a landscape assessment of other literature on the topic, an explanation of the novel analysis or policy approach being suggested or assessed in the report, and a conclusion with a list of recommendations. Chapter 6 covered how these reports often had a consistent design theme, branding, and layout, sometimes with an evocative picture on the cover and always sporting PEN's logo on the front and the back.

In addition to the formal analysis and coding of the main set of materials in Atlas.ti, during the primary research phase from 2011–2013 I also reviewed a wide range of additional documents and multimedia material outside of the Atlas.ti software to further augment the findings. These additional supplementary materials that were studied include:

- a review of all 14 hard copy quarterly reports that PEN produced over its history for The Pew Charitable Trusts. These quarterly reports included high-level summaries of PEN's work, a list of key meetings held during the period, a presentation of PEN's web statistics, and copies of all media coverage PEN received during the reporting period. Aspects of the media analysis presented in Chapter 6 emerged from information contained in these internal quarterly reports;
- an exploration of all eight online, publicly available inventories PEN hosted on its website. While the background materials and inventory summaries were included in the documents reviewed in Atlas.ti, the web-based inventories themselves were explored outside of the Atlas.ti software;
- virtual observations of select audio podcasts, radio interviews, television interviews, archived event webinars, and videos of PEN presentations. This included listening to the six podcasts PEN produced as part of its *NanoFrontiers* series with leading nanotechnology scientists and radio interviews conducted by Andrew Maynard. The videos that were reviewed included excerpts from some of the public perception focus groups PEN arranged, clips from recorded Congressional testimony, videos of public events held at the Wilson Center, and television interviews with PEN staff conducted at the Wilson Center and elsewhere;
- a review of the event listings and photograph archive posted on the PEN website. This included a review of the many pictures, images, and graphics that PEN used in its reports, on its website, and that it made available for public use;
- reviews of select published materials by PEN staff and additional publications written by organizations referencing or referring to PEN work. These included:
  - hard copies of ancillary materials PEN printed and distributed, such as informational flyers, event handouts, and promotional postcards;
  - leading blogs in the field that wrote about or provided perspectives about PEN;
  - inventories tracking nanotechnology consumer products that followed the methodologies of those produced by PEN, particularly those produced by the European Consumer Organisation;
  - electronic records of Congressional committee and subcommittee hearings, along with the texts of bills introduced that potentially drew on PEN testimony.

Coupled with the other two complementary data collection approaches, the document analysis component of this research served as a rich and diverse resource base from which to examine multiple aspects of the organizations assessed here and to draw both theoretically- and practically-oriented conclusions.

Semi-structured interviews

A second strand of data collection that was undertaken involved a number of semi-structured interviews related to the role of the NGOs examined here that served to confirm, challenge, and generate findings that are presented throughout the book. The interviews were primarily focused on discussing the influence of each institution and covered a range of topics, such as how they operated, getting perspective on their strengths and weaknesses, and discussing relevant lessons emerging from their respective efforts over time.

I conducted a total of 53 semi-structured interviews with 47 individuals, as some individuals were interviewed more than once. A total of 44 interviews, with 41 different respondents, took place during the primary research phase, mostly in 2012. An additional nine interviews, with six new respondents, occurred during the supplementary research phase in the second half of 2015. I used a snowball sampling approach toward selecting interviewees, beginning with a list of suggested contacts culled from a review of documents, suggestions from experts in the field, and personal experience. I recruited subsequent interviewees based on recommendations from respondents and additional research into key thought leaders in the field. This sampling method yielded a total of 58 interview prospects. The 47 respondents represent completed interviews with over 80 percent of that roster. Interviewees included current and former staff from the organizations studied (7 people), members of their advisory networks (5), non-governmental representatives (7), former and current government officials at the federal and local levels in the United States (7), academic scholars (6), private sector actors (5), print journalists and web-based reporters (4), non-US based experts (3), and foresight professionals who provided a helpful cross-cutting perspective (3). Many respondents had experience working in multiple sectors that went beyond their current professional affiliations presented above.

One interviewee, PEN and the Synthetic Biology Project Director David Rejeski, was interviewed four times during the primary research phase due to his central familiarity with the examined institutions. Three other respondents were interviewed twice over the first and second research phases. Of the 11 interview targets that I was not able to engage, I received no response from five individuals during the recruitment process after three attempts at making contact with them. Three other individuals indicated that they were not allowed to participate given their current professional positions or affiliations. The remaining three individuals declined to participate, citing a lack of knowledge or sufficient familiarity with the subject area.

Since all of the interviewees worked in some professional capacity in the field—and, in some instances, occupied senior positions in their respective organizations—I originally scheduled each interview for 30 minutes, with the actual interview length ranging from 25 to 60 minutes. I conducted the majority of the interviews (39) by phone, with 12 conducted in-person and the remaining two interviews preferring to submit written responses to interview questions. Of the 51 interviews I conducted by phone or in person, all but four were recorded, producing nearly 27 hours of audio content.

I took detailed notes for all the interviews conducted by phone or in-person, regardless of whether they were recorded. The audio files were transcribed professionally, and I checked them for accuracy. The interview transcripts were analyzed, in conjunction with the notes taken during the interviews, outside of the Atlas.ti software. While many interviewees provided consent to be quoted by name, a decision to protect anonymity was nevertheless made in an effort to respect respondent privacy. All individuals quoted by name either provided consent to do so or had quotes drawn from previous events or written statements that were already available in the public domain.

Media analyses

The final strand of data collection was a multidimensional media analysis consisting of a variety of different elements. The media analyses were primarily directed at examining PEN's communications and engagement efforts, and the results of these findings are mainly discussed in Chapter 6. Multiple media analysis strategies were utilized because no single source of information is capable of providing a sufficiently complete picture for this dimension of interest. This is largely due to the challenge of tracking media coverage and the dissemination of outputs across a wide range of platforms, such as print, online, television, and radio. Additionally, many reports from entities such as PEN, ICON, and the Synthetic Biology Project were published on their websites as stand-alone documents and not in more easily trackable journals. Therefore, a number of proxy indicators helped provide a better grasp on the scope of these activities.

The primary component of the media analysis strand of research was tracking coverage of PEN in leading American newspapers. This research was based on searching through a database of articles focused on nanotechnology that contained over 20 years of newspaper coverage. The nanotechnology newspaper article database was compiled by Dietram Scheufele and graciously shared by Doo-Hun Choi at the University of Wisconsin-Madison. Newspaper articles were obtained through a search of the LexisNexis Academic database. This database culled nanotechnology related articles from 21 daily US newspapers that "were strategically chosen to create variance in both circulation size and geographic location" (Dudo, Dunwoody, and Scheufele, 2011: 60). Large, medium, and small-scale circulation newspapers were contained in this sample, which included leading national newspapers such as *The New York*

Times, *The Washington Post*, and *USA Today*, along with more regionally focused newspapers in geographic areas with substantial nanotechnology research activity, such as the *Houston Chronicle*, *Boston Globe*, and *Star Tribune* in Minneapolis. To construct this database, the researchers "created a complex Boolean search term designed to maximize the retrieval of nanotechnology-related stories while simultaneously limiting the number of false positives" (Dudo, Dunwoody, and Scheufele, 2011: 60). Subsequently, the researchers assembling this database manually screened articles to identify any remaining false positives, and all articles were then exported and stored in text files. This process led to the creation of a set of 2,132 newspaper articles published from 1998 to 2011. These raw data files were made available by the researchers for this time period, and I used keywords to search a subset of the database, 1,303 articles covering the period of 2003—two years before PEN was formed—through 2011, a year after PEN drew to a close. The articles were searched for the names of ten NGOs: PEN and the nine other organizations mentioned in Chapter 6 that were involved in nanotechnology policy issues during the time period when PEN was active. The results from this analysis are presented in Figure 6.1.

Tracking coverage in newspaper articles tells only part of the story, albeit an important part, related to media and public engagement activities. Three additional media analysis components were also undertaken to provide a more well-rounded view of this issue. First, in order to gain more perspective about how PEN tried to frame the messages it disseminated in the media, I conducted a high-level content review of all available PEN press releases. I individually reviewed all 117 press releases from PEN's website; it is only a coincidence that this is the same as the number of documents analyzed in Atlas.ti. Chapter 6 describes two aspects of the press releases that were analyzed. The first was whether the overall message of each press release was positive, negative, or neutral in tone. The second was whether the press release predominantly focused on nanotechnology's benefits, risks, or both. The intention of this analysis was to assess the tenor and thrust of PEN's overall messaging strategy.

Another researcher independently categorized and assessed the tone and risk–benefit framing of the press releases, with both researchers discussing the results following the independent coding process. The intention of engaging a second researcher on this aspect of the research was to ensure a macro-level consistency in categorizing the tone and framing of the press releases overall, not to dwell on the message of any one press release in particular. The primary researcher made the final decision on all categorization, with close agreement in the overall final assessment for both researchers. Both researchers agreed 95 percent on categorization of message tone and 94 percent on the categorization of risk–benefit framing. Among the six coded categories, no difference in assessment between the two researchers was greater than five press releases within any one category, and most categories had differences in assessment of three press releases or fewer.

Second, in order to better understand PEN's online efforts, I reviewed and synthesized the user statistics and web analytics featured in each of PEN's internal quarterly reports. This data resulted in the construction of the timeline shown in Figure 6.2 that tracks the total number of page views and unique users visiting PEN's website. Despite a few gaps owing to missing information, the resulting data provided a useful means by which to gauge PEN's web presence.

Third, in order to estimate how PEN contributed to the academic literature, I conducted a citation analysis for two peer-reviewed journal articles that were co-authored by Andrew Maynard, appearing respectively in *Nature* (Maynard et al., 2006) and *Nature Nanotechnology* (Poland et al., 2008). I used the Scopus citation database to determine the citation rank, as of December 2012, of both papers that Maynard co-authored. Two peer-reviewed scientific papers do not a comprehensive analysis make, but the citation counts presented in Chapter 6 are still telling. While it remained a challenge to track the citations of outputs not published in peer-reviewed venues, such as the 19 major reports PEN released during its history, concerted efforts are made throughout the preceding chapters to indicate the likely influence that these materials had by drawing on interview findings and noting mentions and uses in other high profile documents and settings.

Data analysis and quality assurance

Codes are produced in qualitative research to organize and structure insights arising from an investigation of documents, interviews, and other materials. Saldana (2009: 3) describes that codes are "most often a word or short phrase that symbolically assigns a summative, salient, and essence-capturing, and/or evocative attribute for a portion of language-based or visual data." In doing so, they help in organizing, interpreting, and presenting large volumes of qualitative information. Codes can be created by a deductive, top-down approach that can be advantageous in connecting findings back to concepts or theories of interest. Alternatively, codes can also come from an inductive, bottom-up approach and be more descriptive or free-form in nature. These bottom-up codes often directly borrow from language or phrases drawn from documents or can be taken verbatim from quotations that emerge during participant interviews.

Table 8.1 shows how both deductive and inductive approaches to coding were employed in this research, with codes drawn from a range of different sources. The coding structure evolved over time, which is expected as qualitative research progresses and deepens. It began with an initial list of 15 codes, arising from a consideration of the primary research questions, review of the literature related to anticipatory governance, and drawing on salient ideas derived from the documents and interviews. For instance, the codes "Better Foresight," "Better Oversight," and "Strategic Research" were derived

Table 8.1 Code source and role in analysis

Code source	Role in analysis	Examples of codes
Reports and strategy documents	Phrases used in documents helped to direct overall analysis.	• Neutral tone—"Strike a Balance" • "Better Foresight" • "Better Oversight" • "Strategic Research" • "Lack of Information Breeds Mistrust"
Interview quotations	Quotations served as inspiration for key insights about organizational practices.	• Future in the Present—"Getting There Early" • "Watching the Watchdogs" • "Dark Horse" • "Get it Right"
Conceptual framework	Concepts and terminology from anticipatory governance provided guidance and structure for this research.	• Anticipatory governance • Public value • Boundary object • Honest broker • Accelerating technologies
Media analysis	Patterns emerging from the media analysis examined in conjunction with the document analysis and interview findings.	• Systems thinking • Products as touchstones • Design and branding • Voice and participation used as evidence • Repetition
Functional considerations	Procedural and functional elements highlight key points that cut across all dimensions.	• Case study approach • Definition of nanotechnology • Critiqued • Inventory and map • EHS implications • Policy influence

straight from phrases used in PEN's quarterly reports. Codes such as "Watching the Watchdogs," "Dark Horse," and "Get it Right" were taken from quotations provided in some of the initial interviews. Codes such as "Foresight—Frameworks and Wildcards," "Public Engagement," "Cross Sector Collaboration," and "Lesson Learning" came from reflecting on the implications of the conceptual framework underlying this research.

Additional codes were regularly added as more documents were reviewed and as additional interviews were conducted. A handful of papers also proved valuable as sources of codes. These include Barben et al. (2008), the primary academic description of anticipatory governance, and two articles from the public value mapping literature, Jorgensen and Bozeman (2007) and Fisher et al. (2010), which provided an extensive list of relevant keywords that could be used as codes. For instance, codes drawn from the lists presented in these two papers include phrases such as "Transparency" and "Risk Management." A set of cross-cutting conceptual and functional codes were also added as the analysis progressed, including "Future in the Present—'Getting There Early,'" "Prototype/Models," "Systems Thinking," "Dialogue and Convening," and "Experimentation and Outlier."

The code list reached its most expansive range at 126 codes in September 2012. Efforts were then taken to consolidate and group together similar codes as the findings became more convergent. This resulted in a final list of 60 codes as of May 2013, corresponding to a total of 1,902 textual elements coded in the Atlas.ti document database in the primary research phase. Following rough guidelines and rules-of-thumb provided in Saldana (2009), this total number of resulting codes is in line with what is typical for a qualitative exploration of this scope. To ensure that the codes accurately mirrored the content of the documents in the database, I produced a frequency count of the top codes to compare against a frequency count of the top words that appear throughout the documents in the database. The most frequently used codes and the most frequent substantive words that appear in the documents generally were in close alignment: nine of the top 11 codes corresponded to seven of the top 11 substantive words (and their variations) that appear in the document set. Once this manageable set of codes was achieved, codes were then clustered together, using the three different dimensions of anticipatory governance to organize findings and to facilitate analysis.

Following Bowen (2009: 32), the document analysis and coding component involved a series of phases that included "skimming (superficial examination), reading (thorough examination), and interpretation." The process of reading and coding the documents led to the generation of short narrative memorandums that gathered together insights and helped in identifying key discoveries. Over time, these memos and other notes became more detailed, eventually forming the core of the book's empirical chapters and contributed to creating the table and figure visualizations (Miles and Huberman, 1994). Simultaneously, the figures and charts were created to help convey theoretical relationships and summarize the emerging results.

Finally, maintaining quality assurance of the ultimate conclusions was paramount, which was accomplished following the relevant quality assurance criteria laid out in Tracy (2010). These criteria include undertaking a close reading of the evidence to inform eventual interpretations and triangulating findings across different types of source materials and different points of view. For these reasons, close attention was paid to connections that arose from both the semi-structured interviews and document analysis components of the research. Thick description was used throughout to report on the central outcomes and findings to provide a nuanced presentation of the main ideas. Rhetorical devices, such as presenting illustrative vignettes and anecdotes, were also adopted in order to help highlight essential findings. Instances in which my interpretations as a researcher may have differed from alternative views expressed by others—or where I have offered diverging interpretations to what was suggested elsewhere—are indicated appropriately to ensure transparency. The intention throughout was to paint a compelling yet analytical picture that makes evident how the studied organizations actually operated and what their work implies for future efforts of this kind to better understand the societal implications of emerging technologies that may yet arise both in the United States and around the world.

Bibliography

Barben, D., Fisher, E., Selin, C., and Guston, D. H. (2008). Anticipatory Governance of Nanotechnology: Foresight, Engagement, Integration. In E. J. Hackett, O. Amsterdamska, M. Lynch, and J. Wajcman (Eds.), *The Handbook of Science and Technology Studies*, (3rd ed.). (pp. 979–1000). Cambridge, MA: The MIT Press.

Bowen, G. (2009). Document Analysis as a Qualitative Research Method. *Qualitative Research Journal*, 9(2), 27–40.

Dudo, A., Dunwoody, S., and Scheufele, D. A. (2011). The Emergence of Nano News: Tracking Thematic Trends and Changes in U.S. Newspaper Coverage of Nanotechnology. *Journalism and Mass Communication Quarterly*, 88(1), 55–75.

Fisher, E., Slade, C. P., Anderson, D., and Bozeman, B. (2010). The Public Value of Nanotechnology. *Scientometrics*, 85(1), 29–39.

Friese, S. (2012). *Qualitative Data Analysis with ATLAS.ti*. Thousand Oaks, CA: SAGE Publications.

Jorgensen, T. B., and Bozeman, B. (2007). Public Values: An Inventory. *Administration and Society*, 39(1), 354–381.

Lincoln, Y. S., and Guba, E. G. (1985). *Naturalistic Inquiry*. Newbury Park, CA: SAGE Publications.

Maynard, A. D., Aitken, R. J., Butz, T., Colvin, V., Donaldson, K., Oberdorster, G., Philbert, M. A., Ryan, J., Seaton, A., Tinkle, S. A., Tran, L., Walker, N. J., Warheit, D. B. (2006, November). Safe Handling of Nanotechnology. *Nature*, 444(7117), 267–269.

Miles, M. B., and Huberman, A. M. (1994). *Qualitative Data Analysis: An Expanded Sourcebook*, 2nd ed. Thousand Oaks, CA: SAGE Publications.

Mogalakwe, M. (2006). The Use of Documentary Research Methods in Social Research. *African Sociological Review*, 10(1), 221–230.

Poland, C. A., Duffin, R., Kinloch, I., Maynard, A., Wallace, W. A., Seaton, A., Stone, V., Brown, S., MacNee, W., Donaldson, K. (2008). Carbon Nanotubes Introduced into the Abdominal Cavity of Mice Show Asbestos-like Pathogenicity in a Pilot Study. *Nature Nanotechnology*, 3(7), 423–428.

Prior, L. (2003). *Using Documents in Social Research*. Thousand Oaks, CA: SAGE Publications.

Saldana, J. (2009). *The Coding Manual for Qualitative Researchers*. Thousand Oaks, CA: SAGE Publications.

Scott, J. (1990). *A Matter of Record: Documentary Sources in Social Research*. Cambridge, UK: Polity Press.

Stake, R. E. (1995). *The Art of Case Study Research*. Thousand Oaks, CA: Sage Publications.

Tracy, S. J. (2010). Qualitative Quality: Eight "Big Tent" Criteria for Excellent Qualitative Research. *Qualitative Inquiry*, 16(10), 837–851.

Ventresca, M. J., and Mohr, J. W. (2001). Archival Research Methods. In J. A. Baum (Ed.), *The Blackwell Companion to Organizations*. Chichester, UK.

Yanow, D. (1996). *How Does a Policy Mean? Interpreting Policy and Organizational Actions*. Washington, DC: Georgetown University Press.

Yanow, D. (2000). *Conducting Interpretive Policy Analysis*. Thousand Oaks, CA: SAGE Publications.

Yin, R. (2003). *Case Study Research: Design and Methods*, (3rd ed.). Thousand Oaks, CA: SAGE Publications.

Index

For Product Safety Concerns and Information please contact our EU
representative GPSR@taylorandfrancis.com
Taylor & Francis Verlag GmbH, Kaufingerstraße 24, 80331 München, Germany

* 9 7 8 0 8 1 5 3 5 5 7 8 6 *